*The*

*Dictionary*

*of*

*Humorous Quotations*

# The Dictionary of Humorous Quotations

EDITED BY
EVAN ESAR

DORSET PRESS
New York

This edition published by Dorset Press,
a division of Marboro Books Corporation,
by arrangement with Doubleday,
a division of Bantam Doubleday Dell
1989 Dorset Press

ISBN 0-88029-290-3

Printed in the United States of America
M 9 8 7 6 5 4 3 2

# Foreword

I DON'T KNOW why, but dictionaries of quotations and treasuries of humor generally ignore comic sayings. This became apparent to me while doing research in humorology. I had encountered many comic sayings, but when I tried to check them in such reference books I found that most of them were omitted. So I decided to compile an anthology of witticisms, and here it is—a combination treasury of humor and dictionary of quotations. Because of its dual nature, this anthology supplements the excellent works in these fields. It does not pretend to compete with them.

After having collected thousands of comic items, my problem was to organize them for ready reference. I knew that quotation dictionaries are usually arranged according to subject, and humor treasuries according to author. This collection, it seemed to me, belonged in structure to the latter type. So I put its contents in a frame of author reference. And to enhance its usefulness I added a subject index.

When authors are listed with their own sayings grouped under them, their personalities become clear to us at once. We notice their individual styles, how they achieve their comic effects, and how their wit differs from others. We observe quickly and easily the sweet of Thoreau, the sour of Nietzsche, the salt of Samuel Butler, and the bitter of Bierce.

Sometimes authors reveal themselves by the subjects they choose. As wise old Goethe learned from his own lack of humor: "Men show their character in nothing more clearly than by what they find laughable." But more often than subject, it is by temperament they reveal themselves. The wit of Swift is chiefly satire, but in Lamb it is wordplay, in Hazlitt it is skepticism, and in Sydney Smith it is drollery.

And each of these styles bears its own individual bias. Compare Americans to these Britons and note how their temperaments vary. The satire of Swift differs from the satire of Mencken. The wordplay of Lamb from the wordplay of Oliver Herford. The skepticism of

Hazlitt from the skepticism of Robert Frost. And the drollery of Smith from the drollery of Don Herold.

> Lord, what fools these immortals be,
> But how immortal their foolery.

If brevity is the soul of wit, variety is the mark of it. And you will find ample evidence of this variety here. You will find fun in the profundity of Anatole France, and jests in the suggestions of Douglas Jerrold. You will even find wit in Whitman, and in other such humorless spirits who occasionally struck comic effects by accident. All types of comic quotations are included in this collection. The wit of humor—nonsense, satire, caricature, et cetera. And the humor of wit—paradoxes, wellerisms, reversibles, et cetera.

This work is made up roughly of three parts: one century of American wit, two centuries of English wit, and the rest of a more ancient and foreign vintage. My emphasis on modern humor is easily understood. The older the wit, the less quotable it. Many an excellent "wit-crack" of older writers like Shakespeare has been omitted because proverbial overuse has destroyed its original comic appeal. Benjamin Franklin's saying, for example, "We must all hang together or we shall all hang separately," was once a great epigram; but it has long ago lost its laughable point and is remembered now only for its historic association. Thomas Marshall's classic comment, "What this country needs is a good five-cent cigar," is another witticism that has lost its mirth through reiteration and parody. These random examples illustrate an important distinction between comic and non-comic quotations. The former lose their piquancy by frequent repetition whereas the latter acquire acceptance by it. Familiarity breeds serious quotations but buries comic ones.

There are other reasons why I have stressed modern humor in this collection. I shall not go into them here, for they would make dull reading. One point, though, is worth mentioning. The older literary wit was largely expressed in rigid verse patterns. Not until the eighteenth century did it finally shake off these shackles and become enormously more flexible. My desire to make this book as quotable as possible led me to omit verse, with the occasional exception of a couplet in prose form. This in turn meant the omission of most pre-eighteenth-century wit, which consisted largely of verse.

The inclusion of contemporaries presented several problems. Since a notable is more quotable than a nonentity, it is common practice in periodical literature to tag anonymous flashes of wit onto famous names. This applies particularly to radio and Hollywood comedians. Fortunately my familiarity with gag-file wit has enabled me to exclude most of these false credits. I have also excluded many apocryphal quotations customarily attached to wits like Wilson Mizner, malaprop-makers like Samuel Goldwyn, and columnists like Walter Winchell, who give wide currency to comedy lines.

Another problem of handling the wit of contemporaries is the difficulty of doing justice to them. I cannot pretend even to have approximated justice. Nevertheless, I have included far more contemporary items than any other collection of quotations or humor. In a future edition I hope to make amends, and I shall be grateful to readers for suitable comic quotations sent to me in care of the publishers.

When I began this work I considered confining it to original English quotations, for translation is the sworn enemy of wit. *Traduttori, traditori* applies as much to the comic as to the poetic. But there were always Voltaire and a host of others whose salty sayings even in translation I would not willingly forego. So I decided to include them. Of these, the French are the most numerous, for theirs is the wittiest tradition of all European tongues; and among them La Rochefoucauld is tops, though he is less witty than wise. As for other foreigners, two individuals are worth passing notice here, for they underscore the translation limitations of wit and they deserve as many pages in this book as they are given lines. Heine, one of the wittiest of the moderns, seems to lose his sparkle when converted into English, and this is as true of his smiling prose as of his poetry. And Martial, one of the wittiest of the ancients, must not only battle the barriers of verse and translation but two millennia as well—an impossible task.

Although I have tried to check the contents of this book for verbal accuracy, there may be a number of items which are not reproduced here perfectly. Misquotations of language persist because they are briefer or sharper or more rhythmic than their originals. For example, Shakespeare wrote: "A young man married is a man that's marred." But some unknown misquoter bettered it to: "A young man married is a young man marred," and that's the way it is usually expressed. I am tempted to misquote Emerson myself: "Next to the originator of a good sentence is the first misquoter of it."

The greater evil lies not with misquotations of language, as Byron thought, but with misquotations of source. Every epigrammatist finds some of his bon mots attributed to others, and naturally resents it. But fourth-century Donatus gave this matter an unexpected turnabout. "Damn those," he exclaimed, "who have made my remarks before me!" And in modern times that twist-wit Samuel Butler gave the idea of misquotation another twirl: "It is bad enough," he said, "to see one's own good things fathered on other people, but it is worse to have other people's rubbish fathered upon oneself." Fortunate was Butler indeed to have lived before the age of columnists and digest-magazine fillers!

A point should be made here about identical quotations from different sources. Under the law of levity, as under the law of gravity, things tend to move toward each other. Thus we occasionally find famous men passing off as original the same epigrams. For example, both Robert Ingersoll and Samuel Butler hit upon the identical reversible: "An honest God is the noblest work of man." I have generally avoided such duplication by entering only the quotation from the earlier source.

By the same token, much that is wittily expressed is unwittingly borrowed. Bill Nye said: "Be virtuous and you will be happy, but you will be lonesome sometimes." And Mark Twain said after him: "Be good and you will be lonesome." Nor is this the only instance where the greater unconsciously borrowed from the lesser wit, though more often it is the other way around. Dr. Johnson said: "If he does really think there is no distinction between vice and virtue, when he leaves our houses let us count our spoons." And Emerson said after him: "The louder he talked of his honor, the faster we counted our spoons." Such pairs of pared satire are inevitable in the nature of humor, and they occur more frequently than is realized. I have usually included such parallel items in this dictionary.

Identity of idea rather than language is, of course, another matter, and we need no Ecclesiastes come from the grave Old Testament to tell us that nothing is said that has not been said before. Certain subjects, like man and woman, husband and wife, love and marriage, lend themselves eternally to caricature and ridicule. What wonder, then, that the same ideas are expressed by satirists of every generation! The same ideas, but every expression of them different. For example, to Wilde a gentleman was "one who never hurts anyone's feelings unintentionally," whereas to Mencken he is "one who never strikes a woman without provocation." I cannot resist citing another illustration here out of the many included in this dictionary. Kin Hubbard took the Aesopian proverb, "Those who seek to please everybody, please nobody." He particularized the general idea, adapted it to the present, and put it into his typical climactic style: "He was over to the poor farm the other day to see an old friend that used to publish a newspaper that pleased everybody."

Occasionally clever ideas are cleverly paraphrased. Such items have been included only when I thought the rewording sufficiently rewarding and not too close to the original. Thus you will find here Shakespeare's "I am not only witty in myself but the cause that wit is in other men," as well as Foote's "He is not only dull himself but the cause of dullness in others."

I have similarly included proverbial paraphrases, though these always follow the original closely because they are puns. For example, Addison Mizner's "Absinthe makes the heart grow fonder," and "Poets are born, not paid." Most wits indulge in this type of wordplay, and pun-loving Shakespeare was one of them. He revised the proverb "Comparison are odious" into "Comparisons are odorous"— a pun that would be in bad odor if authored by a lesser wit. A number of proverb twisters will be found in this book, punsters like Ethel Watts Mumford who made an unwholesome hobby of it, but I have included only the best of their parodies.

I have taken the liberty of changing into orthodox orthography the intentional misspelling of important American humorists. Men like Artemus Ward, Josh Billings, Finley Peter Dunne, and others. This corrective seems to me necessary if they are to be rescued from the oblivion to which their eccentric spelling is rapidly consigning them. We alter the unintentional spelling of Shakespeare and bring him closer to us and make him more readable. Surely we need not hesitate to do so with these lesser lights.

The letter of wit, like the letter of the law, is often in sharp conflict with its spirit. So it was with these men. They were unaware that phonetic wit is auditory and not visual, and simply followed the tradition of their time. Yet how amusingly they defended it from attack. Artemus Ward declared: "It is a pity that Chawcer, who had geneyus, was so unedicated; he's the wuss speller I know of." And Billings argued: "I hold that a man haz az much rite tew spell a word az it iz pronounsed az he haz tew pronounse it the way it ain't spelt." On another occasion Billings defended his errorthography in correct spelling: "Noah Webster was a good speller; he had better spells than Billings."

Unintentional humor has generally been omitted from this book because the element of awareness is the *sine qua non* of wit. Nevertheless, for reasons too tedious to detail, here and there an exception has enabled a humorless creature to creep into these pages. Whitman has already been mentioned, and Shelley is a good illustration too, he who wrote: "I am convinced that there can be no regeneration of mankind until laughter is put down." Even with humorous creatures I have made an occasional exception of unintentional humor, but only when I thought such items quotable for reverse laughs. For example, Dr. Johnson's polysyllabic definition of network.

The contents of this book have been restricted to quoteworthy items from noteworthy authors. Thus comic sayings which derive from obscure authors have been omitted. Also all items of anonymous origin, whether proverbs or not. This has necessitated the exclusion of famous proverbialists like Heywood, Clarke, and others. An exception has been made of Franklin, whose merry personality animated many a proverbial saying.

The contents have also been restricted to quotations of single-sentence length, generally to twenty-five words. To this rule, as to others, I have admitted exceptions. But I have constantly borne in mind that these quotations must be comic laconics, that their brevity is as essential as their wit, and their wit as essential as their famous authors. In detaching many a quotation from its context so that it could stand alone—brief, complete, and epigrammatic—I have sometimes had to alter punctuation, omit qualifying phrases, delete proper because unknown names, et cetera. But all such liberties I have taken have been minor ones, and in no case do they violate the original spirit or meaning.

Many immortals who flourish in quotation dictionaries and humor treasuries are missing from this book. Poets like Milton, Keats, Wordsworth, Browning, Swinburne, and others have been omitted because they had no humor in them. Other poets, like Burns and Dryden, have been omitted because they clothed their wit solely in verse, and therefore have no place in this collection. Famous prose writers, too, will not be found here—humorless ones like Bacon and Bunyan, for example. Still others are absent, as already explained, due to the barriers of time and translation, and the difficulty of covering contemporaries. As for the great humorists, many of them are only slightly represented here. Rabelais is one of these, and Lewis Carroll, and Cervantes, and Dickens, and even Shakespeare. The nature of this work prevents it from doing justice to authors whose humor does not reside chiefly in witty sentences.

Conversely, I am aware of having included much witty-worded trivia. Salt and substance, like quantity and quality, do not always make laughing companions here. If certain lightweights, like Austin O'Malley and Helen Rowland, appear like heavyweights in these pages, it is due solely to their uncommon quotability. The eminently quotable are not always the quotably eminent. Or, to put it in another way, proportional representation may be valid in politics, but politics, unlike comics, is not always a laughing matter.

This may partly explain why Oscar Wilde stands here quantitatively so far ahead of Mark Twain and Bernard Shaw. "In all pointed sentences," declared the Great Cham of Literature, "some degree of accuracy must be sacrificed to conciseness." To Wilde the right angle was not some degree but more often ninety degrees, which makes so many of his witty-pretty comments more false than true. Yet they are no less quotemirthy for being less quoteworthy. When Shaw said, "When a thing is funny, search it for a hidden truth," he was referring to Shavian shafts rather than the wit of Wilde. One need not go beyond this compilation for proof that much truth is said in jest—and much untruth as well. "My way of joking," said Shaw again, "is telling the truth; that is the funniest joke in the world." But it is not the way of all flashes of wit. Will Rogers, too, knew that "a gag to be good has to be fashioned about some truth. The rest you get by your slant on it, and perhaps by a wee bit of exaggeration, so's people won't miss the point."

The special nature of these contents throws light on many matters in the field of humor. A few of these highlights are worth pointing out, but without any extended comment.

Scattered among the comic quotations are the opinions famous people have flung at others equally famous. These are often biting biographies-in-one-sentence, and every whit as revealing as every wit is amusing. Under Oscar Wilde alone are listed verbal caricatures of Browning, Frank Harris, Henry James, Meredith, George Moore, Shaw, Wagner, and Whistler. If you are interested in biography, you will find the subject index profitable.

This collection also covers the facetious fancies of both sexes. It includes more examples of the wit of women than any other reference book. By this proof, it clarifies a subject of unfailing interest—the place in humor of the daughters of Eve, the first rib-tickler. The funny females who parade through these pages range alphabetically from Sophie Arnould and Jane Austin to Carolyn Wells and Rebecca West. And they represent many types of quotable notables: humorists, journalists, letter writers, novelists, et cetera.

Another subject of endless interest among Americans and Englishmen is the difference between their humor. A comparison of their leading wits, as exemplified here, points up this difference. The top liner in this collection is Oscar Wilde, who is generally considered the world's greatest wit. He leads the Englishmen, followed by two great men of culture and letters, Bernard Shaw and Samuel Butler. Mark Twain is the high-water mark of American humor, and he is followed here by two provincials, Kin Hubbard and Josh Billings. Naturally this quantitative comparison is more suggestive than exact. Wilde and Shaw, for example, are of Irish origin, while Billings and Hubbard never reach the heights of witty wisdom. Moreover, this collection cannot throw light on those wider differences between American and English humor which exceed the single-sentence limit of epigrams.

One final word. Although this dictionary of comic quotations will be enjoyed by the random reader, it is intended even more for the reference user. Its arrangement and index make it a convenient tool for amateur wit-lovers and professional humorists. As for others, I am reminded of Bovée: "Next to being witty yourself, the best thing to do is to be able to quote another's wit."

EVAN ESAR

# The
# Dictionary
# of
# Humorous Quotations

**ADAMS, Franklin Pierce ("F.P.A."),** born 1881, *American journalist, poet, and humorous writer.*

1. Accustomed as I am to public speaking, I know the futility of it.
2. A first edition of his work is a rarity but a second is rarer still.
3. The best part of the fiction in many novels is the notice that the characters are all purely imaginary.
4. Count that day won when, turning on its axis, this earth imposes no additional taxes.
5. Don't tell me what you dream'd last night for I've been reading Freud.
6. Dunking is bad taste but tastes good.
7. Health is the thing that makes you feel that now is the best time of the year.
8. If a man keep his trap shut, the world will beat a path to his door.
9. Insomniacs don't sleep because they worry about it, and they worry about it because they don't sleep.
10. In the order named, these are the hardest to control: Wine, Women and Song.
11. Middle age occurs when you are too young to take up golf and too old to rush up to the net.
12. She was suffering from fallen archness.
13. There are seventy stanzas in the Uruguay national anthem, which fact may account for the Uruguay standing army.
14. There's no accounting for tastes, as the woman said when somebody told her her son was wanted by the police.
15. What this country needs is a good five-cent nickel.
16. You never know what you can do without until you try.
17. The best you get is an even break.

**ADAMS, Henry,** 1838–1918, *American historian.*

1. It is impossible to underrate human intelligence—beginning with one's own.
2. Philosophy: unintelligible answers to insoluble problems.

3. Practical politics consists in ignoring facts.

4. They also serve who only stand and cheer.

## ADDISON, Joseph, 1672–1719, *English essayist, statesman, and poet.*

1. A moneylender serves you in the present tense, lends you in the conditional mood, keeps you in the subjunctive, and ruins you in the future.

2. Authors have established it as a kind of rule that a man ought to be dull sometimes.

3. Nothing is capable of being well set to music that is not nonsense.

4. There is not so variable a thing in nature as a lady's headdress.

5. We are always doing something for posterity, but I would fain see posterity do something for us.

6. A woman seldom asks advice before she has bought her wedding clothes.

## ADE, George, 1866–1944, *American humorous author and playwright.*

1. Anybody can win, unless there happens to be a second entry.

2. Early to bed and early to rise, and you'll meet very few of our best people.

3. For parlor use, the vague generality is a lifesaver.

4. A good folly is worth whatever you pay for it.

5. A good musical comedy consists largely of disorderly conduct occasionally interrupted by talk.

6. He had been kicked in the head by a mule when young, and believed everything he read in the Sunday papers.

7. Here's to man: he can afford anything he can get; here's to woman: she can afford anything she can get a man to get for her.

8. The house was more covered with mortgages than with paint.

9. If it were not for the presents, an elopement would be preferable.

10. My father sent me to an engineering school to prepare me for a literary career.

11. She was a town-and-country soprano of the kind often used for augmenting the grief at a funeral.

12. She was short on intellect, but long on shape.

13. There are only three basic jokes, but since the mother-in-law joke is not a joke but a very serious question, there are only two.

14. After being turned down by numerous publishers, he decided to write for posterity.

15. Her features did not seem to know the value of teamwork.

16. The time to enjoy a European trip is about three weeks after unpacking.

17. "Whom are you?" said he, for he had been to night school.

18. Don't try to marry an entire family or it may work out that way.

19. A friend who is very near and dear may in time become as useless as a relative.

20. He had heard that one is permitted a certain latitude with widows, and went in for the whole 180 degrees.

21. The music teacher came twice each week to bridge the awful gap between Dorothy and Chopin.

22. She invariably was first over the fence in the mad pursuit of culture.

23. She told him it was terrible to hear such things as he told her and to please go ahead.

24. Those who marry to escape something usually find something else.

**ADLER, Alfred,** 1870–1937, *Austrian psychologist and psychiatrist.*

It is easier to fight for one's principles than to live up to them.

**AGAR, Herbert,** born 1897, *American poet, journalist, and miscellaneous writer.*

Snobs talk as if they had begotten their own ancestors.

**AGASSIZ, Louis J. R.,** 1807–1873, *Swiss-American zoologist and geologist.*

I cannot afford to waste my time making money.

**AGATE, James,** born 1877, *English dramatic critic.*

1. The English instinctively admire any man who has no talent and is modest about it.

2. To force myself to earn more money, I determined to spend more.

**AINSLIE, Douglas,** born 1865, *English poet, critic, and philosopher.*

You can never trust a woman; she may be true to you.

**ALDINGTON, Richard,** born 1892, *English poet, novelist, and critic.*

Nationalism is a silly cock crowing on its own dunghill.

**ALEXANDER the Great,** 356–323 B.C., *King of Macedonia, conqueror of Greece, Egypt, Persia, et cetera.*

I am dying with the help of too many physicians.

**ALLEN, Fred,** born 1894, *American radio wit.*

1. Advertising agency: eighty-five per cent confusion and fifteen per cent commission.

2. An associate producer is the only guy in Hollywood who will associate with a producer.

3. California is a fine place to live in—if you happen to be an orange.

4. A conference is a gathering of important people who singly can do nothing, but together can decide that nothing can be done.

5. He dreamed he was eating Shredded Wheat and woke up to find the mattress half gone.

6. He is so narrow-minded that if he fell on a pin, it would blind him in both eyes.

7. He pasted picture postcards around goldfish bowls to make the goldfish think they were going places.

8. Her hat is a creation that will never go out of style; it will just look ridiculous year after year.

9. He was not brought by the stork; he was delivered by a man from the Audubon Society personally.

10. His hobby is collecting old echoes.
11. Hollywood is a place where people from Iowa mistake each other for movie stars.
12. Hollywood is no place for a professional comedian; the amateur competition is too great.
13. If a circus is half as good as it smells, it's a great show.
14. What's on your mind—if you'll forgive the overstatement?
15. I have never seen a pair of slacks that had very much slack in them.
16. I like long walks, especially when they are taken by people who annoy me.
17. I play a musical instrument some, but only for my own amazement.
18. Man has made his bedlam; let him lie in it.
19. The man was so small, he was a waste of skin.
20. My agent gets ten per cent of everything I get, except my blinding headaches.
21. The only thing he ever takes out on a moonlit night is his upper plate.
22. On ships they call them barnacles; in radio they attach themselves to desks, and are called vice-presidents.
23. Some movie stars wear their sunglasses even in church; they're afraid God might recognize them and ask for autographs.
24. When you smoke cigarettes you're likely to burn yourself to death; with chewing tobacco the worst thing you can do is drown a midget.
25. Sense doesn't make sense in radio.

**ALLEN, Grant,** 1848–1899, *British author of voluminous fiction.*

1. All men are born free and unequal.
2. Cockroaches think that kitchens were created to afford a convenient home for cockroaches.

**ARBUTHNOT, John,** 1667–1735, *Scottish physician and witty political pamphleteer.*

1. All political parties die at last of swallowing their own lies.
2. Biography is one of the new terrors of death.

**ARETINO, Pietro,** 1492-1556, *Italian satirist.*

1. If you want to annoy your neighbors, tell the truth about them.
2. Wise is the young man who is always thinking of taking a wife, and never takes one.

**ARISTOTLE,** 384-322 B.C., *Greek philosopher, student of Plato, and teacher of Alexander the Great.*

1. Homer has taught all other poets the art of telling lies skillfully.
2. My friends! There are no friends.

**ARLEN, Michael,** born 1895, *British novelist and playwright.*

1. It is amazing how nice people are to you when they know you are going away.
2. She not only expects the worst, but makes the worst of it when it happens.

**ARNOULD, Sophie,** 1744-1802, *French opera star and wit.*

1. Oh! the good old days when I was so unhappy.
2. Women give themselves to God when the devil wants nothing more to do with them.

**ARP, Bill,** 1826-1903, *pseudonym of Charles Henry Smith, American humorist.*

I joined the army, and succeeded in killing about as many of the enemy as they of me.

**AUDEN, Wystan Hugh,** born 1907, *English poet.*

A professor is one who talks in someone else's sleep.

**AUERBACH, Berthold,** 1812-1882, *German novelist.*

What's all our knowledge worth? We don't even know what the weather will be tomorrow.

**AUGUSTINE, Saint,** A.D. 354-430, *one of the leaders in the early Christian church.*

1. Give me chastity and self-restraint, but do not give it yet.
2. The playthings of our elders are called business.

3. To abstain from sin when a man cannot sin is to be forsaken by sin, not to forsake it.

## AUSTEN, Jane, 1775-1817, *English novelist.*

1. I have been a selfish being all my life, in practice, though not in principle.
2. A woman, especially, if she have the misfortune of knowing anything, should conceal it as well as she can.

## BAER, Arthur ("Bugs"), born 1897?, *American comic columnist and short-story writer.*

1. Alimony is like buying oats for a dead horse.
2. Although it is a far cry from there to here, he laughed all the way.
3. An empty cab drove up, and Sarah Bernhardt got out.
4. She used to diet on any kind of food she could lay her hands on.
5. A good neighbor is a fellow who smiles at you over the back fence but doesn't climb over it.
6. He had insomnia so bad that he couldn't sleep when he was working.
7. He had reasons for not working; he said your body was only a machine and he was no mechanic.
8. He is an adventurer who traces leaky plumbing to its source.
9. Hello! We heard you at the door, but just thought you were part of the bad weather.
10. His family were the largest dandruff manufacturers in France.
11. He was so ugly, the last time I saw him he was the top of a totem pole in Seattle.
12. He was thrown out trying to steal second; his head was full of larceny but his feet were honest.
13. How much would you charge to haunt a house?
14. If you do big things they print your face, and if you do little things they only print your thumbs.

15. If you laid all our laws end to end, there would be no end.

16. I paused like a woodpecker at timber line.

17. It arrived by first-class mail in second-class condition.

18. It is impossible to tell where the law stops and justice begins.

19. It was as helpful as throwing a drowning man both ends of a rope.

20. The ladies looked one another over with microscopic carelessness.

21. She was a brunette by birth but a blonde by habit.

22. A newspaper is a circulating library with high blood pressure.

23. Do incubator chickens love their mother?

24. He doesn't remember any silent days in motion pictures—the director always yelled.

25. She was always crying; in fact, she wept so much she made everybody's corns ache.

26. He was born silly and had a relapse.

27. He writes dialogues by cutting monologues in two.

28. It was so quiet, you could hear a pun drop.

29. What did the storm at sea say to the passenger's lunch?

30. She's always in a triangle—like Napoleon's hat.

31. She's generous to a fault—if it's her own.

32. You can always judge a man by what he eats, and therefore a country in which there is no free lunch is no longer a free country.

33. You can take a boy out of the country but you can't take the country out of a boy.

**BAGEHOT, Walter,** 1826–1877, *English economist, essayist, and journalist.*

1. The cure for admiring the House of Lords is to go and look at it.

2. The greatest mistake is trying to be more agreeable than you can be.

3. Human nature is not a high thing, but at least it has a high idea of itself.

4. An inability to stay quiet is one of the most conspicuous failings of mankind.

5. It is good to be without vice, but it is not good to be without temptations.

6. Poverty is an anomaly to rich people; it is very difficult to make out why people who want dinner do not ring the bell.

7. Men who do not make advances to women are apt to become victims to women who make advances to them.

8. A parliament is nothing less than a big meeting of more or less idle people.

9. The great pleasure in life is doing what people say you cannot do.

**BAILEY, James Montgomery,** 1841–1894, *American humorous journalist.*

1. Any young man with good health and a poor appetite can save up money.

2. A blunderer is a man who starts a meat market during Lent.

3. The dearest object to a married man should be his wife but it is not infrequently her clothes.

4. I hear quite frequently of civil engineers, and wonder if there is no one to say a good word for conductors.

5. The longest funeral I ever heard of took place a week ago; my hired girl went to it and hasn't got back yet.

6. She was completely unmanned by the loss of her husband.

7. When a couple of young people strongly devoted to each other commence to eat onions, it is safe to pronounce them engaged.

**BAILEY, Philip James,** 1816–1902, *English poet and lawyer.*

The worst men often give the best advice.

**BALDWIN, Faith,** born 1893, *American novelist and short-story writer.*

She was torn between love and booty.

**BALZAC, Honoré de,** 1799–1850, *French novelist.*

1. Believe everything you hear about the world; nothing is too impossibly bad.

2. Friendships last when each friend thinks he has a slight superiority over the other.

3. A good husband is never the first to go to sleep at night or the last to awake in the morning.

4. A husband should always know what is the matter with his wife, for she always knows what is not.

5. I do not regard a broker as a member of the human race.

6. If we all said to people's faces what we say behind each other's backs, society would be impossible.

7. Marriage is the end of man.

8. Money brings everything to you, even your daughters.

9. Nature makes only dull animals; we owe the fool to society.

10. One of the first conditions of learning in a woman is to keep the fact a profound secret.

11. When a woman gets too old to be attractive to man she turns to God.

12. When in Turkey, do as the turkeys do.

13. When there is an old maid in the house, a watchdog is unnecessary.

14. Women, when they have made a sheep of a man, always tell him that he is a lion with a will of iron.

**BANGS, John Kendrick**, 1862–1922, *American humorous writer and lecturer*.

1. All press agents belong to a club of which Ananias is the honorary president.

2. Although man is already ninety per cent water, the Prohibitionists are not yet satisfied.

3. Being an Episcopalian interferes neither with my business nor my religion.

4. I can't tell a lie—not even when I hear one.

5. Pandemonium did not reign; it poured.

6. She would rather fool with a bee than be with a fool.

**BANNING, Margaret Culkin**, born 1891, *American novelist*.

She never quite leaves her children at home, even when she doesn't take them along.

**BARNUM, Phineas Taylor,** 1810–1891, *American showman.*

1. Every crowd has a silver lining.

2. There's a sucker born every minute.

**BARRIE, James Matthew,** 1860–1937, *Scottish dramatist and novelist.*

1. Every man who is high up loves to think that he has done it all himself; and the wife smiles, and lets it go at that.

2. God gave us our memories so that we might have roses in December.

3. Have you ever noticed that many jewels make women either incredibly fat or incredibly thin?

4. His lordship may compel us to be equal upstairs, but there will never be equality in the servants' hall.

5. I am not young enough to know everything.

6. If *Hamlet* had been written in these days it would probably have been called *The Strange Affair at Elsinore.*

7. If you have charm, you don't need to have anything else; and if you don't have it, it doesn't matter what else you have.

8. It is not true that woman was made from man's rib; she was really made from his funny bone.

9. Never ascribe to an opponent motives meaner than your own.

10. The printing press is either the greatest blessing or the greatest curse of modern times, one sometimes forgets which.

11. She was a large woman who seemed not so much dressed as upholstered.

12. We are all of us failures—at least, the best of us are.

13. The God to whom little boys say their prayers has a face very like their mother's.

**BARRYMORE, John,** 1882–1942, *American actor.*

1. America is the country where you buy a lifetime supply of aspirin for one dollar, and use it up in two weeks.

2. The good die young—because they see it's no use living if you've got to be good.

3. One of my chief regrets during my years in the theater is that I couldn't sit in the audience and watch me.

4. If it isn't the sheriff, it's the finance company; I've got more attachments on me than a vacuum cleaner.

5. In Genesis it says that it is not good for a man to be alone, but sometimes it is a great relief.

6. I've read some of your modern free verse and wonder who set it free.

7. Love is the delightful interval between meeting a beautiful girl and discovering that she looks like a haddock.

8. My wife was too beautiful for words, but not for arguments.

9. My wife is the kind of girl who'll not go anywhere without her mother, and her mother will go anywhere.

10. I am thinking about taking a fifth wife; why not? Solomon had a thousand wives and he is a synonym for wisdom.

11. Paper napkins never return from a laundry, nor love from a trip to the law courts.

12. There's something about a closet that makes a skeleton terribly restless.

13. The thing that takes up the least amount of time and causes the most amount of trouble is Sex.

14. The trouble with life is that there are so many beautiful women —and so little time.

15. The way to fight a woman is with your hat—grab it and run.

16. You never realize how short a month is until you pay alimony.

**BARUCH, Bernard Mannes,** born 1870, *American statesman and financier.*

To me, old age is always fifteen years older than I am.

**BAUDELAIRE, Pierre Charles,** 1821-1867, *French poet and critic.*

1. Life is a hospital in which every patient is possessed by the desire to change his bed.

2. The man who gets on best with women is the one who knows best how to get on without them.

3. A sweetheart is a bottle of wine; a wife is a wine bottle.

4. What is love? The need to escape from oneself.

**BEAUMARCHAIS, Caron de,** 1732-1799, *French playwright.*

It is not necessary to understand things in order to argue about them.

**BECKFORD, William,** 1759-1844, *English writer and art collector.*

He did not think that it was necessary to make a hell of this world to enjoy paradise in the next.

**BEECHER, Henry Ward,** 1813-1887, *American preacher, lecturer, and reformer.*

1. The cynic puts all human actions into two classes: openly bad and secretly bad.

2. Every man should have a fair-sized cemetery in which to bury the faults of his friends.

3. Flowers are the sweetest things that God ever made and forgot to put a soul into.

4. Men are called fools in one age for not knowing what they were called fools for averring in the age before.

5. Next to ingratitude, the most painful thing to bear is gratitude.

6. Poverty is very good in poems but very bad in the house; very good in maxims and sermons but very bad in practical life.

7. Selfishness is that detestable vice which no one will forgive in others and no one is without in himself.

8. Some people are so dry that you might soak them in a joke for a month and it would not get through their skins.

9. The monkey is an organized sarcasm upon the human race.

10. There are many people who think that Sunday is a sponge to wipe out all the sins of the week.

**BEECHER, Lyman,** 1775-1863, *American preacher and theologian.*

Oh Lord, grant that we may not despise our rulers; and grant, oh Lord, that they may not act so we can't help it.

**BEERBOHM, Max,** born 1872, *English essayist and caricaturist.*

1. After all, as a pretty girl once said to me, women are a sex by themselves, so to speak.

2. Fate wrote her a most tremendous tragedy, and she played it in tights.

3. I was a modest, good-humored boy; it is Oxford that has made me insufferable.

4. People are either born hosts or born guests.

5. To give an accurate and exhaustive account of that period would need a far less brilliant pen than mine.

**BEHN, Aphra,** 1640–1689, *English dramatist and novelist.*

1. Come away! Poverty's catching.

2. He that will live in this world must be endowed with the three rare qualities of dissimulation, equivocation, and mental reservation.

3. Money speaks sense in a language all nations understand.

**BENCHLEY, Robert,** 1889–1945, *American humorous editor, critic, actor, and author.*

1. Drawing on my fine command of language, I said nothing.

2. Drinking makes such fools of people, and people are such fools to begin with, that it's compounding a felony.

3. I do most of my work sitting down; that's where I shine.

4. In America there are two classes of travel—first class, and with children.

5. It took me fifteen years to discover I had no talent for writing, but I couldn't give it up because by that time I was too famous.

6. It was one of those plays in which all the actors unfortunately enunciated very clearly.

**BENÉT, Stephen Vincent,** 1898–1943, *American poet and short-story writer.*

As for what you're calling hard luck—well, we made New England out of it, that and codfish.

**BENNETT, Arnold,** 1867–1931, *English novelist and playwright.*

1. Good taste is better than bad taste, but bad taste is better than no taste at all.

2. It is well, when one is judging a friend, to remember that he is judging you with the same godlike and superior impartiality.

3. Journalists say a thing that they know isn't true, in the hope that if they keep on saying it long enough it will be true.

4. Make love to every woman you meet; if you get five per cent on your outlay, it's a good investment.

5. Pessimism, when you get used to it, is just as agreeable as optimism.

6. Women are strange and incomprehensible, a device invented by Providence to keep the wit of man well sharpened by constant employment.

7. It is only people of small moral stature who have to stand on their dignity.

8. It is a profound truth that women as a sex are vain; it is also a profound truth that men as a sex are vain.

9. A man of sixty has spent twenty years in bed and over three years in eating.

**BENNETT, James Gordon,** 1841–1918, *newspaper editor.*

I have made mistakes, but I have never made the mistake of claiming that I never made one.

**BENTHAM, Jeremy,** 1748–1832, *English philosopher, jurist, and political scientist.*

Lawyers are the only persons in whom ignorance of the law is not punished.

**BENTON, Thomas Hart,** born 1889, *American painter.*

An art school is a place for young girls to pass the time between high school and marriage.

**BIERCE, Ambrose,** 1842–1914?, *American short-story writer and journalist.*

1. Abstainer: a weak person who yields to the temptation of denying himself a pleasure.

2. Acquaintance: a degree of friendship called slight when its object is poor or obscure, and intimate when he is rich or famous.

3. Acquaintance: a person whom we know well enough to borrow from, but not well enough to lend to.

4. Admiration: our polite recognition of another man's resemblance to ourselves.

5. Applause is the echo of a platitude.

6. Architect: one who drafts a plan of your house, and plans a draft of your money.

7. Armor is the kind of clothing worn by a man whose tailor was a blacksmith.

8. Bore: a person who talks when you wish him to listen.

9. Brain: the apparatus with which we think we think.

10. Cabbage: a familiar kitchen-garden vegetable about as large and wise as a man's head.

11. Calamities are of two kinds: misfortune to ourselves, and good fortune to others.

12. Christians and camels receive their burdens kneeling.

13. A clergyman is a man who undertakes the management of our spiritual affairs as a method of bettering his temporal ones.

14. A conservative is a statesman who is enamored of existing evils, as distinguished from the liberal who wishes to replace them with others.

15. Coward: one who in a perilous emergency thinks with his legs.

16. Cynic: a blackguard whose faulty vision sees things as they are, not as they ought to be.

17. Dentist: a prestidigitator who, putting metal into your mouth, pulls coins out of your pocket.

18. Diaphragm: a muscular partition separating disorders of the chest from disorders of the bowels.

19. Discussion: a method of confirming others in their errors.

20. Education: that which discloses to the wise and disguises from the foolish their lack of understanding.

21. Egotist: a person of low taste, more interested in himself than in me.

22. Empty wine bottles have a bad opinion of women.

23. The fact that boys are allowed to exist at all is evidence of a remarkable Christian forbearance among men.

24. Faith: belief without evidence in what is told by one who speaks without knowledge, of things without parallel.

25. Fashion: a despot whom the wise ridicule and obey.

26. The first man you meet is a fool; if you do not think so ask him, and he will prove it.

27. The gambling known as business looks with austere disfavor upon the business known as gambling.

28. Genealogy: an account of one's descent from an ancestor who did not particularly care to trace his own.

29. The hardest tumble a man can make is to fall over his own bluff.

30. Here's to woman! Would that we could fall into her arms without falling into her hands.

31. History: an account mostly false, of events unimportant, which are brought about by rulers mostly knaves, and soldiers mostly fools.

32. Hospitality: the virtue which induces us to feed and lodge certain persons who are not in need of food and lodging.

33. In each human heart are a tiger, a pig, an ass, and a nightingale; diversity of character is due to their unequal activity.

34. Lecturer: one with his hand in your pocket, his tongue in your ear, and his faith in your patience.

35. Marriage: the state or condition of a community consisting of a master, a mistress, and two slaves, making, in all, two.

36. Of two evils, choose to be the least.

37. Opportunity: a favorable occasion for grasping a disappointment.

38. Our vocabulary is defective; we give the same name to woman's lack of temptation and man's lack of opportunity.

39. Peace: in international affairs, a period of cheating between two periods of fighting.

40. Positive: being mistaken at the top of one's voice.

41. A prejudice is a vagrant opinion without visible means of support.

42. Revolution: in politics, an abrupt change in the form of mis-government.

43. A saint is a dead sinner revised and edited.

44. Slang is the speech of him who robs the literary garbage cans on their way to the dump.

45. Take not God's name in vain; select a time when it will have effect.

46. To apologize is to lay the foundation for a future offense.

47. Total abstainer: one who abstains from everything but absten-tion, and especially from inactivity in the affairs of others.

48. You are not permitted to kill a woman who has injured you, but nothing forbids you to reflect that she is growing older every minute.

49. All are lunatics, but he who can analyze his delusion is called a philosopher.

50. The author of the best seller of last week is thought by the police of repeating his offense.

51. Experience is a revelation in the light of which we renounce our errors of youth for those of age.

52. To the small part of ignorance that we arrange and classify we give the name knowledge.

53. When Eve saw her reflection in a pool, she sought Adam and accused him of infidelity.

54. When you are ill make haste to forgive your enemies, for you may recover.

BILLINGS, Josh, 1818–1885, *pseudonym of Henry Wheeler Shaw, American humorist.*

1. Adam invented love at first sight, one of the greatest labor-saving machines the world ever saw.

2. Advice is like castor oil, easy enough to give but dreadful uneasy to take.

3. As long as we are lucky we attribute it to our smartness; our bad luck we give the gods credit for.

4. As scarce as truth is, the supply has always been in excess of the demand.

5. Beauty that don't make a woman vain makes her very beautiful.

6. Be kind to your mother-in-law, and if necessary pay for her board at some good hotel.

7. The best bait for bedbugs is to sleep three in a bed.

8. The best medicine I know for rheumatism is to thank the Lord it ain't the gout.

9. The best way to convince a fool that he is wrong is to let him have his own way.

10. The biggest fool in the world hasn't been born yet.

11. The choicest compliment that can be paid to virtue is that the best lies we have are those which most resemble the truth.

12. Confess your sins to the Lord, and you will be forgiven; confess them to men, and you will be laughed at.

13. A congregation who can't afford to pay a clergyman enough want a missionary more than they do a clergyman.

14. Consider the postage stamp: its usefulness consists in the ability to stick to one thing till it gets there.

15. Credit is like chastity: both of them can stand temptation better than they can suspicion.

16. Debt is a trap which a man sets and baits himself, and then deliberately gets into.

17. The devil is the father of lies, but he neglected to patent the idea, and the business now suffers from competition.

18. A dog is the only thing on this earth that loves you more than he loves himself.

19. The dog that will follow everybody ain't worth a curse.

20. Do not put off till tomorrow what can be enjoyed today.

21. Don't borrow or lend; but if you must do one, lend.

22. Don't despise your poor relations; they may become suddenly rich someday, and then it will be awkward to explain things to them.

23. Don't ever prophesy; for if you prophesy wrong, nobody will forget it; and if you prophesy right, nobody will remember it.

24. Don't lay any certain plans for the future; it is like planting toads and expecting to raise toadstools.

25. Don't undertake to live with your mother-in-law, but if worst comes to worst, let your mother-in-law live with you.

26. Every man has a perfect right to his opinion, provided it agrees with ours.

27. Every man should know something of law; if he knows enough to keep out of it, he is a pretty good lawyer.

28. Eve was the first woman who fooled her man.

29. Experience increases our wisdom but doesn't reduce our follies.

30. Experience is a school where a man learns what a big fool he has been.

31. Experience teaches us much, but learns us little.

32. Flattery is like cologne water, to be smelt of, not swallowed.

33. Give the devil his due, but be very careful that there ain't much due him.

34. God save the fools, and don't let them run out, for if it weren't for them, wise men couldn't get a living.

35. Honesty is the rarest wealth anyone can possess, and yet all the honesty in the world ain't lawful tender for a loaf of bread.

36. I am a poor man, but I have this consolation: I am poor by accident, not by design.

37. I am poor, and I am glad that I am, for I find that wealth makes more people mean than it does generous.

38. I am willing to admit that man is my brother, but I contend at the same time that I have got a lot of cursed relations.

39. I don't know of anything more remorseless on the face of the earth than seven per cent interest.

40. If a man is right, he can't be too radical; if he is wrong, he can't be too conservative.

41. If a man ain't got a well-balanced head, I like to see him part his hair in the middle.

42. If it wasn't for faith, there would be no living in this world; we couldn't even eat hash with any safety.

43. If the animals had reason, they would act just as ridiculous as we menfolks do.

44. If the world despises a hypocrite, what must they think of him in heaven?

45. If you can't get half a loaf take a whole one—a whole loaf is better than no bread.

46. If you want to get a sure crop, and a big yield, sow wild oats.

47. Ignorance is bliss—ignorance of sawing wood, for instance.

48. I have finally come to the conclusion that a good reliable set of bowels is worth more to a man than any quantity of brains.

49. I haven't got as much money as some folks, but I've got as much impudence as any of them, and that's the next thing to money.

50. I haven't much doubt that man sprang from the monkey, but where did the monkey spring from?

51. I never could see any use in making wooden gods male and female.

52. I never knew an auctioneer to lie, unless it was absolutely necessary.

53. In youth we run into difficulties, in old age difficulties run into us.

54. It ain't so much trouble to get rich as it is to tell when we have got rich.

55. It is the little bits of things that fret and worry us; we can dodge an elephant, but we can't a fly.

56. It is very easy to manage our neighbor's business, but our own sometimes bothers us.

57. It's a wise man who profits by his own experience, but it's a good deal wiser one who lets the rattlesnake bite the other fellow.

58. Keep a cow, and the milk won't have to be watered but once.

59. Laughing is the sensation of feeling good all over, and showing it principally in one spot.

60. Laziness is a good deal like money; the more a man has of it the more he seems to want.

61. A learned fool is one who has read everything, and simply remembered it.

62. Life is short, but it is long enough to ruin any man who wants to be ruined.

63. Live within your income, even if you have to borrow money to do so.

64. Love is like the measles; we can have it but once, and the later in life we have it, the tougher it goes with us.

65. Love is said to be blind, but I know lots of fellows in love who can see twice as much in their sweethearts as I can.

66. Man is my brother, and I am nearer related to him through his vices than I am through his virtues.

67. Man was created a little lower than the angels, and has been getting a little lower ever since.

68. The man who ain't got an enemy is really poor.

69. The man who can get fat on baloney sausage has got a good deal of dog in him.

70. The man who gets bit twice by the same dog is better adapted for that kind of business than any other.

71. A man with a small head is like a pin without any, very apt to get into things beyond his depth.

72. Men ain't apt to get kicked out of good society for being rich.

73. Men mourn for what they have lost, women for what they ain't got.

74. The miser and the glutton are two facetious buzzards: one hides his store and the other stores his hide.

75. Misfortunes and twins never come singly.

76. The more humble a man is before God, the more he will be exalted; the more humble he is before man, the more he will get rode roughshod.

77. Most everyone seems to be willing to be a fool himself, but he can't bear to have anybody else one.

78. Most men are like eggs, too full of themselves to hold anything else.

79. Most of the happiness in this world consists in possessing what others can't get.

80. Most people repent of their sins by thanking God they ain't so wicked as their neighbors.

81. The mule is half horse and half jackass, and then comes to a full stop, nature discovering her mistake.

82. Music hath charms to soothe a savage; this may be so, but I would rather try a revolver on him first.

83. Nature never makes any blunders; when she makes a fool she means it.

84. Necessity is the mother of invention, but patent right is the father.

85. Never run into debt, not if you can find anything else to run into.

86. Never work before breakfast; if you have to work before breakfast, get your breakfast first.

87. A new milk-cow is stepmother to every man's baby.

88. Nobody really loves to be cheated, but it does seem as though everyone is anxious to see how near he could come to it.

89. No man is so poor that he can't afford to keep one dog, and I've seen them so poor that they could afford to keep three.

90. One half the troubles of this life can be traced to saying "yes" too quick, and not saying "no" soon enough.

91. One of the best temporary cures for pride and affectation is sea-sickness: a man who wants to vomit never puts on airs.

92. One of the hardest things for any man to do is to fall down on the ice when it is wet and then get up and praise the Lord.

93. The only profit there is in keeping more than one dog is what you can make on the board.

94. Pity costs nothing, and ain't worth nothing.

95. Politeness looks well in every man, except an undertaker.

96. The quickest way to take the starch out of a man who is always blaming himself is to agree with him.

97. Remember the poor—it costs nothing.

98. The road to ruin is always kept in good repair, and the travelers pay the expense of it.

99. Rum is good in its place, and hell is the place for it.

100. Self-made men are most always apt to be a little too proud of the job.

101. Self-preservation is the first law of nature; so says Blackstone, and he is the best judge of law.

102. Seven per cent has no rest, nor no religion; it works nights, and Sundays, and even wet days.

103. Silence is one of the hardest arguments to refute.

104. Silence is said to be golden, but the best fools the world has ever produced had nothing to say on the subject.

105. Some folks in this world spend their whole time hunting after righteousness and can't find any time to practice it.

106. Success is not always a sure sign of merit, but it is a first-rate way to succeed.

107. Suicide is cheating the doctors out of a job.

108. Take all the fools out of this world, and there wouldn't be any fun or profit living in it.

109. Take the humbug out of this world, and you haven't much left to do business with.

110. There ain't anything that will completely cure laziness, but I have known a second wife to hurry it some.

111. There are but few men who have character enough to lead a life of idleness.

112. There are people so addicted to exaggeration that they can't tell the truth without lying.

113. There is two things in this life for which we are never fully prepared, and that is—twins.

114. There are very few good judges of humor, and they don't agree.

115. There is one advantage in a plurality of wives; they fight each other instead of their husbands.

116. There is only one good substitute for the endearments of a sister, and that is the endearments of some other fellow's sister.

117. There may come a time when the lion and the lamb will lie down together, but I am still betting on the lion.

118. There's lots of people in this world who spend so much time watching their health that they haven't the time to enjoy it.

119. There's nothing that you and I make so many blunders about, and the world so few, as the actual amount of our importance.

120. The thinner the ice, the more anxious is everyone to see whether it will bear.

121. Threescore years and ten is enough; if a man can't suffer all the misery he wants in that time, he must be numb.

122. Time is money, and many people pay their debts with it.

123. To enjoy a good reputation, give publicly, and steal privately.

124. To learn your offspring to steal, make them beg hard for all that you give them.

125. The trouble with most folks isn't so much their ignorance, as knowing so many things that ain't so.

126. Truth is said to be stranger than fiction; it is to most folks.

127. Waiting to be whipped is the most uninteresting period in boyhood life.

128. When a man comes to me for advice, I find out the kind of advice he wants, and I give it to him.

129. When a man makes up his mind to become a rascal, he should examine himself closely and see if he isn't better constructed for a fool.

130. When I see a man of shallow understanding extravagantly clothed, I always feel sorry—for the clothes.

131. The wicked work harder to reach hell than the righteous do to get to heaven.

132. Woman's influence is powerful, especially when she wants anything.

133. A woman will sometimes confess her sins, but I never knew one to confess her faults.

134. Young man, sit down and keep still; you will have plenty of chances yet to make a fool of yourself before you die.

**BISMARCK, Otto von**, 1815–1898, *German statesman.*

1. I have seen three emperors in their nakedness, and the sight was not inspiring.

2. Be polite; write diplomatically; even in a declaration of war one observes the rules of politeness.

**BLACKIE, John Stuart**, 1809–1895, *Scottish author and translator.*

Wine is the drink of the gods, milk the drink of babies, tea the drink of women, and water the drink of beasts.

**BOSSUET, Jacques,** 1627-1704, *French theologian and pulpit orator.*

The cruelest revenge of a woman is to remain faithful to a man.

**BOUCICAULT, Dion,** 1820?-1890, *Irish-Anglo-American dramatist and actor.*

I wish Adam had died with all his ribs in his body.

**BOURGET, Paul,** 1852-1935, *French poet, novelist, and critic.*

The proof that experience teaches us nothing is that the end of one love does not prevent us from beginning another.

**BRADLEY, Francis Herbert,** 1846-1924, *English writer on philosophy.*

1. Everything comes to him who waits—among other things, death.
2. His mind is open; yes, it is so open that nothing is retained; ideas simply pass through him.
3. Optimism: the world is the best of all possible worlds, and everything in it is a necessary evil.
4. Pessimism: where everything is bad, it must be good to know the worst.
5. The propriety of some persons seems to consist in having improper thoughts about their neighbors.
6. There are those who so dislike the nude that they find something indecent in the naked truth.

**BRANDEIS, Louis Dembitz,** 1856-1941, *American lawyer and jurist.*

Behind every argument is someone's ignorance.

**BRILLAT-SAVARIN, Anthelme,** 1755-1826, *French politician and writer on gastronomy.*

The table is the only place where a man is never bored during the first hour.

**BRISBANE, Arthur,** 1864-1936, *American journalist and columnist.*

The fence around a cemetery is foolish, for those inside can't come out and those outside don't want to get in.

**BROUGHAM, Henry,** 1778-1868, *British statesman, author, and scholar.*

A lawyer is a learned gentleman who rescues your estate from your enemies and keeps it himself.

**BROUN, Heywood,** 1888-1939, *American journalist and columnist.*

1. The ability to make love frivolously is the chief characteristic which distinguishes human beings from the beasts.
2. Christian ethics are seldom found save in the philosophy of some unbeliever.
3. God is always on the side which has the best football coach.
4. If anyone corrects your pronunciation of a word in a public place, you have every right to punch him in the nose.
5. It is always safe to be dogmatic about tomorrow.
6. The urge to gamble is so universal and its practice so pleasurable that I assume it must be evil.
7. What a dull world this would be if every imaginative maker of legends was stigmatized as a liar!
8. Repartee is what you wish you'd said.

**BROWNE, Thomas,** 1605-1682, *English writer and physician.*

1. The long habit of living indisposeth us for dying.
2. We all labor against our own cure, for death is the cure of all diseases.
3. The world, which took but six days to make, is like to take us six thousand years to make out.

**BRUSH, Katharine,** born 1893, *American novelist.*

1. Many a girl has gotten into trouble by obeying that boyological urge.
2. New Yorkers are nice about giving you street directions; in fact, they seem quite proud of knowing where they are themselves.
3. One woman's poise is another woman's poison.

**BRYCE, James,** 1838–1922, *British statesman, diplomat, historian, and writer on government.*

Medicine is the only profession that labors incessantly to destroy the reason for its own existence.

**BUCHAN, John,** 1875–1940, *Scottish writer and historian.*

An atheist is a man who has no invisible means of support.

**BUCK, Pearl,** born 1892, *American novelist.*

We send missionaries to China so the Chinese can get to heaven, but we won't let them into our country.

**BUNNER, Henry Cuyler,** 1855–1896, *American humorous writer of short stories and light verse.*

Shakespeare was a dramatist of note who lived by writing things to quote.

**BURBANK, Luther,** 1849–1926, *American naturalist, originator of new fruits and flowers.*

1. For those who do not think, it is best at least to rearrange their prejudices once in a while.
2. It is well for people who think to change their minds occasionally in order to keep them clean.

**BURDETTE, Robert Jones,** 1844–1914, *American clergyman, humorous journalist, and lecturer.*

1. Don't believe the world owes you a living; the world owes you nothing—it was here first.
2. I will be so polite to my wife as though she were a perfect stranger.
3. There are two days about which nobody should ever worry, and these are yesterday and tomorrow.
4. When you are climbing a mountain, don't talk; silence gives ascent.

**BURGESS, Gelett,** born 1866, *American humorous writer and illustrator.*

1. Bad manners simply indicate that you care a good deal more for the food than for the society at the table.

2. If the Lord would only send something interesting, I wouldn't mind if it was only a plaid pig.

3. Many people live alone and like it, but most of them live alone and look it.

4. Men like to pursue an elusive woman, like a cake of wet soap in a bathtub—even men who hate baths.

5. She was only sixteen; but what does that matter when one is young.

6. Some men give their blood to their country; others their spleen.

7. To be two years a widow exceedeth a college education.

8. With a man, a lie is a last resort; with women, it's First Aid.

**BURKE, Edmund, 1729-1797, *British statesman and orator*.**

1. He was not merely a chip off the old block, but the old block itself.

2. It is a general popular error to suppose the loudest complainers for the public to be the most anxious for its welfare.

3. Strip majesty of its exteriors (the first and last letters) and it becomes a jest.

4. They defend their errors as if they were defending their inheritance.

**BURTON, Robert, 1577-1640, *English clergyman and author*.**

1. Diogenes struck the father when the son swore.

2. One was never married, and that's his hell; another is, and that's his plague.

3. They are proud in humility, proud in that they are not proud.

**BUTLER, Nicholas Murray, 1862-1947, *American educator*.**

1. An expert is one who knows more and more about less and less.

2. One of the embarrassments of being a gentleman is that you are not permitted to be violent in asserting your rights.

**BUTLER, Samuel, 1835-1902, *English novelist and satirist*.**

1. All of the animals except man know that the principal business of life is to enjoy it.

2. Any fool can paint a picture, but it takes a wise man to be able to sell it.

3. Any fool can tell the truth, but it requires a man of some sense to know how to lie well.

4. An apology for the devil: it must be remembered that we have heard only one side of the case; God has written all the books.

5. The artist drew a great many lines and saved the best of them.

6. At any rate there will be no wedding presents in heaven.

7. The better part of valor is indiscretion.

8. The body is but a pair of pincers set over a bellows and a stew-pan, and the whole fixed upon stilts.

9. Books should be tried by a judge and jury as though they were crimes, and counsel should be heard on both sides.

10. Brevity is very good when we are, or are not, understood.

11. Brigands demand your money or your life; women require both.

12. Cleanliness is almost as bad as godliness.

13. Cooking is half digesting; we do half our digestion, therefore, outside our own bodies.

14. The dead being the majority, it is natural that we should have more friends among them than among the living.

15. A degenerate nobleman, or one that is proud of his birth, is like a turnip; there is nothing good of him but that which is underground.

16. The devil tempted Christ, but it was Christ who tempted the devil to tempt him.

17. The dons are too busy educating the young men to be able to teach them anything.

18. For the better cure of vice they think it necessary to study it, and the only efficient study is through practice.

19. The giraffe must get up at six in the morning if it wants to have its breakfast in its stomach by nine.

20. God cannot alter the past; that is why he is obliged to connive at the existence of historians.

21. Greater luck hath no man than this, that he lay down his wife at the right moment.

22. He is considered the most graceful speaker who can say nothing in most words.

23. A hen is only an egg's way of making another egg.

24. He was an unprincipled, principle-ridden prig.

25. He was born stupid, and greatly increased his birthright.

26. He was capable of bringing out an expurgated edition of Wordsworth.

27. "Home, Sweet Home" must surely have been written by a bachelor.

28. I do not mind lying, but I hate inaccuracy.

29. If God considered woman a helpmeet for man, he must have had a very poor opinion of man.

30. If I were to say all the unpleasant things that occur to me about posthumous memoirs, I should have nothing left for my posthumous memoirs.

31. If you aim at imperfection, there is some chance of your getting it; whereas if you aim at perfection, there is none.

32. If you follow reason far enough it always leads to conclusions that are contrary to reason.

33. I keep my books at the British Museum and at Mudie's.

34. Invention is the mother of necessity.

35. I should like to add an eighth sacrament to those of the Roman Church—the sacrament of Divorce.

36. I take it that all plants feel, but some make more fuss about their feelings than others.

37. It costs a lot of money to die comfortably.

38. It is my relations with my relations that I sometimes find embarrassing.

39. Life is one long process of getting tired.

40. Life is the art of drawing sufficient conclusions from insufficient premises.

41. A little cooking is good because it unsettles the meat's mind and prepares it for new ideas.

42. A little knowledge is a dangerous thing, but a little want of knowledge is also a dangerous thing.

43. Lord, I do not believe; help thou my unbelief.

44. Man is the only animal that can remain on friendly terms with the victims he intends to eat until he eats them.

45. A man should be just cultured enough to be able to look with suspicion upon culture.

46. Men should not try to overstrain their goodness more than any other faculty.

47. The money that men make lives after them.

48. The most important service rendered by the press is that of educating people to approach printed matter with distrust.

49. Most of those who call themselves artists are in reality picture dealers, only they make the pictures themselves.

50. Nothing is potent against love save only impotence.

51. Nothing makes a man or woman look so saintly as seasickness.

52. Not only is there a skeleton in every closet, but there is a screw loose in every skeleton.

53. The oldest books are only just out to those who have not read them.

54. The one serious conviction that a man should have is that nothing is to be taken too seriously.

55. People should learn to lie as they learn anything else—from very small beginnings.

56. Peter remained on friendly terms with Christ notwithstanding Christ's having healed his mother-in-law.

57. Providence itself could not be more absolutely improvident.

58. The public do not know enough to be experts, yet know enough to decide between them.

59. She is a very fascinating woman, and he is very fond of fascinating with her.

60. She looks as if her soul had got the better of her.

61. She ought never to have been a mother, but she'll make a rare mother-in-law.

62. She went up the Nile as far as the first crocodile.

63. The tendency of modern science is to reduce proof to absurdity by continually reducing absurdity to proof.

64. There is nothing so unthinkable as thought, unless it be the absence of thought.

65. There should be asylums for habitual teetotalers, but they would probably relapse into teetotalism as soon as they came out.

66. There should be some schools called deformatories to which people are sent if they are too good to be practical.

67. This age will serve to make a very pretty farce for the next.

68. 'Tis better to have loved and lost than never to have lost at all.

69. To live is like to love; all reason is against it, and all healthy instinct for it.

70. To the lexicographer, God is simply the word that comes next to "gocart."

71. Two are better than one, but the man who said that did not know my sisters.

72. Vaccination is the medical sacrament corresponding to baptism.

73. Vouchsafe, O Lord, to keep us this day without being found out.

74. We are all miscarriages, but some miscarry at three months after conception and some at 100 years after birth.

75. We ought to have books teaching us not how to compose music but how to decompose it.

76. We should so use the next world that it should advance us in that which is before it.

77. What I want to write is songs without words—or music.

78. You can do very little with faith, but you can do nothing without it.

**BYRON, George Gordon, 1788-1824,** *English poet.*

1. All tragedies are finished by death; all comedies are ended by a marriage.

2. After all, what is a lie? 'Tis but the truth in masquerade.

3. Believe a woman or an epitaph, or any other thing that's false, before you trust in critics.

4. The English winter—ending in July, to recommence in August.

5. He was the mildest-manner'd man that ever scuttled ship or cut a throat.

6. I hate to hunt down a tired metaphor.

7. I hope to merit Heaven by making earth a Hell.

8. I wish he would explain his explanation.

9. One of the pleasures of reading old letters is the knowledge that they need no answer.

10. Pleasure's a sin, and sometimes sin's a pleasure.

11. Since Eve ate apples, much depends on dinner.

12. Society is now one polished horde, form'd of two mighty tribes, the Bores and Bored.

13. There is a tide in the affairs of women which, taken at the flood, leads—God knows where.

14. There's naught, no doubt, so much the spirit calms as rum and true religion.

15. Though I love my country, I do not love my countrymen.

16. 'Tis pleasant, sure, to see one's name in print; a book's a book, although there's nothing in't.

17. What men call gallantry, and gods adultery, is much more common where the climate's sultry.


**CABELL, James Branch, born 1879, *American novelist.***

1. The optimist proclaims that we live in the best of all possible worlds, and the pessimist fears this is true.

2. The religion of Hell is patriotism, and the government is an enlightened democracy.

**CAMERON, Simon, 1799–1889, *American politician.***

An honest politician is one who when he is bought will stay bought.

**CANNING, George, 1770–1827, *English statesman and prime minister.***

Nothing is so fallacious as facts, except figures.

**ČAPEK, Karel, 1890–1938, *Czech journalist, playwright, and short-story writer.***

If dogs could talk, perhaps we'd find it just as hard to get along with them as we do with people.

**CARLYLE, Thomas,** 1795–1881, *Scotch essayist, historian, and biographer.*

1. Four thousand people cross London Bridge daily, mostly fools.
2. The greatest of faults, I should say, is to be conscious of none.
3. If you are ever in doubt as to whether or not you should kiss a pretty girl, always give her the benefit of the doubt.
4. Love is not altogether a delirium, yet it has many points in common therewith.
5. Make yourself an honest man and then you may be sure there is one rascal less in the world.
6. There is a great discovery still to be made in literature, that of paying literary men by the quantity they do not write.
7. A well-written life is almost as rare as a well-spent one.

**CARROLL, Lewis,** 1832–1898, *pseudonym of Charles Lutwidge Dodgson, English writer and mathematician.*

1. It's a poor sort of memory that only works backwards.
2. That's the reason they're called lessons, because they lessen from day to day.

**CATO, Marcus Porcius ("the Censor"),** 234–149 B.C., *Roman statesman.*

1. I had rather men should ask why no statue has been erected in my honor, than why one has.
2. Wise men learn more from fools than fools from wise men.
3. It is a difficult matter, my fellow citizens, to argue with the belly since it has no ears.

**CAVOUR, Benso di,** 1810–1861, *Italian statesman.*

I have discovered the art of fooling diplomats; I speak the truth and they never believe me.

**CERVANTES, Miguel de,** 1547–1616, *Spanish author.*

1. All women are good—good for nothing, or good for something.
2. Between a woman's "yes" and "no," I would not venture to stick a pin.

3. Everyone is as God made him, and often a great deal worse.

4. I drink when there is an occasion, and sometimes when there is no occasion.

5. The most difficult character in comedy is the fool, and he must be no fool who plays that part.

6. The rich widow cries with one eye and rejoices with the other.

7. When a man says, "Get out of my house! What do you want with my wife?"—there's no answer to be made.

**CHAMBERS, Robert W.,** 1865-1933, *American novelist.*

All the world may not love a lover but all the world watches him.

**CHAMFORT, Nicholas,** 1741-1794, *French wit and writer.*

1. Bachelors' wives and old maids' children are always perfect.

2. A beautiful woman is paradise for the eyes, hell for the soul, and purgatory for the purse.

3. Change in fashion is the tax which the industry of the poor levies on the vanity of the rich.

4. Fame: the advantage of being known to those who do not know us.

5. If a woman were on her way to her execution, she would demand a little time to put on make-up.

6. If it were not for the government, we should have nothing left to laugh at in France.

7. In France we leave unmolested those who set fire to the house, and persecute those who sound the alarm.

8. In love, everything is true, everything is false; it is the one subject on which one cannot express an absurdity.

9. A lover is a man who tries to be more amiable than it is possible for him to be.

10. The loves of some people are but the result of good suppers.

11. Many men and women enjoy popular esteem, not because they are known, but because they are not known.

12. Most contemporary books give the impression of having been manufactured in a day, out of books read the day before.

13. One would risk being disgusted if one saw politics, justice, and one's dinner in the making.

14. Paris is a city of gaieties and pleasures where four fifths of the inhabitants die of grief.

15. The public! The public! How many fools does it take to make up a public?

16. Society is composed of two great classes: those who have more dinners than appetite, and those who have more appetite than dinners.

17. The success of many books is due to the affinity between the mediocrity of the author's ideas and those of the public.

18. There are more fools than wise men and even in the wise man himself there is more folly than wisdom.

19. There are well-dressed foolish ideas just as there are well-dressed fools.

20. The threat of a neglected cold is for doctors what the threat of purgatory is for priests—a gold mine.

21. 'Tis easier to make certain things legal than to make them legitimate.

22. A woman is like your shadow—follow her, she flies; fly from her, she follows.

**CHAPMAN, George,** 1559?–1634, *English poet and dramatist.*

1. Flatterers look like friends, as wolves like dogs.

2. When a man dies, the last thing that moves is his heart; in a woman, her tongue.

3. Young men think old men are fools; but old men know young men are fools.

**CHASE, Ilka,** born 1905?, *American actress and author.*

1. America's best buy for a nickel is a telephone call to the right man.

2. George Moore unexpectedly pinched my behind; I felt rather honored that my behind should have drawn the attention of the great master of English prose.

3. He's all buttoned up in an impenetrable little coat of complacency.

4. When he said we were trying to make a fool of him, I could only murmur that the Creator had beat us to it.

**CHASE, Salmon P.,** 1808–1873, *American statesman and jurist.*

I would rather that the people should wonder why I wasn't President than why I am.

**CHEKHOV, Anton,** 1860–1904, *Russian writer of short stories, plays, and novels.*

1. If you are afraid of loneliness do not marry.

2. A man and a woman marry because both of them don't know what to do with themselves.

3. The university brings out all abilities including incapability.

4. What a lot of idiots there are among ladies; people have got so used to it that they no longer notice it.

5. When an actor has money, he doesn't send letters but telegrams.

6. A woman is fascinated not by art, but by the noise made by those who are in the art field.

**CHESTERFIELD, Lord (4th Earl of),** 1694–1773, *English statesman and man of letters.*

1. He and I have been dead these two years, but we don't choose to have it known.

2. If a fool knows a secret, he tells it because he is a fool.

3. If people are unwilling to hear you, better it is to hold your tongue than them.

4. If the multitude ever deviate into the right, it is always for the wrong reason.

5. The less one has to do, the less time one finds to do it in.

6. The manner of a vulgar man has freedom without ease; the manner of a gentleman has ease without freedom.

7. Most people enjoy the inferiority of their best friends.

8. Nature has hardly formed a woman ugly enough to be insensible to flattery upon her person.

9. The only solid and lasting peace between a man and his wife is doubtless a separation.

10. To govern mankind one must not overrate them.

11. I look upon opera as a magic scene contrived to please the eyes and the ears at the expense of the understanding.

12. Very ugly or very beautiful women should be flattered on their understanding, mediocre ones on their beauty.

13. We, my lords, may thank Heaven that we have something better than our brains to depend on.

**CHESTERTON, Gilbert Keith**, 1874-1936, *English journalist, author, and critic.*

1. An adventure is only an inconvenience, rightly considered.

2. All our schools are finishing schools; they finish what has never been begun.

3. The artistic temperament is a disease that afflicts amateurs.

4. Art, like morality, consists in drawing the line somewhere.

5. The Bible tells us to love our neighbors, and also to love our enemies; probably because they are generally the same people.

6. Christianity has not been tried and found wanting; it has been found difficult and not tried.

7. Companionate marriage is so-called because the people involved are not married and will very rapidly cease to be companions.

8. The dipsomaniac and the abstainer both make the same mistake: they both regard wine as a drug and not as a drink.

9. The doctrine of human equality reposes on this: that there is no man really clever who has not found that he is stupid.

10. The evolutionists seem to know everything about the missing link except the fact that it is missing.

11. Farce creates people who are so intellectually simple as to hide in packing cases or pretend to be their own aunts.

12. Free verse is like free love; it is a contradiction in terms.

13. The full potentialities of human fury cannot be reached until a friend of both parties tactfully intervenes.

14. Heaven sent us soda water as a torment for our crimes.

15. I believe in getting into hot water; it keeps you clean.

16. I do not believe in a fate that falls on men however they act; but I do believe in a fate that falls on them unless they act.

17. If a thing is worth doing, it is worth doing badly.

18. I gravely doubt whether women were ever married by capture; I think they pretended to be, as they do still.

19. I hate a quarrel because it interrupts an argument.

20. Inspiration at its best means breath, and only too frequently means wind.

21. I think I will not hang myself today.

22. It is a pity that people travel in foreign countries; it narrows their minds so much.

23. It is better to speak wisdom foolishly like the saints than to speak folly wisely like the deans.

24. A man knows what style of book he wants to write when he knows nothing else about it.

25. A man must be orthodox upon most things or he will never have time to preach his own heresy.

26. The men who really believe in themselves are all in lunatic asylums.

27. Merely having an open mind is nothing; the object of opening the mind, as of opening the mouth, is to shut it again on something solid.

28. The modern humanitarian can love all opinions, including the opinion that men are unlovable.

29. "My country, right or wrong" is like saying, "My mother, drunk or sober."

30. The old religionists tortured men physically for a moral truth; the new realists torture men morally for a physical truth.

31. Once men sang together round a table in chorus; now one man sings alone for the absurd reason that he can sing better.

32. The only way of catching a train I ever discovered is to miss the train before.

33. Optimism: the noble temptation to see too much in everything.

34. Our wisdom, whether expressed in public or private, belongs to the world, but our follies belong to those we love.

35. A puritan is a person who pours righteous indignation into the wrong things.

36. Science in the modern world has many uses; its chief use, however, is to provide long words to cover the errors of the rich.

37. Silence is the unbearable repartee.

38. Some men never feel small, but these are the few men who are.

39. The success of the marriage comes after the failure of the honeymoon.

40. There are only three things in the world that women do not understand, and they are Liberty, Equality, and Fraternity.

41. There is a great deal of difference between the eager man who wants to read a book and the tired man who wants a book to read.

42. There is nothing the matter with Americans except their ideals; the real American is all right; it is the ideal American who is all wrong.

43. There is only one thing that requires real courage to say, and that is a truism.

44. Thieves respect property; they merely wish the property to become their property that they may more perfectly respect it.

45. The two things that a healthy person hates most between heaven and hell are a woman who is not dignified and a man who is.

46. What a glorious garden of wonders the lights of Broadway would be to anyone lucky enough to be unable to read.

47. The wickedest work in this world is symbolized not by a wine glass, but by a looking glass.

48. A yawn is a silent shout.

49. Youth is always too serious, and just now it is too serious about frivolity.

**CHOATE, Joseph Hodges,** 1832–1917, *American lawyer, diplomat, and after-dinner speaker.*

You cannot live without lawyers, and certainly you cannot die without them.

**CHURCHILL, Winston,** born 1874, *English statesman, writer, and prime minister.*

1. In those days he was wiser than he is now; he used frequently to take my advice.

2. It is a socialist idea that making profits is a vice; I consider the real vice is making losses.

3. It saves a lot of trouble if, instead of having to earn money and save it, you can just go and borrow it.

4. Men occasionally stumble over the truth, but most of them pick themselves up and hurry off as if nothing had happened.

5. Russia is a riddle wrapped in a mystery inside an enigma.

6. They are decided only to be undecided, resolved to be irresolute, adamant for drift, all-powerful for impotence.

**CICERO, Marcus Tullius,** 106–43 B.C., *Roman orator, statesman, and philosopher.*

1. When you have no basis for an argument, abuse the plaintiff.

2. There is no opinion so absurd but that some philosopher will express it.

**CLARKE, James Freeman,** 1810–1888, *American clergyman and writer.*

A politician thinks of the next election; a statesman, of the next generation.

**CLAUDEL, Paul,** born 1868, *French diplomat, poet, and dramatist.*

It is fortunate that diplomats have long noses since they usually cannot see beyond them.

**CLEMENCEAU, Georges,** 1841–1929, *French statesman, premier, and author.*

1. Everything I know I learned after I was thirty.

2. War is much too important a matter to be left to the generals.

**COBB, Irvin Shrewsbury,** 1876–1944, *American journalist, humorous short-story writer, and raconteur.*

1. A capacity for self-pity is one of the last things that any woman surrenders.

2. Epitaph: a belated advertisement for a line of goods that has been permanently discontinued.

3. Every line in her face is the line of least resistance.

4. A good storyteller is a person who has a good memory and hopes other people haven't.

5. He has more kinfolk than a microbe.

6. His words were long enough to run in serials.

7. I couldn't write the things they publish now, with no beginning and no end, and a little incest in the middle.

8. I once knew a fellow who spoke a dialect with an accent.

9. I've just learned about his illness; let's hope it's nothing trivial.

10. Learn all the rules, every one of them, so that you will know how to break them.

11. Men are vain, but they won't mind women working so long as they get smaller salaries for the same job.

12. Middle age: when you begin to exchange your emotions for symptoms.

13. Save whatever is current at the moment, except currency.

14. What is a croquette but hash that has come to a head?

15. Why should a worm turn? It's probably just the same on the other side.

16. Women now insist on having all the prerogatives of the oak and all the perquisites of the clinging vine.

17. You couldn't tell if she was dressed for an opera or an operation.

**COCTEAU, Jean,** born 1891, *French novelist, poet, and playwright.*

1. The course of a river is almost always disproved of by the source.

2. The eyes of the dead are closed gently; we also have to open gently the eyes of the living.

3. The speed of a runaway horse counts for nothing.

4. Tact consists in knowing how far we may go too far.

5. The worst tragedy for a poet is to be admired through being misunderstood.

**COLBERT, Jean Baptiste, 1619–1683,** *French statesman and financial reformer.*

The art of taxation consists in so plucking the goose as to obtain the largest amount of feathers with the least amount of hissing.

**COLBY, Frank Moore, 1865–1925,** *American editor, essayist, and encyclopedist.*

1. Never burn an uninteresting letter is the first rule of British aristocracy.

2. A "new thinker," when studied closely, is merely a man who does not know what other people have thought.

3. Satire is a lonely and introspective occupation, for nobody can describe a fool to the life without much patient self-inspection.

4. Self-esteem is the most voluble of the emotions.

5. When a young American writer seems mad, it is usually because an old one drives him crazy.

**COLERIDGE, Samuel Taylor, 1772–1834,** *English poet, literary critic, and philosopher.*

1. Only the wise possess ideas; the greater part of mankind are possessed by them.

2. Plagiarists are always suspicious of being stolen from.

3. Some men are like musical glasses: to produce their finest tones you must keep them wet.

4. Swans sing before they die; 'twere no bad thing should certain persons die before they sing.

5. There are three classes of elderly women: first, that dear old soul; second, that old woman; third, that old witch.

6. Until you understand a writer's ignorance, presume yourself ignorant of his understanding.

7. You abuse snuff! Perhaps it is the final cause of the human nose.

**COLLINS, John Churton, 1848–1908,** *English literary critic.*

1. Half our mistakes in life arise from feeling where we ought to think, and thinking where we ought to feel.

2. The secret of success in life is known only to those who have not succeeded.

3. Suicide is the worst form of murder, because it leaves no opportunity for repentance.

4. There can be only one end to marriage without love, and that is love without marriage.

5. To profit from good advice requires more wisdom than to give it.

6. Truth is the object of philosophy, but not always of philosophers.

7. We make more enemies by what we say than friends by what we do.

8. The world, like an accomplished hostess, pays most attention to those whom it will soonest forget.

**COLMAN, George (the elder),** 1732–1794, *English dramatist.*

What a pity it is that nobody knows how to manage a wife but a bachelor.

**COLMAN, George (the younger),** 1762–1836, *English dramatist.*

I have henceforth the privilege of adding to my name the honorable title of A double S.

**COLTON, Charles Caleb,** 1780?–1832, *English clergyman, sportsman, and aphorist.*

1. Many speak the truth when they say that they despise riches, but they mean the riches possessed by other men.

2. Genius, in one respect, is like gold; numbers of persons are constantly writing about both, who have neither.

3. If you would be known, and not know, vegetate in a village; if you would know, and not be known, live in a city.

4. Law and equity are two things which God hath joined, but which man has put asunder.

5. Lawyers are the only civil delinquents whose judges must of necessity be chosen from themselves.

6. Many books require no thought from those who read them, and for a very simple reason—they made no such demand upon those who wrote them.

7. Marriage is a feast where the grace is sometimes better than the dinner.

8. Men will wrangle for religion; write for it; fight for it; die for it; anything but live for it.

9. Most of our misfortunes are more supportable than the comments of our friends upon them.

10. Never join with your friend when he abuses his horse or his wife, unless the one is about to be sold and the other to be buried.

11. There are three difficulties in authorship: to write anything worth the publishing, to find honest men to publish it, and to get sensible men to read it.

12. When the million applaud, you ask yourself what harm you have done; when they censure you, what good.

13. Some read to think, these are rare; some to write, these are common; and some read to talk, and these form the great majority.

14. Some reputed saints that have been canonized ought to have been cannonaded.

## CONGREVE, William, 1670-1729, *English dramatist.*

1. I am always of the opinion with the learned, if they speak first.

2. I came upstairs into the world, for I was born in a cellar.

3. I confess freely to you, I could never look long upon a monkey without very mortifying reflections.

4. In my conscience I believe the baggage loves me, for she never speaks well of me herself nor suffers anybody else to rail at me.

5. She is chaste who was never asked the question.

6. Though marriage makes man and wife one flesh, it leaves them still two fools.

7. A wit should be no more sincere than a woman constant.

8. You are a woman: you must never speak what you think; your words must contradict your thoughts, but your actions may contradict your words.

9. Every man plays the fool once in his life, but to marry is playing the fool all one's life long.

**CONRAD, Joseph,** 1857-1924, *English novelist.*

1. The belief in a supernatural source of evil is not necessary; men alone are quite capable of every wickedness.
2. Being a woman is a terribly difficult trade, since it consists principally of dealing with men.
3. Gossip is what no one claims to like—but everybody enjoys.
4. I can't imagine a human being so hard up for something to do as to quarrel with me.
5. Neither his fellows, nor his gods, nor his passions will leave a man alone.

**COOLIDGE, Calvin,** 1872-1933, *President of the United States.*

1. The business of America is business.
2. If you don't say anything, you won't be called on to repeat it.
3. I sometimes wish that people would put a little more emphasis upon the observance of the law than they do upon its enforcement.
4. Patriotism is easy to understand in America; it means looking out for yourself by looking out for your country.

**COWARD, Noel,** born 1899, *English actor, composer, and playwright.*

Alfred Lunt has his head in the clouds and his feet in the box office.

**COWLEY, Hannah,** 1743-1809, *English dramatist.*

What is woman? Only one of nature's agreeable blunders.

**COWPER, William,** 1731-1800, *English poet.*

1. A fool must now and then be right by chance.
2. A life of ease is a difficult pursuit.
3. A noisy man is always in the right.
4. A self-made man? Yes—and worships his creator.

**CRANE, Stephen,** 1871-1900, *American novelist.*

Every sin is the result of a collaboration.

**CUPPY, Will,** born 1884, *American humorous writer.*

All modern men are descended from wormlike creatures, but it shows more on some people.

**CURTIS, Cyrus H. K.,** 1850–1933, *American publisher.*

There are two kinds of men who never amount to much: those who cannot do what they are told, and those who can do nothing else.

**DALI, Salvador,** born 1904, *Spanish-American painter.*

I do not paint a portrait to look like the subject, rather does the person grow to look like his portrait.

**DARROW, Clarence,** 1857–1938, *American lawyer.*

1. Depressions may bring people closer to the church, but so do funerals.
2. The first half of our lives is ruined by our parents and the second half by our children.
3. I am a friend of the workingman, and I would rather be his friend than be one.
4. I am an agnostic; I do not pretend to know what many ignorant men are sure of.
5. I have suffered from being misunderstood, but I would have suffered a hell of a lot more if I had been understood.
6. I never wanted to see anybody die, but there are a few obituary notices I have read with pleasure.
7. The trouble with law is lawyers.
8. When I was a boy I was told that anybody could become President; I'm beginning to believe it.
9. If a man is happy in America it is considered he is doing something wrong.
10. My constitution was destroyed long ago; now I'm living under the bylaws.
11. Someday I hope to write a book where the royalties will pay for the copies I give away.

**DARWIN, Charles,** 1809–1882, *English scientist.*

I love fools' experiments; I am always making them.

**DAVIES, William H.,** 1871–1940, *English poet and author.*

The more help a man has in his garden, the less it belongs to him.

**DAVIS, Richard Harding,** 1864–1916, *American journalist, war correspondent, and writer.*

No civilized person ever goes to bed the same day he gets up.

**DAWES, Charles Gates,** born 1865, *American financier and statesman.*

American diplomacy is easy on the brain but hell on the feet.

**DEEPING, Warwick,** born 1877, *English novelist.*

1. He sat on the edge of his suspense.
2. He was a simple soul who had not been introduced to his own subconscious.
3. I spent a year in that town, one Sunday.

**DEFFAND, Marquise du,** 1697–1780, *French society leader and letter writer.*

Women are never stronger than when they arm themselves with their weakness.

**DELAVIGNE, Casimir,** 1793–1843, *French poet and playwright.*

Ever since Adam fools have been in the majority.

**DEPEW, Chauncey,** 1834–1928, *American lawyer and after-dinner speaker.*

1. Benefactor: one who makes two smiles grow where one grew before.
2. I get my exercise acting as a pallbearer to my friends who exercise.

**DEWAR, Thomas Robert,** 1864–1930, *British distiller and raconteur.*

1. Confessions may be good for the soul but they are bad for the reputation.

2. Four fifths of the perjury in the world is expended on tombstones, women, and competitors.

3. A husband should tell his wife everything that he is sure she will find out, and before anyone else does.

4. If Adam came on earth again the only thing he would recognize would be the old jokes.

5. It is only the people with push who have a pull.

6. Judge a man not by his clothes, but by his wife's clothes.

7. Lions of society are tigers for publicity.

8. Love is an ocean of emotions, entirely surrounded by expenses.

9. Minds are like parachutes: they only function when open.

10. Nothing deflates so fast as a punctured reputation.

11. No wife can endure a gambling husband unless he is a steady winner.

12. The one thing that hurts more than paying an income tax is not having to pay an income tax.

13. The road to success is filled with women pushing their husbands along.

**DICKENS, Charles, 1812–1870, *English novelist.***

1. Anything for a quiet life, as the man said when he took the situation at the lighthouse.

2. Business first, pleasure afterward, as King Richard said when he stabbed the other king in the Tower, before he smothered the babies.

3. Charity begins at home, and justice begins next door.

4. Credit: a person who can't pay, gets another person who can't pay, to guarantee that he can pay.

5. Do other men, for they would do you; that's the true business precept.

6. Every baby born into the world is a finer one than the last.

7. He'd make a lovely corpse.

8. He had but one eye, and the popular prejudice runs in favor of two.

9. If a pig could give his mind to anything he would not be a pig.

10. If the law thinks it can make a woman do what she's made up her mind not to do, then the law is a bloomin' hass.

11. If there were no bad people, there would be no good lawyers.

12. It is a melancholy truth that even great men have their poor relations.

13. The virtues of mothers shall occasionally be visited upon the children, as well as the sins of the fathers.

14. Regrets are the natural property of gray hairs.

15. She still aims at youth, though she shot beyond it years ago.

16. There are books of which the backs and covers are by far the best parts.

17. There are only two styles of portrait painting: the serious and the smirk.

**DIDEROT, Denis,** 1713–1784, *French philosopher, critic, and encyclopedist.*

The best doctor is the one you run for and can't find.

**DISRAELI, Benjamin,** 1804–1881, *English statesman, novelist, and prime minister.*

1. The author who speaks about his own books is almost as bad as the mother who talks about her own children.

2. The best way to become acquainted with a subject is to write a book about it.

3. The disappointment of manhood succeeds to the delusion of youth.

4. Every man has a right to be conceited until he is successful.

5. Every woman should marry—and no man.

6. He was distinguished for ignorance; for he had only one idea and that was wrong.

7. I am bound to furnish my antagonists with arguments, but not with comprehension.

8. If every man were straightforward in his opinions, there would be no conversation.

9. If you are not very clever, you should be conciliatory.

10. In politics, nothing is contemptible.

11. It is much easier to be critical than to be correct.

12. It is well known what a middleman is: he is a man who bamboozles one party and plunders the other.

13. It often happens that worthless people are merely people who are worth knowing.

14. The magic of first love is our ignorance that it can ever end.

15. A majority is always better than the best repartee.

16. My idea of an agreeable person is a person who agrees with me.

17. Plagiarists, at least, have the merit of preservation.

18. Romance has been elegantly defined as the offspring of fiction and love.

19. She is an excellent creature, but she never can remember which came first, the Greeks or the Romans.

20. Talk to a man about himself and he will listen for hours.

21. There are amusing people who do not interest, and interesting people who do not amuse.

22. There are three kinds of lies: lies, damned lies, and statistics.

23. When a man falls into his anecdotage, it is a sign for him to retire.

24. When I want to read a book I write one.

25. You know who critics are?—the men who have failed in literature and art.

26. Youth is a blunder, manhood a struggle, old age a regret.

**DOUGLAS, Norman,** born 1868, *English author.*

1. Justice is too good for some people, and not good enough for the rest.

2. Many a man who thinks to found a home discovers that he has merely opened a tavern for his friends.

**DUMAS, Alexandre (père),** 1803-1870, *French novelist and dramatist.*

1. The chain of wedlock is so heavy that it takes two to carry it, sometimes three.

2. Economy: the wealth of the poor and the wisdom of the rich.

3. I prefer the wicked rather than the foolish; the wicked sometimes rest.

4. It is often woman who inspires us with the great things that she will prevent us from accomplishing.

5. My father was a Creole, his father a Negro, and his father a monkey; my family, it seems, begins where yours left off.

6. We blame in others only the faults by which we do not profit.

**DUMAS, Alexandre (fils),** 1824-1895, *French dramatist and novelist.*

1. All generalizations are dangerous, even this one.

2. Business? It's quite simple; it's other people's money.

3. A husband is always a sensible man; he never thinks of marrying.

4. The Bible says that the last thing God made was woman; He must have made her on a Saturday night—it shows fatigue.

**DUNNE, Finley Peter,** 1867-1936, *American humorist, creator of "Mr. Dooley."*

1. The American nation in the sixth ward is a fine people; they love the eagle—on the back of a dollar.

2. Capital still pats Labor on the back—with an ax.

3. The Democratic Party ain't on speaking terms with itself.

4. If a man is wise, he gets rich, and if he gets rich, he gets foolish, or his wife does.

5. If Christian Scientists had more science and doctors more Christianity, it wouldn't make any difference which you called in —if you had a good nurse.

6. I think if people marry it ought to be for life; the laws are altogether too lenient with them.

7. A lie with a purpose is one of the worst kind, and the most profitable.

8. Life would not be worth living if we didn't keep our enemies.

9. Many a man that can't direct you to a corner drugstore will get a respectful hearing when age has further impaired his mind.

10. No matter whether the Constitution follows the flag or not, the Supreme Court follows the election returns.

11. One of the strangest things about life is that the poor, who need money the most, are the very ones that never have it.

12. The only good husbands stay bachelors; they're too considerate to get married.

13. The past always looks better than it was; it's only pleasant because it isn't here.

14. Theodore Roosevelt was president of the society of the first man up San Juan Hill.

15. Trust everybody, but cut the cards.

16. Vice is a creature of such hideous mien that the more you see it, the better you like it.

17. What's fame after all? 'Tis apt to be what someone writes on your tombstone.

18. The wise people are in New York because the foolish went there first; that's the way the wise men make a living.

19. Work is work if you're paid to do it, and it's pleasure if you pay to be allowed to do it.

20. You can refuse to love a man or to lend him money, but if he wants to fight you have got to oblige him.

21. A man never becomes an orator if he has anything to say.

22. There are no friends at cards or world politics.

**EASTMAN, Max**, born 1883, *American editor and writer.*

1. A poet in history is divine, but a poet in the next room is a joke.
2. Repartee is a duel fought with the points of jokes.

**EDISON, Thomas Alva**, 1847–1931, *American inventor.*

1. Genius is one per cent inspiration and ninety-nine per cent perspiration.

2. When down in the mouth, remember Jonah: he came out all right.

3. Everything comes to him who hustles while he waits.

**EINSTEIN, Albert,** born 1879, *German-American physicist, developed theory of relativity.*

1. Isn't it strange that I who have written only unpopular books should be such a popular fellow?

2. An empty stomach is not a good political adviser.

**ELDRIDGE, Paul,** born 1888, *American short-story writer, novelist, and poet.*

1. Man is ready to die for an idea, provided that idea is not quite clear to him.

2. Many a crown of wisdom is but the golden chamberpot of success, worn with pompous dignity.

3. Many a necklace becomes a noose.

4. Never to have sinned is the unpardonable sin.

5. Reading the epitaphs, our only salvation lies in resurrecting the dead and burying the living.

6. There are those whose sole claim to profundity is the discovery of exceptions to rules.

**ELIOT, George,** 1819–1880, *pen name of Mary Ann Evans, English novelist.*

1. Animals are such agreeable friends; they ask no questions, they pass no criticisms.

2. An ass may bray a good while before he shakes the stars down.

3. Blessed is the man who, having nothing to say, abstains from giving wordy evidence of the fact.

4. He was like a cock who thought the sun had risen to hear him crow.

5. Ignorance is not so damnable as humbug, but when it prescribes pills it may happen to do more harm.

6. I'm not denying that women are foolish; God Almighty made them to match the men.

7. I'm not one of those as can see the cat in the dairy, and wonder what she's come after.

8. It's hard work to tell which is Old Harry when everybody's got boots on.

9. I've never any pity for conceited people because I think they carry their comfort about with them.

10. She is like the rest of the women—thinks two and two'll come to make five, if she cries and bothers enough about it.

11. There is nothing will kill a man so soon as having nobody to find fault with but himself.

**ELLIS, Havelock,** 1859-1939, *English scientist and writer.*

1. Civilized men arrived in the Pacific, armed with alcohol, syphilis, trousers, and the Bible.

2. Heroes exterminate each other for the benefit of people who are not heroes.

3. The place where optimism most flourishes is the lunatic asylum.

4. A religion can no more afford to degrade its Devil than to degrade its God.

5. To be a leader of men one must turn one's back on men.

6. What we call progress is the exchange of one nuisance for another nuisance.

7. The whole religious complexion of the modern world is due to the absence from Jerusalem of a lunatic asylum.

**EMERSON, Ralph Waldo,** 1803-1882, *American essayist, poet, and philosopher.*

1. And what is a weed? A plant whose virtues have not been discovered.

2. Conversation is an art in which a man has all mankind for competitors.

3. We do not count a man's years until he has nothing else to count.

4. Culture is one thing and varnish another.

5. Cunning egotism: if I cannot brag of knowing something, then I brag of not knowing it; at any rate, brag.

6. Democracy becomes a government of bullies tempered by editors.

7. Do what we can, summer will have its flies.

8. The end of the human race will be that it will eventually die of civilization.

9. Every hero becomes a bore at last.

10. Every man is an impossibility until he is born.

11. Every man is wanted, and no man is wanted much.

12. Every Stoic was a Stoic; but in Christendom, where is the Christian?

13. Fame is proof that the people are gullible.

14. Few envy the consideration enjoyed by the oldest inhabitant.

15. The first lesson of history is the good of evil.

16. A hero is no braver than an ordinary man, but he is brave five minutes longer.

17. If a man own land, the land owns him.

18. It is an amiable illusion, which the shape of our planet prompts, that every man is at the top of the world.

19. It is easy to live for others; everybody does.

20. Keep cool: it will be all one a hundred years hence.

21. Let us treat men and women well; treat them as if they were real; perhaps they are.

22. The louder he talked of his honor, the faster we counted our spoons.

23. A man of no conversation should smoke.

24. Many might go to heaven with half the labor they go to hell.

25. Men are conservative after dinner.

26. Men lose their tempers in defending their taste.

27. Men wish to be saved from the mischiefs of their vices, but not from their vices.

28. Money often costs too much.

29. My cow milks me.

30. People do not deserve to have good writing, they are so pleased with the bad.

31. A person seldom falls sick, but the bystanders are animated with a faint hope that he will die.

32. Society is a hospital of incurables.

33. The solar system has no anxiety about its reputation.

34. Speech is better than silence; silence is better than speech.

35. Take egotism out, and you would castrate the benefactors.

36. That which we call sin in others is experiment for us.
37. There is this benefit in brag, that the speaker is unconsciously expressing his own ideal.
38. Truth is beautiful without doubt, and so are lies.
39. We are always getting ready to live, but never living.
40. The people are to be taken in very small doses.
41. Once we had wooden chalices and golden priests; now we have golden chalices and wooden priests.

**ERSKINE, John,** born 1879, *American educator and writer.*

Most people have some sort of religion, at least they know which church they're staying away from.

**ERTZ, Susan,** born 1894?, *American novelist and short-story writer.*

1. He talked with more claret than clarity.
2. Millions long for immortality who do not know what to do with themselves on a rainy Sunday afternoon.

**ERVINE, St. John,** born 1883, *Irish playwright, novelist, and miscellaneous writer.*

1. American motion pictures are written by the half-educated for the half-witted.
2. No one can fully appreciate the fatuity of human nature until he has spent some time in a box office.

**FABRE, Jean Henri,** 1823–1915, *French entomologist.*

History records the names of royal bastards, but cannot tell us the origin of wheat.

**FADIMAN, Clifton,** born 1904, *American editor, writer, lecturer, and radio entertainer.*

1. Born in a log cabin, Ambrose Bierce defied Alger's Law and did not become President.
2. It is of such stuff and nonsense that dreams are made on.
3. Gertrude Stein is the mama of dada.

**FARQUHAR, George,** 1678–1707, *British dramatist.*

1. There's no form of prayer in the liturgy against bad husbands.

2. 'Tis a strange thing that among us people can't agree the whole week because they go different ways upon Sundays.

3. When the blind lead the blind, they both fall into—matrimony.

**FÉNELON, François,** 1651–1715, *French archbishop and writer.*

The more you say, the less people remember.

**FERBER, Edna,** born 1887, *American novelist, short-story writer, and playwright.*

Being an old maid is like death by drowning, a really delightful sensation after you cease to struggle.

**FIELD, Eugene,** 1850–1895, *American journalist, poet, and humorist.*

1. The actor who took the role of King Lear played the king as though he expected someone to play the ace.

2. The biggest fish he ever caught were those that got away.

3. He is so mean, he won't let his little baby have more than one measle at a time.

4. The size of a woman's stomach depends largely on her surroundings.

5. Any color, so long as it's red, is the color that suits me best.

**FIELDING, Henry,** 1707–1754, *English novelist.*

1. Beauty seldom recommends one woman to another.

2. Every physician almost hath his favorite disease.

3. His designs were strictly honorable; that is, to rob a lady of her fortune by way of marriage.

4. How easy it is for a man to die rich, if he will but be contented to live miserable.

5. Love and scandal are the best sweeteners of tea.

6. Money is the fruit of evil as often as the root of it.

7. Money will say more in one moment than the most eloquent lover can in years.

8. There's one fool at least in every married couple.

9. Some folks rail against other folks because other folks have what some folks would be glad of.

10. When children are doing nothing, they are doing mischief.

**FISCHER, Martin Henry,** born 1879, *American scientist, author, and educator.*

1. The greatest discoveries of surgery are anesthesia, asepsis, and roentgenology—and none was discovered by a surgeon.

2. Half the modern drugs could well be thrown out the window, except that the birds might eat them.

3. I teach only the truth—but that shouldn't make you believe it.

4. Many a diabetic has stayed alive by stealing the bread denied him by his doctor.

5. The popular concept of a strengthening diet is a chicken wrung out in hot water.

6. We humans are the greatest of the earth's parasites.

**FISHBEIN, Morris,** born 1889, *American medical editor and writer.*

He is an expert surgeon, brilliant pathologist, and an uncanny diagnostician, but he is somewhat rusty on advanced cigarette testimonials.

**FLAMMARION, Camille,** 1842–1925, *French astronomer.*

There are men who would even be afraid to commit themselves on the doctrine that castor oil is a laxative.

**FONTENELLE, Le Bovier de,** 1657–1757, *French writer.*

1. There are three things I have always loved and never understood —art, music, and women.

2. A philosopher will not believe what he sees because he is too busy speculating about what he does not see.

**FOOTE, Samuel,** 1720–1777, *English actor and dramatist.*

He is not only dull himself but the cause of dullness in others.

**FORBES, Esther,** born 1894?, *American novelist.*

He was so narrow-minded he could see through a keyhole with two eyes.

**FORD, Corey,** born 1902, *American author.*

1. I would rather fish than eat, particularly eat fish.
2. She's learned to say things with her eyes that others waste time putting into words.

**FRANCE, Anatole,** 1844–1924, *pen name of Jacques Anatole Thibault, French novelist and critic.*

1. The absurdity of a religious practice may be clearly demonstrated without lessening the number of persons who indulge in it.
2. Chance is the pseudonym of God when He did not want to sign.
3. Everything is not known but everything is said.
4. He despises men with tenderness.
5. History books which contain no lies are extremely dull.
6. If fifty million people say a foolish thing, it is still a foolish thing.
7. It is better to understand a little than to misunderstand a lot.
8. It is in the ability to deceive oneself that the greatest talent is shown.
9. The law, in its majestic equality, forbids the rich as well as the poor to sleep under bridges, to beg in the streets, and to steal bread.
10. Never lend books, for no one ever returns them; the only books I have in my library are books that other folk have lent me.
11. Of all the ways of defining man, the worst is the one which makes him out to be a rational animal.
12. Only men who are not interested in women are interested in women's clothes; men who like women never notice what they wear.
13. People who have no faults are terrible; there is no way of taking advantage of them.

14. Religion has done love a great service by making it a sin.

15. There are very honest people who do not think that they have had a bargain unless they have cheated a merchant.

16. We do not know what to do with this short life, yet we want another which will be eternal.

17. We reproach people for talking about themselves; but it is the subject they treat best.

18. A woman must choose: with a man liked by women, she is not sure; with a man disliked by women, she is not happy.

19. The books that everybody admires are those that nobody reads.

20. A writer is rarely so well inspired as when he talks about himself.

**FRANKLIN**, Benjamin, 1706–1790, *American statesman, author, scientist, inventor, and philosopher.*

1. The absent are never without fault, nor the present without excuse.

2. All would live long, but none would be old.

3. Anger is never without a reason, but seldom with a good one.

4. Clean your finger before you point at my spots.

5. Clearly spoken, Mr. Fogg; you explain English by Greek.

6. Creditors have better memories than debtors.

7. The first mistake in public business is the going into it.

8. God heals, and the doctor takes the fee.

9. God works wonders now and then; behold, a lawyer, an honest man.

10. Here comes the orator, with his flood of words and his drop of reason.

11. He's the best physician that knows the worthlessness of the most medicines.

12. He that falls in love with himself will have no rivals.

13. He that is good for making excuses is seldom good for anything else.

14. He that teaches himself hath a fool for a master.

15. He was so learned that he could name a horse in nine languages; so ignorant that he bought a cow to ride on.

16. His conversation does not show the minute hand, but he strikes the hour very correctly.

17. If a man could have half his wishes, he would double his troubles.

18. If men are so wicked with religion, what would they be without it?

19. If your riches are yours, why don't you take them with you to the other world?

20. If you would keep a secret from an enemy, tell it not to a friend.

21. If you would know the value of money, go and try to borrow some.

22. If you would lose a troublesome visitor, lend him money.

23. An infallible remedy for toothache: wash the root of an aching tooth in vinegar, and let it dry half an hour in the sun.

24. Keep your eyes wide open before marriage, and half-shut afterwards.

25. The learned fool writes his nonsense in better language than the unlearned, but still 'tis nonsense.

26. Love your enemies, for they tell you your faults.

27. Love your neighbor, yet don't pull down your hedge.

28. Mankind are very odd creatures: one half censure what they practice, the other half practice what they censure.

29. Many a man would have been worse if his estate had been better.

30. Ne'er take a wife till thou hast a house (and a fire) to put her in.

31. Neither a fortress nor a maidenhead withhold out long after they begin to parley.

32. None preaches better than the ant, and she says nothing.

33. One good husband is worth two good wives; for the scarcer things are, the more they're valued.

34. Onions can make even heirs and widows weep.

35. Rich widows are the only secondhand goods that sell at first-class prices.

36. Samson with his strong body had a weak head, or he would not have laid it in a harlot's lap.

37. Savages we call them because their manners differ from ours.

38. She laughs at everything you say. Why? Because she has fine teeth.

39. Strange that a man who has wit enough to write a satire should have folly enough to publish it.

40. Teach your child to hold his tongue; he'll learn fast enough to speak.

41. There are more old drunkards than old doctors.

42. There are three faithful friends—an old wife, an old dog, and ready money.

43. There is much difference between imitating a good man and counterfeiting him.

44. Three may keep a secret if two of them are dead.

45. 'Tis against some men's principle to pay interest, and seems against others' interest to pay the principal.

46. To bear other people's afflictions, everyone has courage and enough to spare.

47. To find out a girl's faults, praise her to her girl friends.

48. What maintains one vice would bring up two children.

49. The proud hate pride—in others.

## FRAZER, James George, 1854-1941, *Scottish anthropologist.*

Men make Gods, and women worship them.

## FREDERICK the Great, 1712-1786, *King of Prussia.*

1. A German singer! I should as soon expect to get pleasure from the neighing of my horse.

2. If I wished to punish a province, I would have it governed by philosophers.

3. They say kings are made in the image of God; I feel sorry for God if that is what he looks like.

## FROST, Robert, born 1875, *American poet.*

1. A bank is a place where they lend you an umbrella in fair weather and ask for it back again when it begins to rain.

2. The best way out is always through.

3. The brain is a wonderful organ; it starts working the moment you get up in the morning, and does not stop until you get into the office.

4. By working faithfully eight hours a day, you may eventually get to be a boss and work twelve hours a day.

5. The difference between a man and his valet: they both smoke the same cigars, but only one pays for them.

6. A diplomat is a man who always remembers a woman's birthday but never remembers her age.

7. Half the world is composed of people who have something to say and can't, and the other half who have nothing to say and keep on saying it.

8. Home is the place where, when you have to go there, they have to take you in.

9. It's a funny thing that when a man hasn't got anything on earth to worry about, he goes off and gets married.

10. A jury consists of twelve persons chosen to decide who has the better lawyer.

11. A man will sometimes devote all his life to the development of one part of his body—the wishbone.

12. A mother takes twenty years to make a man of her boy, and another woman makes a fool of him in twenty minutes.

13. The reason why worry kills more people than work is that more people worry than work.

14. A receiver is appointed by the court to take what's left.

15. A successful lawsuit is the one worn by a policeman.

16. There is one thing more exasperating than a wife who can cook and won't, and that's the wife who can't cook and will.

17. Time and tide wait for no man, but time always stands still for a woman of thirty.

18. The world is full of willing people; some willing to work, the rest willing to let them.

19. Writing free verse is like playing tennis with the net down.

**GALSWORTHY, John,** 1867–1933, *English novelist, playwright, and short-story writer.*

1. For a man who can't see an inch into human nature, give me a psychological novelist.
2. The French cook; we open tins.
3. He's not worth my wiles.
4. Idealism increases in direct proportion to one's distance from the problem.

**GALTON, Francis,** 1822–1911, *English scientist.*

Well-washed and well-combed domestic pets grow dull; they miss the stimulus of fleas.

**GAY, John,** 1685–1732, *English poet and dramatist.*

1. The comfortable estate of widowhood is the only hope that keeps up a wife's spirits.
2. Men were born to lie, and women to believe them.
3. Those who in quarrels interpose must often wipe a bloody nose.
4. Do you think your mother and I should have lived comfortably so long together if ever we had been married?

**GERALDY, Paul,** born 1885, *French poet and playwright.*

1. As soon as you cannot keep anything from a woman, you love her.
2. Generally the woman chooses the man who will choose her.
3. It is well to love; not to love any more is well also.
4. Love is the effort a man makes to be satisfied with only one woman.
5. Women are not virtuous but they have given us the idea of virtue.
6. You leave your family for the sake of love to create another family which you may leave someday for another love.

**GIBBON, Edward,** 1737–1794, *English historian.*

1. The appellation of heretics has always been applied to the less numerous party.

2. Unprovided with original learning, unformed in the habits of thinking, unskilled in the arts of composition, I resolved—to write a book.

**GIBBS, Philip,** born 1877, *English journalist and novelist.*

It's better to give than to lend, and it costs about the same.

**GIBBS, Wolcott,** born 1902, *American writer and critic.*

He wasn't exactly hostile to facts but he was apathetic about them.

**GIBRAN, Kahlil,** 1883–1931, *Syrian-American poet and painter.*

An exaggeration is a truth that has lost its temper.

**GIDE, André,** born 1869, *French critic, translator, and miscellaneous writer.*

Art is a collaboration between God and the artist, and the less the artist does the better.

**GILBERT, William Schwenck,** 1836–1911, *English humorous poet and playwright, collaborator in operas with Arthur Sullivan.*

1. He did nothing in particular, and did it very well.

2. In all the woes that curse our race, there is a lady in the case.

3. Isn't your life extremely flat with nothing whatever to grumble at?

4. It isn't so much what's on the table that matters, as what's on the chairs.

5. Life's perhaps the only riddle that we shrink from giving up.

6. Man is nature's sole mistake.

7. No one can have a higher opinion of him than I have—and I think he is a dirty little beast.

8. She may very well pass for forty-three in the dusk with a light behind her.

9. You've no idea what a poor opinion I have of myself, and how little I deserve it.

**GLASGOW, Ellen,** born 1874, *American novelist.*

1. In her single person she managed to produce the effect of a majority.

2. The only difference between a rut and a grave is their dimensions.

**GLASS, Montague,** 1877–1934, *English-American playwright and short-story writer.*

She was a singer who had to take any note above A with her eyebrows.

**GOETHE, Johann Wolfgang von,** 1749–1832, *German poet, dramatist, and miscellaneous writer.*

1. Children, like dogs, have so sharp a scent that they detect everything—the bad before all the rest.
2. Everything in the world may be endured except continual prosperity.
3. I give presents to the mother, but I think of the daughter.
4. Of the best society it used to be said: its conversation affords instruction, but its silence imparts culture.
5. Some people spend the day in complaining of a headache, and the night in drinking the wine that gives it.
6. What must the English and French think of the language of our philosophers when we Germans do not understand it ourselves?
7. If children grew up according to early indications, we should have nothing but geniuses.

**GOLDBERG, Isaac,** 1887–1938, *American critic, essayist, biographer, and short-story writer.*

1. Diplomacy is to do and say the nastiest thing in the nicest way.
2. A gigolo is a fee-male.
3. The Good, the True, the Beautiful! Alas, the Good is so often untrue, the True so often unbeautiful, the Beautiful so often not good.
4. Grammar school never taught me anything about grammar.
5. I do not believe today everything I believed yesterday; I wonder will I believe tomorrow everything I believe today.
6. We spend half our lives unlearning the follies transmitted to us by our parents, and the other half transmitting our own follies to our offspring.

7. A woman tries to get all she can out of a man, and a man tries to get all he can into a woman.

**GOLDSMITH, Oliver,** 1728–1774, *British poet, novelist, and playwright.*

1. Every absurdity has a champion to defend it.
2. He writes indexes to perfection.
3. I always get the better when I argue alone.
4. People seldom improve when they have no model but themselves to copy.
5. There is nothing so absurd or ridiculous that has not at some time been said by some philosopher.

**GONCOURT, Edmond de,** 1822–1896, *French author and artist.*

Genius is the talent of a man who is dead.

**GOURMONT, Remy de,** 1858–1915, *French novelist, critic, and philosopher.*

1. Before undergoing a surgical operation arrange your temporal affairs—you may live.
2. For two thousand years Christianity has been telling us: life is death, death is life; it is high time to consult the dictionary.
3. God is not all that exists; God is all that does not exist.
4. Good books are irrefutable, and bad books refute themselves.
5. It happens in life, as in grammar, that the exceptions outnumber the rules.
6. Man begins by making love and ends by loving a woman; woman begins by loving a man and ends by loving love.
7. Man has made use of his intelligence; he invented stupidity.
8. Most men who run down women are only running down a certain woman.
9. Of all sexual aberrations, perhaps the most peculiar is chastity.
10. Property is necessary, but it is not necessary that it should remain forever in the same hands.
11. Religions revolve madly around sexual questions.
12. The terrible thing about the quest for truth is that you find it.

13. To know what everybody knows is to know nothing.

14. Very simple ideas lie within the reach only of complex minds.

15. The woman one loves always smells good.

16. A woman sometimes feels pity for the sorrows that she causes without remorse.

17. Women are like the gentlemen of Molière's time; they know everything without having learned anything.

18. Women still remember the first kiss after men have forgotten the last.

**GRANT, Ulysses Simpson,** 1822-1885, *American general and President of the United States.*

I know only two tunes; one of them is "Yankee Doodle," and the other isn't.

**GREELEY, Horace,** 1811-1872, *American journalist.*

1. I never said all Democrats were saloonkeepers; what I said was all saloonkeepers were Democrats.

2. Journalism will kill you, but it will keep you alive while you're at it.

**GUEDALLA, Philip,** 1889-1944, *English biographer and historian.*

1. Any stigma will do to beat a dogma.

2. Biography is a region bounded on the north by history, on the south by fiction, on the east by obituary, and on the west by tedium.

3. History repeats itself; historians repeat each other.

4. The twentieth century is only the nineteenth speaking with a slightly American accent.

5. He gives thanks that Britons never will be Slavs.

6. He holds the mirror up to Nietzsche.

7. Henry James had three reigns: James I, James II, and the Old Pretender.

**GUNTHER, John,** born 1901, *American journalist and author.*

The famous politician was trying to save both his faces.

**HALDANE, John B. S.,** born 1892, *British scientist.*

1. Even the ugliest human exteriors may contain the most beautiful viscera.

2. I've never met a healthy person who worried much about his health, or a good person who worried much about his soul.

**HALIBURTON, Thomas Chandler,** 1796-1865, *Canadian jurist and humorist, creator of "Sam Slick."*

1. A college education shows a man how little other people know.

2. Every woman is wrong until she cries, and then she is right, instantly.

3. Some people have a perfect genius for doing nothing, and doing it assiduously.

4. The Spaniards have it that a buxom widow must be either married, buried, or shut up in a convent.

5. Time is like a woman and pigs; the more you want it to go, the more it won't.

**HALIFAX, George Savile, Marquis of,** 1633-1695, *English statesman and essayist.*

1. The best qualification of a prophet is to have a good memory.

2. By the time men are fit for company, they see the objections to it.

3. Education is what remains when we have forgotten all that we have been taught.

4. If the laws could speak for themselves, they would complain of the lawyers in the first place.

5. The struggling for knowledge hath a pleasure in it like that of wrestling with a fine woman.

6. There are hardly two creatures of a more differing species than the same man when pretending to a place and when in possession of it.

7. When the people contend for their liberty they seldom get anything by their victory but new masters.

8. A wife is to thank God her husband has faults; a husband without faults is a dangerous observer.

9. The vanity of teaching doth oft tempt a man to forget that he is a blockhead.

**HALSEY, Margaret,** born 1910, *American writer.*

1. He must have had a magnificent build before his stomach went in for a career of its own.

2. His handshake ought not to be used except as a tourniquet.

**HARDY, Thomas,** 1840–1928, *English novelist and poet.*

That man's silence is wonderful to listen to.

**HARRIS, Joel Chandler,** 1848–1908, *American writer, creator of "Uncle Remus."*

1. Liquor talks mighty loud when it gets loose from the jug.

2. The rooster makes more racket than the hen that lays the egg.

3. Watch out when you're getting all you want; fattening hogs ain't in luck.

**HAY, Ian,** born 1876, *pen name of John Hay Beith, Scottish novelist and dramatist.*

Marriage is a ghastly public confession of a strictly private intention.

**HAY, John,** 1838–1905, *American statesman and writer.*

There are three species of creatures who when they seem coming are going, when they seem going they come: diplomats, women, and crabs.

**HAYS, Arthur Garfield,** born 1881, *American lawyer.*

1. Desertion—the poor man's method of divorce.

2. When there's a rift in the lute, the business of the lawyer is to widen the rift and gather the loot.

**HAZLITT, William,** 1778–1830, *English critic, essayist, and lecturer.*

1. Actors are the only honest hypocrites.

2. Discussing the characters and foibles of common friends is a great sweetener and cementer of friendship.

3. Fashion is gentility running away from vulgarity, and afraid of being overtaken.

4. The greatest offense against virtue is to speak ill of it.

5. He who comes up to his own idea of greatness must always have had a very low standard of it in his mind.

6. If mankind had wished for what is right, they might have had it long ago.

7. If the world were good for nothing else, it is a fine subject for speculation.

8. I like a friend the better for having faults that one can talk about.

9. It is better to be able neither to read nor write than to be able to do nothing else.

10. It is essential to the triumph of reform that it should never succeed.

11. Silence is one great art of conversation.

12. Some persons make promises for the pleasure of breaking them.

13. There are names written in her immortal scroll at which Fame blushes.

14. There is a division of labor, even in vice; some persons addict themselves to the speculation only, others to the practice.

15. Those who are fond of setting things to rights have no great objection to seeing them wrong.

16. The vices are never so well employed as in combating one another.

17. We are not satisfied to be right, unless we can prove others to be quite wrong.

18. There is nothing so pedantic as pretending not to be pedantic.

**HECHT, Ben,** born 1894, *American novelist, playwright, short-story writer, and motion-picture director.*

1. Any views are unimportant, if they are held about women by a man past forty.

2. I'm a Hollywood writer; so I put on a sports jacket and take off my brain.

**HEGEL, Georg Wilhelm Friedrich,** 1770–1831, *German philosopher.*

1. The people are that part of the state which does not know what it wants.

2. We learn from history that we do not learn from history.

**HEINE, Heinrich,** 1797–1856, *German poet, critic, wit, and miscellaneous writer.*

1. A blaspheming Frenchman is a spectacle more pleasing to the Lord than a praying Englishman.

2. As soon as Eve ate the apple of wisdom, she reached for the fig leaf; when a woman begins to think, her first thought is of a new dress.

3. God will forgive me; that's his business.

4. I fell asleep reading a dull book, and I dreamt that I was reading on, so I awoke from sheer boredom.

5. If the Romans had been obliged to learn Latin, they would never have found time to conquer the world.

6. I have never seen an ass who talked like a human being, but I have met many human beings who talked like asses.

7. I will not say that women have no character; rather, they have a new one every day.

8. One should forgive one's enemies, but not before they are hanged.

9. *De mortuis nil nisi bonum;* of the living speak nothing but evil.

10. The Hanoverian squires are asses who can talk of nothing but horses.

11. The music at a marriage procession always reminds me of the music of soldiers marching to battle.

12. She resembles the Venus de Milo: she is very old, has no teeth, and has white spots on her yellow skin.

13. I do not know if she was virtuous, but she was ugly, and with a woman that is half the battle.

14. Ordinarily he was insane, but he had lucid moments when he was merely stupid.

**HELPS, Arthur,** 1813–1875, *English historian.*

1. The absence of humility in critics is something wonderful.
2. The worst use that can be made of success is to boast of it.

**HENDERSON, Leon,** born 1895, *American economist.*

A little inflation is like a little pregnancy—it keeps on growing.

**HENRY, O.,** 1862–1910, *pen name of William Sydney Porter, American short-story writer.*

1. Life is made up of sobs, sniffles, and smiles, with sniffles predominating.
2. A straw vote only shows which way the hot air blows.

**HERBERT, Alan Patrick,** born 1890, *English journalist and writer.*

A highbrow is the kind of person who looks at a sausage and thinks of Picasso.

**HERFORD, Oliver,** 1863–1935, *American humorous writer and illustrator.*

1. Actresses will happen in the best-regulated families.
2. Alas: early Victorian for *oh, hell.*
3. Bigamy is one way of avoiding the painful publicity of divorce and the expense of alimony.
4. Cat: a pygmy lion who loves mice, hates dogs, and patronizes human beings.
5. Charity is the sterilized milk of human kindness.
6. A woman's mind is cleaner than a man's; she changes it more often.
7. Darling: the popular form of address used in speaking to a person of the opposite sex whose name you cannot at the moment recall.
8. Detour: something that lengthens your mileage, diminishes your gas, and strengthens your vocabulary.
9. Dilettante: a philanderer who seduces the several arts and deserts each in turn for another.
10. Diplomacy: lying in state.

11. Zoo: a place devised for animals to study the habits of human beings.
12. A hair in the head is worth two in the brush.
13. I don't recall your name, but your manners are familiar.
14. If some people got their rights they would complain of being deprived of their wrongs.
15. In one's old coterie may one sport the old pantry and vestry.
16. In the midst of life we are in Brooklyn.
17. It's a strong stomach that has no turning.
18. Jade: a semi-precious stone or a semi-precious woman.
19. Jehovah has always seemed to me the most fascinating character in all fiction.
20. Liar: one who tells an unpleasant truth.
21. Lisp: to call a spade a thpade.
22. Junk is anything that has outlived its usefulness.
23. Lots of people have matrimonial troubles and don't know it.
24. A man is known by the silence he keeps.
25. Manuscript: something submitted in haste and returned at leisure.
26. Many are called but few get up.
27. Modesty: the gentle art of enhancing your charm by pretending not to be aware of it.
28. Monaco is the center of the spinning industry of the world.
29. Money makes the mayor go.
30. The more waist, the less speed.
31. My wife has a whim of iron.
32. No one knows the worth of woman's love till he sues for alienation.
33. Nothing succeeds like—failure.
34. Only the young die good.
35. People who live in glass houses should pull down the blinds.
36. Perhaps it was because Nero played the fiddle, they burned Rome.
37. A rolling stone gathers no moss, but it gains a certain polish.

38. A soft drink turneth away company.

39. Song: the licensed medium for bawling in public things too silly or sacred to be uttered in ordinary speech.

40. There are more fish taken out of a stream than ever were in it.

41. There is no time like the pleasant.

42. There's always room at the top—after the investigation.

43. There's none so blind as those who won't fee.

44. What can't be cured must be insured.

45. What is my loftiest ambition? I've always wanted to throw an egg into an electric fan.

**HERODOTUS,** 484?–425 B.C., *Greek historian.*

Very few things happen at the right time, and the rest do not happen at all; the conscientious historian will correct these defects.

**HEROLD, Don,** born 1889, *American humorous writer and artist.*

1. Women give us solace, but if it were not for women we should never need solace.

2. Work is a form of nervousness.

3. At its present cost, life is worth about thirty cents on the dollar.

4. Before the advent of the radio, there were advantages in being a shut-in.

5. Be good, even at the cost of your self-respect.

6. Be kind and considerate to others, depending somewhat upon who they are.

7. Be kind to dumb people.

8. The brighter you are, the more you have to learn.

9. The chief trouble with jazz is that there is not enough of it; some of it we have to listen to twice.

10. Comic-strip artists do not make good husbands, and God knows they do not make good comic strips.

11. Conversation is the slowest form of human communication.

12. Doctors know what you tell them.

13. Doctors think a lot of patients are cured who have simply quit in disgust.

14. Electric fans should be resharpened every season.

15. Everything in life is fairly simple except one's wife.

16. Funerals are a lost art in the big cities.

17. Genius is an infinite capacity for giving pains.

18. Gentlemen prefer blondes, but take what they can get.

19. Guides have annoyed me so, that today I killed one and am having him stuffed for our trophy room.

20. Hollywood—out where the Sex begins.

21. You cannot philosophize your life and live it too.

22. A humorist is a man who feels bad but who feels good about it.

23. I do not believe in doing for pleasure things I do not like to do.

24. I had, out of my sixty teachers, a scant half dozen who couldn't have been supplanted by phonographs.

25. Intellectuals should never marry; they won't enjoy it, and besides, they should not reproduce themselves.

26. Work is the greatest thing in the world, so we should always save some of it for tomorrow.

27. I say banish bridge; let's find some pleasanter way of being miserable together.

28. It is a good thing that life is not as serious as it seems to a waiter.

29. It is but a few short years from diapers to dignity and from dignity to decomposition.

30. It's easier to be a Bernard Shaw to the British or American public than it is to be a Bernard Shaw to your own family.

31. It takes a lot of things to prove you are smart, but only one thing to prove you are ignorant.

32. It takes a lot of time to be sentimental.

33. I wish I were either rich enough or poor enough to do a lot of things that are impossible in my present comfortable circumstances.

34. I would rather sing grand opera than listen to it.

35. Jesus was a bachelor.

36. Women have a wonderful sense of right and wrong, but little sense of right and left.

37. Lord, spare me from sickly women and healthy men!

38. A lot of men think that if they smile for a second, somebody will take advantage of them, and they are right.

39. A lot of women are getting alimony who don't earn it.

40. A man can't have his soul and save it too.

41. Man is the only animal that plays poker.

42. Many people have character who have nothing else.

43. Marriage: a woman's hair net tangled in a man's spectacles on top of the bedroom dresser.

44. Marriage is a mistake of youth—which we should all make.

45. Marriage is an honorable agreement among men as to their conduct toward women, and it was devised by women.

46. Marriage, like death, is nothing to worry about.

47. Married men live longer than single men, or at least they complain more about it.

48. Marry one woman and you get six.

49. Mens' wives are usually their husbands' mental inferiors and spiritual superiors; this gives them double instruments of torture.

50. Methods of locomotion have improved greatly in recent years, but places to go remain about the same.

51. Moralizing and morals are two entirely different things and are always found in entirely different people.

52. "The more articulate, the less said" is an old Chinese proverb which I just made up myself.

53. Most wives are nicer than their husbands, but that's nothing; I am nice to everybody from whom I get money.

54. No woman should have enough clothes to make her ask, "What'll I wear?"

55. Oh, what a tangled web we weave when first we practice to conceive.

56. One thing this country needs is a clearinghouse for coat hangers.

57. Pleasure is more trouble than trouble.

58. Poverty must have many satisfactions, else there would not be so many poor people.

59. The road to hell is thick with taxicabs.

60. She's the kind of person who spends extra money for a stateroom on a Pullman for privacy, and then leaves her door open for publicity.

61. The short skirts of today reveal the malnutrition of yesterday.

62. Some people have had nothing else but experience.

63. Sophistication: knowing enough to keep your feet out of the crack of the theater seat in front of you.

64. Thank God few people live as they believe.

65. There is little use to talk about your child to anyone; other people either have one or haven't.

66. There is more sophistication and less sense in New York than anywhere else on the globe.

67. There is nobody so irritating as somebody with less intelligence and more sense than we have.

68. There is nothing distinctive about living in New York; over eight million other people are doing it.

69. There's no reason why any child should lack a complete knowledge of life, since there is no censorship of drugstore windows.

70. There's one thing about baldness: it's neat.

71. Thought itself is probably a superstition.

72. Unhappiness is in not knowing what we want and killing ourselves to get it.

73. Very few people look the part and are it too.

74. We will hereafter believe less history than ever, now that we have seen how it is made.

75. What do you suppose God thinks of a man (created in His own image) putting on his pants in an upper berth?

76. What is home without a hot-water bottle?

77. When one has had to work so hard to get money, why should he impose on himself the further hardship of trying to save it?

78. When you take baby to church or on the train, be sure to have plenty of cookies and chloroform.

79. Why resist temptation—there will always be more.

80. Women are not much, but they are the best other sex we have.

**HIRSCHFELD, Magnus,** 1868–1935, *German psychiatrist and sexologist.*

Love is a conflict between reflexes and reflections.

**HOBBES, Thomas,** 1588–1679, *English philosopher.*

If I had read as much as other men, I should have known no more than other men.

**HOFFENSTEIN, Samuel,** 1890–1947, *American humorous poet and scenarist.*

1. Breathes there a man with hide so tough, who says two sexes aren't enough?
2. What a lucky thing the wheel was invented before the automobile; otherwise, can you imagine the awful screeching?

**HOLMES, Oliver Wendell,** 1809–1894, *American author, physician, and humorist.*

1. All men are bores, except when we want them.
2. Apology is only egotism wrong side out.
3. The bore is the same eating dates under the cedars of Lebanon as over baked beans in Beacon Street.
4. A child's education should begin at least one hundred years before he is born.
5. Easy-crying widows take new husbands soonest; there's nothing like wet weather for transplanting.
6. Everybody likes and respects self-made men; it's a great deal better to be made that way than not to be made at all.
7. Every library should try to be complete on something, if it were only the history of pinheads.
8. Fate tried to conceal him by naming him Smith.
9. Give us the luxuries of life and we will dispense with necessaries.
10. Heredity is an omnibus in which all our ancestors ride, and every now and then one of them puts his head out and embarrasses us.

11. How many people live on the reputation of the reputation they might have made.

12. Humility is the first of the virtues—for other people.

13. I have always considered my face a convenience rather than an ornament.

14. Life is a fatal complaint, and an eminently contagious one.

15. Man has his will, but woman has her way.

16. Man wants but little here below, but wants that little strong.

17. The man who is always worrying whether or not his soul would be damned generally has a soul that isn't worth a damn.

18. Nature, when she invented, manufactured, and patented her authors, contrived to make critics out of the chips that were left.

19. One has to dismount from an idea and get into saddle again at every parenthesis.

20. Pink Tea: Giggle, Gabble, Gobble, Git.

21. Pretty much all the honest truthtelling there is in the world is done by children.

22. Self-abnegation is a rare virtue that good men preach and good women practice.

23. To be seventy years young is sometimes far more cheerful and hopeful than to be forty years old.

24. Why can't somebody give us a list of things that everybody thinks and nobody says, and another list of things that everybody says and nobody thinks?

25. What I call a good patient is one who, having found a good physician, sticks to him till he dies.

**HOOD, Thomas,** 1799–1845, *English poet and humorist.*

1. Extremes meet, as the whiting said with its tail in its mouth.

2. Holland lies so low, they're only saved by being damned.

3. Homemade dishes drive one from home.

4. I don't set up for being a cosmopolite, which to my mind signifies being polite to every country except your own.

5. There are three things which the public will always clamor for sooner or later, namely, novelty, novelty, novelty.

**HOPE, Anthony,** 1863–1933, *pen name of Anthony Hope Hawkins, English novelist and dramatist.*

1. Economy is going without something you do want, in case you should someday want something which you probably won't want.
2. Good families are generally worse than others.
3. Your ignorance cramps my conversation.
4. Telling the truth to people who misunderstand you is generally promoting a falsehood, isn't it?
5. Unless one is a genius, it is best to aim at being intelligible.

**HOUSMAN, Alfred Edward,** 1859–1936, *English poet and classical scholar.*

He drank like a fish, if drinking nothing but water could be so described.

**HOUSSAYE, Arsène,** 1815–1896, *French writer of fiction, verse, criticism, and history.*

A woman forgives only when she is in the wrong.

**HOWE, Edgar Watson ("Ed"),** 1853–1937, *American journalist and author.*

1. About all some men accomplish in life is to send a son to Harvard.
2. About the only thing on a farm that has an easy time is the dog.
3. The average man's judgment is so poor, he runs a risk every time he uses it.
4. A bad woman raises hell with a good many men while a good woman raises hell with only one.
5. Be careful, and you will save many men from the sin of robbing you.
6. So far as is known, no widow ever eloped.
7. Don't abuse your friends and expect them to consider it criticism.
8. Don't take up a man's time talking about the smartness of your children; he wants to talk to you about the smartness of his children.

9. Don't tell a good story even though you know one; its narration will simply remind your hearers of a bad one.

10. Even if a farmer intends to loaf, he gets up in time to get an early start.

11. Everybody has something; a man has dandruff, and a woman has cold feet.

12. Some people never have anything except ideals.

13. Every time a boy shows his hands, someone suggests that he wash them.

14. Except the Flood, nothing was ever as bad as reported.

15. Families with babies and families without babies are sorry for each other.

16. The flavor of frying bacon beats orange blossoms.

17. A good scare is worth more to a man than good advice.

18. Half the world does not know how the other half lives, but is trying to find out.

19. He belongs to so many benevolent societies that he is destitute.

20. His wife is ten years older than he is, and she calls him "Father."

21. I don't want my friends to die for me; if they will be polite, and let me alone, I will be satisfied.

22. I express many absurd opinions, but I am not the first man to do it; American freedom consists largely in talking nonsense.

23. If all the people in the world should agree to sympathize with a certain man at a certain hour, they could not cure his headache.

24. If a loafer is not a nuisance to you, it is a sign that you are somewhat of a loafer yourself.

25. If a man dies and leaves his estate in an uncertain condition, the lawyers become his heirs.

26. If a man should suddenly be changed to a woman, he couldn't get his clothes off.

27. If the fools do not control the world, it isn't because they are not in the majority.

28. If you want to know how old a woman is, ask her sister-in-law.

29. I never knew a man so mean that I was not willing he should admire me.

30. Instead of loving your enemies, treat your friends a little better.

31. If you think before you speak, the other fellow gets in his joke first.

32. I think I am better than the people who are trying to reform me.

33. There are few grave legal questions involved in a poor estate.

34. Let the heathen go to hell; help your neighbor.

35. A man never does justice to himself as an entertainer when his wife is around.

36. Men have as exaggerated an idea of their rights as women have of their wrongs.

37. The most natural man in a play is the villain.

38. Most people put off till tomorrow that which they should have done yesterday.

39. News is anything that makes a woman say, "For heaven's sake!"

40. No man knows where his business ends and his neighbor's begins.

41. No man's credit is as good as his money.

42. No man would listen to you talk if he didn't know it was his turn next.

43. One of the difficult tasks in this world is to convince a woman that even a bargain costs money.

44. One of the surprising things of this world is the respect a worthless man has for himself.

45. The only way to amuse some people is to slip and fall on an icy pavement.

46. People always say that they are not themselves when tempted by anger into betraying what they really are.

47. Probably a widower enjoys a second wife as much as a widow enjoys her husband's life insurance.

48. Put cream and sugar on a fly, and it tastes very much like a black raspberry.

**HOWELL, James,** 1594?–1666, *English author and lexicographer.*

The creditor hath a better memory than the debtor.

**HOWELLS, William Dean,** 1837–1920, *American novelist, editor, critic, and miscellaneous prose writer.*

Some people can stay longer in an hour than others can in a week.

**HUBBARD, Elbert,** 1856–1915, *American author, editor, and printer.*

1. Charity: a thing that begins at home, and usually stays there.
2. A conservative is a man who is too cowardly to fight and too fat to run.
3. Death: to stop sinning suddenly.
4. Do not take life too seriously; you will never get out of it alive.
5. Don't lose faith in humanity: think of all the people in the United States who have never played you a single nasty trick.
6. Editor: a person employed on a newspaper, whose business it is to separate the wheat from the chaff, and to see that the chaff is printed.
7. Every man is a damn fool for at least five minutes every day; wisdom consists in not exceeding the limit.
8. Every tyrant who has lived has believed in freedom—for himself.
9. Friend: one who knows all about you and loves you just the same.
10. Genius may have its limitations, but stupidity is not thus handicapped.
11. God: the John Doe of philosophy and religion.
12. Heaven: the Coney Island of the Christian imagination.
13. The graveyards are full of people the world could not do without.
14. If you don't advertise yourself you will be advertised by your loving enemies.
15. If you have no enemies, you are apt to be in the same predicament in regard to friends.
16. If you lose in an argument, you can still call your opponent names.
17. Man is Creation's masterpiece; but who says so?—Man.
18. Those whom God has put asunder no man can join together.

19. Lawyer: the only man in whom ignorance of the law is not punished.

20. A man is as good as he has to be, and a woman as bad as she dares.

21. Many a man's reputation would not know his character if they met on the street.

22. A miracle: an event described by those to whom it was told by men who did not see it.

23. No man needs a vacation so much as the person who has just had one.

24. The object of teaching a child is to enable him to get along without a teacher.

25. The only man who makes money following the races is the one who does so with a broom and shovel.

26. The path of civilization is paved with tin cans.

27. Perfume: any smell that is used to drown a worse one.

28. Repartee: any reply that is so clever that it makes the listener wish he had said it himself.

29. Righteous indignation: your own wrath as opposed to the shocking bad temper of others.

30. Secrets are things we give to others to keep for us.

31. You can lead a boy to college but you cannot make him think.

32. To avoid criticism, do nothing, say nothing, be nothing.

33. We are descended not only from monkeys, but from monks.

34. The world is moving so fast these days that the man who says it can't be done is generally interrupted by someone doing it.

35. Wrong no man and write no woman.

**HUBBARD, Frank McKinney ("Kin"),** 1868–1930, *American newspaper humorist and caricaturist, creator of "Abe Martin."*

1. About the only thing we have left that actually discriminates in favor of the plain people is the stork.

2. After a fellow gets famous it doesn't take long for someone to bob up that used to sit by him at school.

3. Anybody that's got time to read half of the new books has got entirely too much time.

4. A bad cold wouldn't be so annoying if it weren't for the advice of our friends.

5. A bee is never as busy as it seems; it's just that it can't buzz any slower.

6. Boys will be boys, and so will a lot of middle-aged men.

7. A chap ought to save a few of the long evenings he spends with his girl till after they're married.

8. The chronic grumbler is a church social compared to the fellow that agrees with everything you say.

9. Classical music is the kind that we keep hoping will turn into a tune.

10. The constable has three sons, two self-sustaining and one employed by the city.

11. Distant relatives are the best kind, and the further the better.

12. Don't knock the weather; nine tenths of the people couldn't start a conversation if it didn't change once in a while.

13. The election isn't very far off when a candidate can recognize you across the street.

14. Ever notice how an office seeker's eyesight fails after he gets what he wants?

15. Every once in a while you meet a fellow in some honorable walk of life that was once admitted to the bar.

16. Everything comes to him who waits except a loaned book.

17. Every time I read where some woman gave a short talk I wonder how she stopped.

18. A fellow never knows what he would have done till he's been married a couple of years.

19. The fellow that brags about how cheap he heats his home always sees the first robin.

20. The fellow that calls you "brother" generally wants something that doesn't belong to him.

21. The fellow that owns his own home is always just coming out of a hardware store.

22. The fellow that's pleased with everything either don't cut any ice or has something up his sleeve.

23. The fellow that tells a good story always has to listen to a couple of poor ones.

24. The fellow that tries to commit suicide with a razor, and fails, would fail at anything.

25. The first one to catch a circus in a lie is a boy.

26. The first thing to turn green in the spring is Christmas jewelry.

27. Florida's all right if you can keep from catching a sailfish and going to the expense of having it mounted.

28. Folks that blurt out just what they think wouldn't be so bad if they thought.

29. A friend that ain't in need is a friend indeed.

30. Fun is like life insurance: the older you get, the more it costs.

31. The hardest thing is to disguise your feelings when you put a lot of relatives on the train for home.

32. The hardest thing is writing a recommendation for someone we know.

33. He took his first holiday in forty years yesterday, and picked out a cemetery plot.

34. Honesty pays, but it don't seem to pay enough to suit some people.

35. Human life and turnips remain cheap and plentiful.

36. I don't know of anything better than a woman if you want to spend money where it'll show.

37. I don't think much of a dance step where the girl looks like she was being carried out of a burning building.

38. If some people didn't tell you, you'd never know they'd been away on a vacation.

39. If there's anything a public servant hates to do it's something for the public.

40. If there were only some shorter and more direct route to the devil, it would save an awful lot of sorrow and anxiety in this world.

41. If you want to get rid of somebody just tell 'em something for their own good.

42. I'll say this for adversity: people seem to be able to stand it, and that's more than I can say for prosperity.

43. I never saw an athletic girl that thought she was strong enough to do indoor work.

44. In order to live off a garden, you practically have to live in it.

45. I think some folks are foolish to pay what it costs to live.

46. It makes no difference what it is, a woman will buy anything she thinks a store is losing money on.

47. It must be great to be rich and let the other fellow keep up appearances.

48. It must be nice to run a boardinghouse and not have to worry about something different for dinner every day.

49. It seems like one of the hardest lessons to be learned in this life is where your business ends and somebody else's begins.

50. It seems to make an auto driver mad if he misses you.

51. It seems like the less a statesman amounts to, the more he loves the flag.

52. It's going to be fun to watch and see how long the meek can keep the earth after they inherit it.

53. It's no disgrace to be poor, but it might as well be.

54. It's pretty hard to tell what does bring happiness; poverty and wealth have both failed.

55. It's sweet to be remembered, but it's often cheaper to be forgotten.

56. It's what a fellow thinks he knows that hurts him.

57. It would be a swell world if everybody was as pleasant as the fellow who's trying to skin you.

58. I wish somebody would make a new Republican speech.

59. Kindness goes a long ways lots of times when it ought to stay at home.

60. Lack of pep is often mistaken for patience.

61. Lots of fellows think a home is only good to borrow money on.

62. Lots of folks confuse bad management with destiny.

63. Many a family tree needs trimming.

64. Married life ain't so bad after you get so you can eat the things your wife likes.

65. Money never made a fool of anybody; it only shows 'em up.

66. Most parents don't worry about a daughter till she fails to show up for breakfast, and then it's too late.

67. My idea of walking into the jaws of death is marrying some woman who's lost three husbands.

68. Next to a city the loneliest place in the world when you're broke is among relatives.

69. Nobody can be as agreeable as an uninvited guest.

70. Nobody ever forgets where he buried a hatchet.

71. Nobody ever grew despondent looking for trouble.

72. Nobody works as hard for his money as the man who marries it.

73. No matter how hard the times get, the wages of sin are always liberal and on the dot.

74. None but the brave can live with the fair.

75. No one can feel as helpless as the owner of a sick goldfish.

76. No self-made man ever did such a good job that some woman didn't want to make a few alterations.

77. Now and then an innocent man is sent to the legislature.

78. No wonder nobody that's got as much money invested in shoes and hose as a woman wants to stick around home.

79. The old-time mother who used to wonder where her boy was now has a grandson who wonders where his mother is.

80. One good thing about having one suit of clothes—you've always got your pencil.

81. One good thing about living on a farm is that you can fight with your wife without being heard.

82. One of the commonest ailments of the present day is premature formation of opinion.

83. Only one fellow in ten thousand understands the currency question, and we meet him every day.

84. The only time some fellows are ever seen with their wives is after they've been indicted.

85. The only way to entertain some folks is to listen to them.

86. Peace has its victories no less than war, but it doesn't have as many monuments to unveil.

87. Politics makes strange postmasters.

88. The reason the way of the transgressor is hard is because it's so crowded.

89. The richer a relative is, the less he bothers you.

90. A rich man and his daughter are soon parted.

91. The safest way to double your money is to fold it over once and put it in your pocket.

92. She treated her hired girl like one of the family—so she quit.

93. So far I haven't heard of anybody who wants to stop living on account of the cost.

94. Some defeated candidates go back to work and others say the fight has just begun.

95. Some folks get what's coming to them by waiting, others while crossing the street.

96. Some folks never begin to figure till there's nothing to add.

97. Some folks pay a compliment like they went down in their pocket for it.

98. Some folks seem to have descended from the chimpanzee much later than others.

99. Some girls get all there is out of life in one summer.

100. Some people are so sensitive that they feel snubbed if an epidemic overlooks them.

101. Some people pay a compliment as if they expected a receipt.

102. Some women seem to be able to entertain everybody but their husbands.

103. Success may go to one's head but the stomach is where it gets in its worst work.

104. A sympathizer is a fellow that's for you as long as it doesn't cost anything.

105. There is nothing so aggravating as a fresh boy who is too old to ignore and too young to kick.

106. There isn't much to be seen in a little town, but what you hear makes up for it.

107. There's another advantage of being poor—a doctor will cure you faster.

108. There seems to be an excess of everything except parking space and religion.

109. There's some folks standing behind the President that ought to get around where he can watch 'em.

110. There's too blamed many ways to spend money and not enough new ways to get it.

111. There's too many folks of limited means who think that nothing's too good for them.

112. 'Tis better to have loved and lost than never to have been sued.

113. A true lady or gentleman remains at home with a grouch same as if they had pneumonia.

114. We like little children because they tear out as soon as they get what they want.

115. We never know how a son is going to turn out or when a daughter is going to turn in.

116. We now have 7,000 beauty preparations, or about 289 for each beauty.

117. We're all pretty much alike when we get out of town.

118. What has become of all the child wonders we used to know in school?

119. When a fellow says, "It ain't the money but the principle of the thing," it's the money.

120. When a woman says, "I don't wish to mention any names," it ain't necessary.

121. When some folks don't know nothing mean about someone, they switch the subject.

122. Where ignorance is bliss, it's foolish to borrow your neighbor's newspaper.

123. Who recalls when folks got along without something if it cost too much?

124. Why doesn't the fellow who says, "I'm no speechmaker," let it go at that instead of giving a demonstration.

125. Why is it that the first gray hairs stick straight out?

126. Why they call a fellow who keeps losing all the time a good sport gets me.

127. Women are just like elephants to me; I like to look at them, but I wouldn't want one.

128. The world gets better every day—then worse again in the evening.

129. The world ain't getting no worse; we've only got better facilities.

130. The worst feature of a new baby is its mother's singing.

131. The worst jolt most of us ever get is when we fall back on our own resources.

132. You won't skid if you stay in a rut.

133. I don't look for much to come out of government ownership as long as we have Democrats and Republicans.

134. Lots of people insist on eating with a knife who were born with a silver spoon in their mouth.

135. Of all the home remedies, a good wife is the best.

136. Some folks get credit for having horse sense that hain't ever had enough money to make fools of themselves.

137. There's somebody at every dinner party who eats all the celery.

**HUGHES, Charles Evans,** 1863–1948, *American statesman and jurist.*

1. The United States is the greatest law factory the world has ever known.

2. We are under a Constitution, but the Constitution is what the judges say it is.

**HUGHES, Rupert,** born 1872, *American novelist, playwright, and editor.*

1. Women's intuition is the result of millions of years of not thinking.

2. Her face was her chaperone.

3. Love is a wonderful thing and highly desirable in marriage.

**HUGO, Victor,** 1802–1885, *French poet, novelist, and dramatist.*

1. Everything bows to success, even grammar.
2. Forty is the old age of youth, fifty is the youth of old age.
3. God created the flirt as soon as He made the fool.
4. If you would civilize a man, begin with his grandmother.
5. Indigestion is charged by God with enforcing morality on the stomach.
6. Melancholy is the pleasure of being sad.
7. The peculiarity of prudery is to multiply sentinels in proportion as the fortress is less threatened.
8. Waterloo was a battle of the first rank won by a captain of the second.
9. When a woman is speaking to you, listen to what she says with her eyes.

**HUME, David,** 1711–1776, *Scottish historian and philosopher.*

I cannot but bless the memory of Julius Caesar, for the great esteem he expressed for fat men, and his aversion to lean ones.

**HUNEKER, James Gibbons,** 1860–1921, *American editor, critic, and biographer.*

1. Berlioz says nothing in his music, but he says it magnificently.
2. A critic is a man who expects miracles.
3. Do married men make the best husbands?
4. Every husband is my enemy.
5. Lawyers earn a living by the sweat of their browbeating.
6. When a woman writes her confessions she is never further from the truth.
7. Life is like an onion: you peel off layer after layer and then you find there is nothing in it.
8. My corns ache, I get gouty, and my prejudices swell like varicose veins.

**HURST, Fannie,** born 1889, *American novelist, playwright, and scenarist.*

1. I'm not happy when I'm writing, but I'm more unhappy when I'm not.

2. It takes a clever man to turn cynic, and a wise man to be clever enough not to.

**HUTCHINS, Robert Maynard**, born 1899, *American educator.*

1. The college graduate is presented with a sheepskin to cover his intellectual nakedness.

2. Whenever I feel like exercise, I lie down until the feeling passes.

**HUXLEY, Aldous**, born 1894, *English novelist, essayist, and critic.*

1. A bad book is as much of a labor to write as a good one.

2. A bilious philosopher's opinion of the world can only be accepted with a pinch of salt, Epsom salt by preference.

3. The silent bear no witness against themselves.

4. Technological progress has merely provided us with more efficient means for going backwards.

5. To his dog, every man is Napoleon; hence the constant popularity of dogs.

6. We are all geniuses up to the age of ten.

7. She was almost too hospitable—she kept open bed.

8. She was a professional athlete—of the tongue.

9. As the influence of religion declines, the social importance of art increases; we must beware of exchanging good religion for bad art.

**HUXLEY, Thomas Henry**, 1825-1895, *English biologist.*

1. If a little knowledge is dangerous, where is the man who has so much as to be out of danger?

2. I have no faith, very little hope, and as much charity as I can afford.

**IBSEN, Henrik**, 1828-1906, *Norwegian dramatist and poet.*

1. It is inexcusable for scientists to torture animals; let them make their experiments on journalists and politicians.

2. You should never wear your best trousers when you go out to fight for freedom and truth.

**INGE, William Ralph,** born 1860, *Anglican prelate and writer.*

1. I am afraid the clergyman's God is too often the head of the clerical profession.

2. I have never understood why it should be considered derogatory to the Creator to suppose that he has a sense of humor.

3. In dealing with Englishmen you can be sure of one thing only, that the logical solution will not be adopted.

4. It is becoming impossible for those who mix with their fellow men to believe that the grace of God is distributed denominationally.

5. It is not easy for Catholics and Protestants to lie in the same bed, unless both are asleep.

6. It is useless for the sheep to pass resolutions in favor of vegetarianism while the wolf remains of a different opinion.

7. It may be doubted whether nature intended the Englishman to be a money-making animal.

8. Originality is undetected plagiarism.

9. Politicians take no interest in eugenics because the unborn have no vote.

10. The proper time to influence the character of a child is about a hundred years before he is born.

11. Religion is caught, not taught.

12. There are two kinds of fools: one says, "This is old, therefore it is good"; the other says, "This is new, therefore it is better."

13. The whole of nature is a conjunction of the verb to eat, in the active and passive.

14. Worry is interest paid on trouble before it falls due.

**INGERSOLL, Robert Green,** 1833–1899, *American lawyer, writer, and lecturer.*

1. Above all things, keep clean; it is not necessary to be a pig in order to raise one.

2. The church has always been willing to swap off treasures in heaven for cash down.

3. An honest God is the noblest work of man.

4. Hope is the only universal liar who never loses his reputation for veracity.

5. If I owe Smith ten dollars, and God forgives me, that doesn't pay Smith.

6. Many people think they have religion when they are merely troubled with dyspepsia.

7. A mule has neither pride of ancestry nor hope of posterity.

8. Religion has not civilized man, man has civilized religion.

9. With soap, baptism is a good thing.

10. If I had my way I'd make health catching instead of disease.

11. Whenever a man lives by prayer you will find that he eats considerable besides.

**IRVING, Washington,** 1783-1859, *American short-story writer and essayist.*

1. I am always at a loss to know how much to believe of my own stories.

2. A sharp tongue is the only edged tool that grows keener with constant use.

3. Whenever a man's friends begin to compliment him about looking young, he may be sure that they think he is growing old.

4. Young lawyers attend the courts, not because they have business there but because they have no business anywhere else.

**IRWIN, Wallace,** born 1876, *American journalist and humorist.*

He grew so proficient in poesy that he could write a sonnet of almost any length on a moment's notice.

**ITURBI, José,** born 1895, *Spanish-American pianist and conductor.*

The only time you realize you have a reputation is when you're not living up to it.

**JACKSON, Holbrook,** born 1874, *English journalist, editor, author, and bibliophile.*

1. As soon as an idea is accepted it is time to reject it.

2. Be contented, when you have got all you want.

3. Fear of corrupting the mind of the younger generation is the loftiest form of cowardice.

4. In democracies, those who lead, follow; those who follow, lead.

5. A lie is that which you do not believe.

6. Man is a dog's ideal of what God should be.

7. Man is the only animal that can be a fool.

8. The marriage system created a new sport—adultery.

9. Only the rich preach content to the poor.

10. The poor are the only consistent altruists; they sell all that they have and give to the rich.

11. Sacrifice is a form of bargaining.

12. Suffer fools gladly; they may be right.

13. There are only two classes in society: those who get more than they earn, and those who earn more than they get.

14. The typical man of any nation is the exception.

15. Why did Nature create man? Was it to show that she is big enough to make mistakes, or was it pure ignorance?

16. Intuition is reason in a hurry.

**JAMES, Henry,** 1843-1916, *American-English novelist.*

1. For a man to pretend to understand women is bad manners; for him really to understand them is bad morals.

2. Life is a predicament which precedes death.

3. Naïveté in art is like zero in a number; its importance depends on the figure it is united with.

**JAMES, William,** 1842-1910, *American psychologist and philosopher.*

1. A great many people think they are thinking when they are merely rearranging their prejudices.

2. The obstinate insisting that tweedledum is not tweedledee is the bone and marrow of life.

3. When you have to make a choice and don't make it, that is in itself a choice.

**JEFFERSON, Thomas,** 1743–1826, *American statesman and President of the United States.*

1. It is the trade of lawyers to question everything, yield nothing, and to talk by the hour.

2. The man who reads nothing at all is better educated than the man who reads nothing but newspapers.

3. Advertisements contain the only truths to be relied on in a newspaper.

**JEROME, Jerome K.,** 1859–1927, *English humorist, dramatist, and novelist.*

1. I like work; it fascinates me; I can sit and look at it for hours.

2. It is always the best policy to speak the truth, unless of course you are an exceptionally good liar.

3. It is impossible to enjoy idling thoroughly unless one has plenty of work to do.

4. Love is like the measles; we all have to go through it.

5. One of the advantages of being poor is that it necessitates the cultivation of the virtues.

6. We drink one another's healths and spoil our own.

**JERROLD, Douglas,** 1803–1857, *English humorist, playwright, and editor.*

1. Australia is so kind that, just tickle her with a hoe, and she laughs with a harvest.

2. The best thing I know between France and England is—the sea.

3. Compared to the city, the country looks like the world without its clothes on.

4. A conservative is a man who will not look at the new moon, out of respect for that ancient institution, the old one.

5. Dogmatism is puppyism come to its full growth.

6. Eve ate the apple that she might dress.

7. Every rose has its thorn: you never find a woman without pins and needles.

8. God said: "Let us make man in our image"; and Man said: "Let us make God in our image."

9. The greatest animal in creation is the animal who cooks.

10. He is one of those wise philanthropists who, in a time of famine, would vote for nothing but a supply of toothpicks.

11. He should have an itch in the Temple of Fame.

12. He was so benevolent, so merciful a man that he would have held an umbrella over a duck in a shower of rain.

13. If an earthquake were to engulf England tomorrow, the English would manage to meet and dine somewhere among the rubbish, just to celebrate the event.

14. If I were a gravedigger, or even a hangman, there are some people I could work for with a great deal of pleasure.

15. In all the wedding cake, hope is the sweetest of the plums.

16. In marriage, as in war, it is permitted to take every advantage of the enemy.

17. In this world, truth can wait; she's used to it.

18. It seems so easy to be good-natured, I wonder anybody takes the trouble to be anything else.

19. I've heard him renounce wine a hundred times a day, but then it has been between as many glasses.

20. A lady, being deserted by one man, has no other remedy than an appeal to twelve.

21. Love is like the measles, all the worse when it comes late in life.

22. Love the sea? I dote upon it—from the beach.

23. My notion of a wife at forty is that a man should be able to change her, like a bank note, for two twenties.

24. The only athletic sport I ever mastered was backgammon.

25. Readers are of two sorts: one who carefully goes through a book, and the other who as carefully lets the book go through him.

26. Self-defense is the clearest of all laws, and for this reason: the lawyers didn't make it.

27. The shirt of Nessus was a shirt not paid for.

28. The sharp employ the sharp; verily, a man may be known by his attorney.

29. Some people are so fond of ill luck that they run halfway to meet it.

30. The surest way to hit a woman's heart is to take aim kneeling.

31. Talk to him of Jacob's ladder, and he would ask the number of the steps.

32. That fellow would vulgarize the Day of Judgment.

33. They say a parson first invented gunpowder, but one cannot believe it till one is married.

34. To reform a man is a tedious and uncertain labor; hanging is the sure work of a minute.

35. Troubles are like babies; they only grow by nursing.

36. Wedlock's like wine—not to be properly judged of till the second glass.

37. Whatever promises a man may make before marriage, the license is as a receipt in full.

38. When a man has nothing in his cupboard, fever is his best guest.

39. Whenever a man exclaims that all mankind are villains, be assured that he contemplates an instant offer of himself as an exception.

40. With women as with warriors, there's no robbery—all's conquest.

**JOAD, C. E. M.**, born 1891, *English author and writer on philosophy.*

When I was eleven, I thought that women were solid from the neck down.

**JOHNSON, Samuel ("Dr.")**, 1709-1784, *English author, lexicographer, editor, and literary leader.*

1. Abstinence is as easy to me as temperance would be difficult.

2. Adversity is the state in which a man most easily becomes acquainted with himself, being especially free from admirers then.

3. Criticism is a study by which men grow important and formidable at very small expense.

4. Every man has a right to utter what he thinks truth, and every other man has a right to knock him down for it.

5. A fishing rod is a stick with a hook at one end and a fool at the other.

6. He talks like a watch which ticks away minutes, but never strikes the hour.

7. He was dull in a new way, and that made many think him great.

8. I am very fond of the company of ladies; I like their beauty, I like their delicacy, I like their vivacity, and I like their silence.

9. I am willing to love all mankind, except an American.

10. If he does really think that there is no distinction between vice and virtue, when he leaves our houses let us count our spoons.

11. I hate mankind, for I think myself one of the best of them, and I know how bad I am.

12. I live in the crowds of jollity, not so much to enjoy company as to shun myself.

13. In lapidary inscriptions a man is not upon oath.

14. The Irish are a fair people; they never speak well of one another.

15. It is better a man should be abused than forgotten.

16. I would be loth to speak ill of any person who I do not know deserves it, but I am afraid he is an attorney.

17. A man in jail has more room, better food, and commonly better company.

18. A man is in general better pleased when he has a good dinner upon his table than when his wife talks Greek.

19. A man seldom thinks with more earnestness of anything than he does of his dinner.

20. Marriage has many pains, but celibacy has no pleasures.

21. Much may be made of a Scotchman, if he be caught young.

22. My diseases are an asthma and a dropsy and, what is less curable, seventy-five.

23. My idea of an agreeable person is one who agrees with me.

24. Nature has given women so much power that the law has very wisely given them little.

25. Network: anything reticulated or decussated at equal intervals, with interstices between the intersections.

26. No human power can deprive the boaster of his own encomiums.

27. No man but a blockhead ever wrote except for money.

28. Nothing flatters a man as much as the happiness of his wife; he is always proud of himself as the source of it.

29. Oats: a grain, which in England is generally given to horses, but in Scotland supports the people.

30. Of all noises, I think music is the least disagreeable.

31. Patron: commonly a wretch who supports with insolence, and is paid with flattery.

32. The rights of nations and of kings sink into questions of grammar if grammarians discuss them.

33. Second marriage: the triumph of hope over experience.

34. The silk stockings and white bosoms of actresses excite my amorous propensities.

35. That fellow seems to me to possess but one idea, and that a wrong one.

36. Treating your adversary with respect is giving him an advantage to which he is not entitled.

37. We are inclined to believe those whom we do not know because they have never deceived us.

38. Were it not for imagination, a man would be as happy in the arms of a chambermaid as of a duchess.

39. When a man knows he is to be hanged in a fortnight, it concentrates his mind wonderfully.

40. When two Englishmen meet, their first talk is of the weather.

41. Whoever thinks of going to bed before twelve o'clock is a scoundrel.

42. Wine makes a man better pleased with himself; I do not say that it makes him more pleasing to others.

43. A woman's preaching is like a dog's walking on his hind legs; it is not done well, but you are surprised to find it done at all.

44. Worth seeing? Yes, but not worth going to see.

45. You raise your voice when you should reinforce your argument.
46. Your manuscript is both good and original; but the part that is good is not original, and the part that is original is not good.
47. There is nothing too little for so little a creature as man.
48. When a man says he had pleasure with a woman he does not mean conversation.

**JONSON, Ben,** 1573?-1637, *English dramatist and poet.*
Man and wife make one fool.

**JOUBERT, Joseph,** 1754-1824, *French writer.*
1. Children have more need of models than of critics.
2. It's better to debate a question without settling it than to settle a question without debating it.
3. We should always keep a spare corner in our heads to give passing hospitality to our friends' opinions.
4. The whisper of a beautiful woman can be heard farther than the loudest call of duty.

**JOWETT, Benjamin,** 1817-1893, *English Greek scholar and translator.*
1. Even the youngest among us is not infallible.
2. Give the clergy your sympathy; don't give them anything else.
3. It is most important in this world to be pushing, but it is fatal to seem so.
4. Nowhere probably is there more true feeling, and nowhere worse taste, than in a churchyard.
5. The time he can spare from the adornment of his person he devotes to the neglect of his duties.

**KARR, Alphonse,** 1808-1890, *French editor and novelist.*
1. If men knew all that women think, they'd be twenty times more daring.

2. If we are to abolish the death penalty, I should like to see the first step taken by my friends the murderers.

3. Some people are always grumbling because roses have thorns; I am thankful that thorns have roses.

4. A woman who writes commits two sins: she increases the number of books, and decreases the number of women.

**KAUFMAN, George S.**, born 1889, *American playwright.*

1. One man's Mede is another man's Persian.

2. Your eyes—they shine like the pants of a blue serge suit.

**KELLAND, Clarence Budington**, born 1881, *American novelist, scenarist, and short-story writer.*

It takes a man twenty-five years to learn to be married; it's a wonder women have the patience to wait for it.

**KETTERING, Charles Franklin**, born 1876, *American inventor.*

My interest is in the future because I am going to spend the rest of my life there.

**KIERKEGAARD, Sören Aabye**, 1813–1855, *Danish philosopher and writer on theology.*

Life can only be understood backwards, but it must be lived forwards.

**KINGSLEY, Charles**, 1819–1875, *English novelist, poet, and clergyman.*

1. A keeper is only a poacher turned outside in, and a poacher a keeper turned inside out.

2. Love is sentimental measles.

3. There are more ways of killing a cat than choking her with cream.

**KIPLING, Rudyard**, 1865–1936, *English poet, novelist, and short-story writer.*

1. Gardens are not made by singing "Oh, how beautiful," and sitting in the shade.

2. Youth had been a habit of hers for so long that she could not part with it.

3. Heaven grant us patience with a man in love!

4. Hit a man an' help a woman, an' ye can't be far wrong anyway.

5. If the aunt of the vicar has never touched liquor, look out when she finds the champagne.

6. I never made a mistake in my life; at least, never one that I couldn't explain away afterwards.

7. It's clever, but is it art?

8. Make 'im take 'er, an' keep 'er; that's hell for 'em both.

9. Man is an imperfectly denatured animal intermittently subject to the unpredictable reactions of an unlocated spiritual area.

10. Never praise a sister to a sister in the hope of your compliments reaching the proper ears.

11. She was as immutable as the hills, but not quite so green.

12. The silliest woman can manage a clever man, but it needs a very clever woman to manage a fool.

13. There's more things told than are true, and more things true than are told.

14. When the clergyman's daughter drinks nothing but water, she's certain to finish on gin.

15. A woman is only a woman, but a good cigar is a smoke.

16. A woman's guess is much more accurate than a man's certainty.

17. Adam was a gardener and God, who made him, sees that half of all good gardening is done upon the knees.

**KORZYBSKI, Alfred,** born 1879, *American scientist and writer.*

God may forgive you your sins, but your nervous system won't.

**KREISLER, Fritz,** born 1875, *Austrian violinist and composer.*

In respect to violins, I am polygamous.

**KRUTCH, Joseph Wood,** born 1893, *American critic and essayist.*

There is no such thing as a dangerous woman; there are only susceptible men.

**LA BRUYÈRE, Jean de,** 1645–1696, *French writer.*

1. At the beginning of love and at its end, lovers are embarrassed if left alone.

2. The best way to get on in the world is to make people believe it's to their advantage to help you.

3. The duty of a judge is to administer justice, but his practice is to delay it.

4. A fool is one whom bigger fools believe to be a man of merit.

5. It is a great misfortune neither to have enough wit to talk well nor enough judgment to be silent.

6. The reason women do not love one another is—men.

7. Next to good judgment, diamonds and pearls are the rarest things in the world.

8. There are no ugly women; there are only women who do not know how to look pretty.

9. There are only two ways of getting on in the world: by one's own industry, or by the stupidity of others.

10. Widows, like ripe fruit, drop easily from their perch.

**LA FONTAINE, Jean de,** 1621–1695, *French poet and writer of fables.*

1. It is difficult for a woman to keep a secret; and I know more than one man who is a woman.

2. It is impossible to please the whole world and your father as well.

3. This beast is very wicked; when it is attacked, it defends itself.

4. What is called discretion in men is called cunning in animals.

**LAMARTINE, Alphonse de,** 1790–1869, *French poet, historian, statesman, and orator.*

The more I see of the representatives of the people, the more I admire my dogs.

**LAMB, Charles,** 1775–1834, *English essayist, critic, punster, and miscellaneous writer.*

1. Borrowers of books—those mutilators of collections, spoilers of the symmetry of shelves, and creators of odd volumes.

2. The first water cure was the Flood, and it killed more than it cured.

3. The greatest pleasure I know is to do a good action by stealth and have it found out by accident.

4. He is no lawyer who cannot take two sides.

5. His life was formal; his actions seemed ruled with a ruler.

6. The human species is composed of two distinct races: the men who borrow, and the men who lend.

7. I am determined my children shall be brought up in their father's religion, if they can find out what it is.

8. If dirt was trumps, what hands you would hold!

9. I have been to a funeral; I can't describe to you the howl which the widow set up at proper intervals.

10. I have not volition enough left to dot my i's, much less to comb my eyebrows.

11. In everything that relates to science, I am a whole encyclopedia behind the rest of the world.

12. May my last breath be drawn through a pipe and exhaled in a pun.

13. A mixture of brandy and water spoils two good things.

14. My bedfellows are cough and cramp; we sleep three in a bed.

15. Nothing puzzles me more than time and space, and yet nothing puzzles me less, for I never think about them.

16. A poor relation is the most irrelevant thing in nature.

17. Positively the best thing a man can have to do is nothing, and next to that, perhaps, good works.

18. Presents endear absents.

19. Satire does not look pretty upon a tombstone.

20. Sentimentally I am disposed to harmony; but organically I am incapable of a tune.

21. Since all the maids are good and lovable, from whence come the evil wives?

22. Tobacco has been my evening comfort and my morning curse.

23. The vices of some men are magnificent.

24. When my sonnet was rejected, I exclaimed: Damn the age; I will write for antiquity.

25. You look wise; pray, correct that error.

26. New Year's Day is every man's birthday.

27. I never knew an enemy to puns who was not an ill-natured man.

28. We read to say that we have read.

**LANDON, Melville D. ("Eli Perkins"), 1839-1910,** *American humorous writer and lecturer.*

1. A bore is a man who spends so much time talking about himself that you can't talk about yourself.

2. I hate the devil and I would kill him, but I see there are several clergymen present and they have their families to support.

3. Levity is the soul of wit.

**LANDOR, Walter Savage, 1775-1864,** *English poet and prose writer.*

I never did a single wise thing in the whole course of my existence, although I have written many which have been thought so.

**LANG, Andrew, 1844-1912,** *Scottish poet, folklorist, biographer, translator, novelist, and scholar.*

1. He missed an invaluable opportunity to hold his tongue.

2. He uses statistics as a drunken man uses lampposts—for support rather than for illumination.

**LARDNER, Ring, 1885-1933,** *American humorist and short-story writer.*

1. He gave her a look that you could have poured on a waffle.

2. He looked at me as if I was a side dish he hadn't ordered.

3. It's the children's night out and I have to stay home with the nurse.

4. The only exercise I get is when I take the studs out of one shirt and put them in another.

5. An optimist is a girl who mistakes a bulge for a curve.

6. They gave each other a smile with a future in it.

**LA ROCHEFOUCAULD, François de**, 1613–1680, *French writer of epigrams.*

1. Conceit causes more conversation than wit.

2. Everyone complains of his memory, no one of his judgment.

3. A fashionable woman is always in love—with herself.

4. Gratitude is merely a secret hope of greater favors.

5. Greater qualities are necessary to bear good fortune than bad.

6. He who is pleased with nobody is much more unhappy than he with whom nobody is pleased.

7. Hypocrisy is the homage which vice pays to virtue.

8. If we had no faults of our own, we should take less pleasure in noticing the faults of others.

9. If we judge love by most of its results, it resembles hatred rather than affection.

10. If we did not flatter ourselves, the flattery of others would not harm us.

11. If we resist our passions, it is more from their weakness than from our strength.

12. In the misfortune of our best friends we find something which is not displeasing to us.

13. It is far better to be deceived than to be undeceived by those whom we love.

14. It is not always for virtue's sake that women are virtuous.

15. It takes much cleverness to know how to conceal cleverness.

16. The love of justice is, in most men, nothing more than the fear of suffering injustice.

17. A man who is always satisfied with himself is seldom satisfied with others.

18. Most of our faults are more pardonable than the means we use to conceal them.

19. Most virtuous women are like hidden treasures, safe only because they are not sought after.

20. Nothing prevents us from being natural so much as the desire to appear so.

21. Old men are fond of giving good advice to console themselves for their inability to give bad examples.

22. One can find women who have never had one love affair, but it is rare indeed to find any who have had only one.

23. A person is never as happy or as unhappy as he thinks he is.

24. Our enemies come nearer the truth in their opinions of us than we do in our opinion of ourselves.

25. People would not long remain in social life if they were not fooled by one another.

26. Philosophy triumphs easily over past and future misfortunes, but present misfortunes triumph over philosophy.

27. The reason lovers are never weary of each other is because they are always talking about themselves.

28. Repentance is not so much remorse for what we have done as the fear of consequences.

29. Solemnity is a trick of the body to hide the faults of the mind.

30. There are bad people who would be less dangerous if they had no good in them.

31. There are crimes which become innocent and even glorious through their splendor, number, and excess.

32. There are few people who are not ashamed of their love affairs when the infatuation is over.

33. There are few people who are more often in the wrong than those who cannot endure to be thought so.

34. There are few virtuous women who do not tire of their role.

35. There are people who would never have fallen in love if they had never heard of love.

36. There are some good marriages, but practically no delightful ones.

37. To establish oneself in the world, one does all one can to seem established there.

38. To love is the least of the faults of a loving woman.

39. To refuse praise is to seek praise twice.

40. True love is like a ghost: everybody talks about it but few have seen it.

41. Truth does not do so much good in the world as the appearance of it does evil.

42. Vanity is the greatest of all flatterers.

43. Virtue in women is often merely love of their reputation and of their peace of mind.

44. Virtue would not go far if vanity did not keep it company.

45. We all have enough strength to bear the misfortunes of others.

46. We always like those who admire us but we do not always like those whom we admire.

47. We are almost always bored in the company of persons with whom we are not permitted to be bored.

48. We are never made as ridiculous through the qualities we have as through those we pretend to.

49. We confess little faults in order to suggest that we have no big ones.

50. We give advice but we cannot give the wisdom to profit by it.

51. We give ourselves credit for the opposite faults of those we have: when we are weak, we boast of being obstinate.

52. We never confess our faults except through vanity.

53. We often do good in order that we may do evil with impunity.

54. We often forgive those who bore us, but we cannot forgive those whom we bore.

55. We often shed tears which deceive ourselves after deceiving others.

56. We prefer to speak evil of ourselves rather than not speak of ourselves at all.

57. We promise according to our hopes, and perform according to our fears.

58. We seldom find people ungrateful so long as we are in a condition to render them service.

59. We should have very little pleasure were we never to flatter ourselves.

60. We sometimes imagine we hate flattery, but we only hate the way we are flattered.

61. We think very few people sensible except those who agree with us.

62. We would often be ashamed of our best actions if the world only knew the motives behind them.

63. What is called liberality is often merely the vanity of giving.

64. What makes the vanity of other people intolerable is that it wounds our own.

65. What makes us so bitter against people who outwit us is that they think themselves cleverer than we are.

66. When our vices leave us, we flatter ourselves that we are leaving them.

67. Why can we remember the tiniest detail that has happened to us, and not remember how many times we have told it to the same persons?

68. Wit sometimes enables us to act rudely with impunity.

69. A woman is faithful to her first lover a long time—unless she happens to take a second.

70. Women in love pardon great indiscretions more easily than little infidelities.

71. You are never so easily fooled as when you are trying to fool someone else.

**LAVATER, Johann Kaspar,** 1741–1801, *Swiss poet, mystic, and philosopher.*

1. If you wish to appear agreeable in society you must consent to be taught many things which you already know.

2. Never say you know a man until you have divided an inheritance with him.

**LAWRENCE, David Herbert ("D. H."),** 1885–1930, *English novelist, poet, and essayist.*

1. The unhappiness of a wife with a good husband is much more devastating than the unhappiness of a wife with a bad husband.

2. When I wish I was rich, then I know I am ill.

**LEACOCK, Stephen,** 1869–1944, *Canadian political economist and humorist.*

1. He flung himself upon his horse and rode madly off in all directions.

2. In a moment the pirates were all around us, rolling their eyes, gnashing their teeth, and filing their nails.

3. It's called political economy because it has nothing to do with either politics or economy.

4. Many a man in love with a dimple makes the mistake of marrying the whole girl.

5. Men are able to trust one another, knowing the exact degree of dishonesty they are entitled to expect.

6. The minute a man is convinced that he is interesting, he isn't.

7. The parent who could see his boy as he really is would shake his head and say, "Willie is no good; I'll sell him."

8. I am a great believer in luck, and I find the harder I work the more I have of it.

**LENCLOS, Ninon de,** 1620–1705, *French lady of fashion and wit.*

1. Love never dies of starvation but often of indigestion.

2. Men lose more conquests by their own awkwardness than by any virtue in the woman.

3. The resistance of a woman is not always a proof of her virtue but more frequently of her experience.

**LESSING, Gotthold,** 1729–1781, *German critic and dramatist.*

A young lady who thinks is like a young man who rouges.

**LEVANT, Oscar,** born 1906, *American pianist, composer, and wit.*

1. An epigram is only a wisecrack that's played Carnegie Hall.

2. In my last movie I played an unsympathetic character—myself.

3. I've given up reading books; I find it takes my mind off myself.

4. My first wife divorced me on grounds of incompatibility, and besides, I think she hated me.

5. The first thing I do in the morning is brush my teeth and sharpen my tongue.

6. A pun is the lowest form of humor—when you don't think of it first.

### LEWIS, Sinclair, born 1885, *American novelist.*

1. Our American professors like their literature clear, cold, pure, and very dead.

2. People will buy anything that's one to a customer.

### LICHTENBERG, Georg Christoph, 1742-1799, *German physicist, satirist, and miscellaneous writer.*

1. Everyone is a genius—at least once a year.

2. Language originated before philosophy, and that's what's wrong with philosophy.

3. What a blessing it would be if we could open and shut our ears as easily as we do our eyes.

4. What astonished him was that cats should have two holes cut in their skins at exactly the same places where their eyes were.

5. What if a man is buried alive from time to time? For every such person there are a hundred dead men walking the earth.

### LINCOLN, Abraham, 1809-1865, *President of the United States.*

1. For people who like that kind of a book, that is the kind of a book they will like.

2. God must have loved the plain people; he made so many of them.

3. He can compress the most words into the smallest ideas of any man I ever met.

4. Honest statesmanship is the wise employment of individual meanness for the public good.

5. I don't know who my grandfather was; I am much more concerned to know what his grandson will be.

6. I fear explanations explanatory of things explained.

7. If this is coffee, please bring me some tea; but if this is tea, please bring me some coffee.

8. It has been my experience that folks who have no vices have very few virtues.

9. My father taught me to work; he did not teach me to love it.

10. My politics are short and sweet, like the old woman's dance.

11. No man has a good enough memory to make a successful liar.

12. The plainest print cannot be read through a gold eagle.

13. It's a good rule never to send a mouse to catch a skunk or a polliwog to tackle a whale.

14. I was not accustomed to flattery; I was like the Hoosier who loved gingerbread better than any man and got less of it.

15. Marriage is neither heaven nor hell; it is simply purgatory.

16. Whenever I hear anyone arguing for slavery, I feel a strong impulse to see it tried on him personally.

17. When I hear a man preach, I like to see him act as if he were fighting bees.

18. When you have got an elephant by the hind legs and he is trying to run away, it's best to let him run.

**LINDSEY, Ben,** 1869–1943, *American jurist.*

Pontius Pilate was the first great censor, and Jesus Christ the first great victim of censorship.

**LIN YUTANG,** born 1895, *Chinese philologist, essayist, and miscellaneous writer.*

All women's dresses are merely variations on the eternal struggle between the admitted desire to dress and the unadmitted desire to undress.

**LIPPMAN, Walter,** born 1899, *American author, editor, and political writer.*

Where all think alike, no one thinks very much.

**LITTLE, Mary Wilson,** born 1880?, *American paragrapher.*

1. Beauty in a woman's face, like sweetness in a woman's lips, is a matter of taste.

2. The bravest toreador in Spain would be nonplused by an Irish bull.

3. He who devotes sixteen hours a day to hard study may become as wise at sixty as he thought himself at twenty.

4. If a mosquito bite thee on one hand, give him the other—palm downward.

5. If a man is only a little lower than the angels, the angels should reform.

6. In some parts of Ireland the sleep which knows no waking is always followed by a wake which knows no sleeping.

7. It is difficult to see why lace should be so expensive; it is mostly holes.

8. It is difficult to tell which gives some couples the most happiness, the minister who marries them or the judge who divorces them.

9. Men who make no pretensions to being good on one day out of seven are called sinners.

10. No man feels like laughing when he bumps his funny bone.

11. The only golden thing that women dislike is silence.

12. The penalty of success is to be bored by the attentions of people who formerly snubbed you.

13. Politeness is one half good nature and the other half good lying.

14. There is a great deal of prose license in Walt Whitman's poetry.

15. There is no pleasure in having nothing to do; the fun is in having lots to do and not doing it.

16. The tombstone is about the only thing that can stand upright and lie on its face at the same time.

17. A youth with his first cigar makes himself sick; a youth with his first girl makes other people sick.

**LLOYD GEORGE, David,** 1863–1945, *British statesman and prime minister.*

A politician is a person with whose politics you don't agree; if you agree with him he is a statesman.

**LONGFELLOW, Henry Wadsworth,** 1807–1882, *American poet.*

1. And so we plough along, as the fly said to the ox.

2. It takes less time to do a thing right than to explain why you did it wrong.

**LOOMIS, Charles Battell,** 1861–1911, *American humorist.*

1. Heaven lies about us in our infancy—and we lie about heaven later on.

2. An old maid has one consolation: she can never be a widow no matter who dies.

**LOUIS XIV ("the Great"),** 1638–1715, *King of France.*

1. Every time I fill a vacant office, I make ten malcontents and one ingrate.

2. I could sooner reconcile all Europe than two women.

**LOVER, Samuel,** 1797–1868, *Irish novelist, portrait painter, and song writer.*

When once the itch of literature comes over a man, nothing can cure it but the scratching of a pen.

**LOWELL, Abbott Lawrence,** 1856–1943, *American political scientist and educator.*

Universities are full of knowledge; the freshmen bring a little in and the seniors take none away, and knowledge accumulates.

**LOWELL, James Russell,** 1819–1891, *American poet, editor, essayist, and diplomat.*

1. Blessed are they who have nothing to say, and who cannot be persuaded to say it.

2. Democracy gives every man the right to be his own oppressor.

3. Don't ever prophesy—unless you know.

4. The foolish and the dead alone never change their opinions.

5. Granting our wish is one of Fate's saddest jokes.

6. Let us be of good cheer, remembering that the misfortunes hardest to bear are those which never come.

7. There is no good in arguing with the inevitable; the only argument available with an east wind is to put on your overcoat.

8. Whatever you may be sure of, be sure of this: that you are dreadfully like other people.

9. What men prize most is a privilege, even if it be that of chief mourner at a funeral.

10. He mastered whatever was not worth the knowing.

**LUCAS, Edward Verrall,** 1868–1938, *English publisher and author.*

1. I am a believer in punctuality though it makes me very lonely.

2. The trouble with marriage is that, while every woman is at heart a mother, every man is at heart a bachelor.

3. People who are late are often so much jollier than the people who have to wait for them.

**LUCE, Clare Boothe,** born 1903, *American editor and playwright.*

The politicans were talking themselves red, white, and blue in the face.

**LUTHER, Martin,** 1483–1546, *leader of the Protestant Reformation in Germany.*

1. If God consulted me I should have advised him to continue the generation of the species by fashioning them of clay.

2. Who loves not women, wine and song remains a fool his whole life long.

**LYTTON, Baron (Edward George Bulwer-Lytton),** 1803–1873, *English novelist and dramatist.*

1. Castles in the air cost a vast deal to keep up.

2. A good cigar is as great a comfort to a man as a good cry to a woman.

3. If you wish to be loved, show more of your faults than your virtues.

4. There is no man so friendless but what he can find a friend sincere enough to tell him disagreeable truths.

5. It is difficult to say who do you the most mischief: enemies with the worst intentions or friends with the best.

6. Just like my luck! If I had been bred a hatter, little boys would have come into the world without heads.

7. Life is like playing a violin solo in public and learning the instrument as one goes on.

8. Life would be tolerably agreeable if it were not for its amusements.

9. Love is the business of the idle, but the idleness of the busy.

10. A man who has ancestors is like a representative of the past.

## MACAULAY, Rose, born 1889?, *English novelist and essayist.*

It was a book to kill time for those who like it better dead.

## MACAULAY, Thomas Babington, 1800–1859, *English historian, essayist, poet, and statesman.*

1. Few of the many wise apothegms which have been uttered have prevented a single foolish action.

2. From Byron they drew a system of ethics in which the two great commandments were to hate your neighbor and to love your neighbor's wife.

3. Perhaps no person can be a poet, or even enjoy poetry, without a certain unsoundness of mind.

4. The Puritan hated bear-baiting not because it gave pain to the bear but because it gave pleasure to the spectators.

5. Richard Steele was a rake among scholars, and a scholar among rakes.

6. We know no spectacle so ridiculous as the British public in one of its periodical fits of morality.

## MACKENZIE, Compton, born 1883, *English playwright and novelist.*

Women do not find it difficult nowadays to behave like men, but they often find it extremely difficult to behave like gentlemen.

## MADARIAGA, Salvador de, born 1886, *Spanish diplomat and writer.*

The Anglo-Saxon conscience does not prevent the Anglo-Saxon from sinning; it merely prevents him from enjoying his sin.

**MAETERLINCK, Maurice,** born 1862, *Belgian poet, dramatist, and essayist.*

1. All our knowledge merely helps us to die a more painful death than the animals that know nothing.
2. The living are the dead on holiday.

**MAHAFFY, John Pentland,** 1839–1919, *Irish scholar.*

Ireland is a country in which the probable never happens and the impossible always does.

**MALLOCK, William H.,** 1849–1923, *English writer.*

Whatever may be God's future, we cannot forget His past.

**MANN, Horace,** 1796–1859, *American educator.*

1. I have never heard anything about the resolutions of the Apostles, but a great deal about their Acts.
2. We go by the major vote, and if the majority are insane, the sane must go to the hospital.

**MANN, Thomas,** born 1875, *German-American novelist and essayist.*

A man's dying is more the survivors' affair than his own.

**MANSFIELD, Katherine,** 1888–1923, *British short-story writer.*

Regret is an appalling waste of energy; you can't build on it; it's only good for wallowing in.

**MARQUAND, John Phillips,** born 1893, *American novelist.*

I know a fellow who's as broke as the Ten Commandments.

**MARQUIS, Don,** 1878–1937, *American journalist and humorist.*

1. The females of all species are most dangerous when they appear to retreat.
2. Fishing is a delusion entirely surrounded by liars in old clothes.
3. He is so unlucky that he runs into accidents which started out to happen to somebody else.

4. He worked like hell in the country so he could live in the city, where he worked like hell so he could live in the country.

5. Hope is all right and so is Faith, but what I would like to see is a little Charity.

6. An idea isn't responsible for the people who believe in it.

7. If you make people think they're thinking, they'll love you; but if you really make them think, they'll hate you.

8. Mankind is being reformed, but conditions among the lower animals are frightful.

9. The more conscious a philosopher is of the weak spots of his theory, the more certain he is to speak with an air of final authority.

10. Most of the people living in New York have come here from the farm to try to make enough money to go back to the farm.

11. Ours is a world where people don't know what they want and are willing to go through hell to get it.

12. Procrastination is the art of keeping up with yesterday.

13. Publishing a volume of verse is like dropping a rose petal down the Grand Canyon and waiting for the echo.

14. The successful people are the ones who can think up things for the rest of the world to keep busy at.

15. There is always a comforting thought in time of trouble when it is not our trouble.

16. Young man, if she asks you if you like her hair that way, beware; the woman has already committed matrimony in her heart.

17. If you want to get rich from writing, write the sort of thing that's read by persons who move their lips when they're reading to themselves.

18. Middle age is the time when a man is always thinking that in a week or two he will feel as good as ever.

**MARSHALL**, Thomas R., 1854–1925, *American lawyer and vice-president of the United States.*

I come from Indiana, the home of more first-rate second-class men than any state in the Union.

**MARTIAL,** A.D. 40?–102?, *Roman poet and epigrammatist.*

1. He does not write at all whose poems no man reads.
2. He was once a doctor but is now an undertaker; and what he does as an undertaker he used to do as a doctor.
3. If fame is to come only after death, I am in no hurry for it.
4. If you want him to mourn, you had best leave him nothing.
5. Lawyers are men who hire out their words and anger.
6. No amount of misfortune will satisfy the man who is not satisfied with reading a hundred epigrams.
7. She has buried all her female friends; I wish she would make friends with my wife.
8. This is now the seventh wife that you have buried in your field; no one gets a better return from his field than you do.
9. The wife should be inferior to the husband; that is the only way to insure equality between the two.

**MASEFIELD,** John, born 1878, *English poet, novelist, and dramatist.*

His face was filled with broken commandments.

**MASSON,** Tom, 1866–1934, *American humorist and editor.*

1. After all, doesn't free love cost the most?
2. The best way to study human nature is when nobody else is present.
3. "Be yourself!" is about the worst advice you can give to some people.
4. To feel themselves in the presence of true greatness many men find it necessary only to be alone.
5. Hamlet is the tragedy of tackling a family problem too soon after college.
6. If Longfellow were alive today he would write: "Sail on, thou Censorship of State."
7. In modern wedlock, too many misplace the key.
8. It must be a hard life to be the child of a psychologist.
9. The love game is never called off on account of darkness.

10. No brain is stronger than its weakest think.

11. Professional charity—the milk of human blindness.

12. Prohibition may be a disputed theory, but none can complain that it doesn't hold water.

13. Reputation: what others are not thinking about you.

14. A senior always feels like the university is going to the kids.

15. Some girls never know just what they are going to do from one husband to another.

16. There are seventy million books in American libraries, but the one you want to read is always out.

17. Think of what would happen to us in America if there were no humorists; life would be one long Congressional Record.

18. What if my trousers are shabby and worn; they cover a warm heart.

19. When billing and cooing results in matrimony, the billing always comes after the cooing.

20. You are not treating a girl right unless you ruin her digestion.

21. You can always get someone to love you—even if you have to do it yourself.

**MATHEWS, Shailer,** 1863–1941, *American educator and writer.*

1. An epigram is a half-truth so stated as to irritate the person who believes the other half.

2. If it is more blessed to give than to receive, then most of us are content to let the other fellow have the greater blessing.

**MATTHEWS, Brander,** 1852–1929, *American educator, novelist, essayist, and playwright.*

A highbrow is a person educated beyond his intelligence.

**MAUGHAM, William Somerset,** born 1874, *English novelist, playwright, and short-story writer.*

1. American women expect to find in their husbands a perfection that English women only hope to find in their butlers.

2. Impropriety is the soul of wit.

3. In heaven when the blessed use the telephone they will say what they have to say and not a word besides.

4. It is a funny thing about life: if you refuse to accept anything but the best you very often get it.

5. Only a mediocre writer is always at his best.

6. To do each day two things one dislikes is a precept I have followed scrupulously: every day I have got up and I have gone to bed.

7. A woman can forgive a man for the harm he does her, but she can never forgive the sacrifices he makes on her account.

**MAUROIS, André,** born 1885, *French biographer and miscellaneous writer.*

1. The only thing experience teaches us is that experience teaches us nothing.

2. To have the license number of one's automobile as low as possible is a social advantage in America.

3. A well-written life will always be rarer than a well-spent one.

4. When you become used to never being alone, you may consider yourself Americanized.

**McFEE, William,** born 1881, *Anglo-American writer.*

The world belongs to the Enthusiast who keeps cool.

**MENCKEN, H. L.,** born 1880, *American editor, critic, biographer, lexicographer, and satirist.*

1. Adultery: democracy applied to love.

2. An anti-vivisectionist is one who gags at a guinea pig and swallows a baby.

3. Archbishop: a Christian ecclesiastic of a rank superior to that attained by Christ.

4. Bachelors know more about women than married men; if they didn't, they'd be married too.

5. The chief knowledge that a man gets from reading books is the knowledge that very few of them are worth reading.

6. Christian endeavor is notoriously hard on female pulchritude.

7. A church is a place in which gentlemen who have never been to heaven brag about it to persons who will never get there.

8. Clergyman: a ticket speculator outside the gates of heaven.

9. Conscience: the inner voice which warns us that someone may be looking.

10. A cynic is a man who, when he smells flowers, looks around for a coffin.

11. A cow goes on giving milk all her life even though what appears to be her self-interest urges her to give gin.

12. Democracy is also a form of religion; it is the worship of jackals by jackasses.

13. The difference between a moral man and a man of honor is that the latter regrets a discreditable act even when it has worked.

14. The dot is simply a bribe designed to overcome the disinclination of the male.

15. Every normal man must be tempted, at times, to spit on his hands, hoist the black flag, and begin slitting throats.

16. Faith may be defined briefly as an illogical belief in the occurrence of the improbable.

17. The first Rotarian was the first man to call John the Baptist Jack.

18. A gentleman is one who never strikes a woman without provocation.

19. Honeymoon: the time during which the bride believes the bridegroom's word of honor.

20. I go on working for the same reason that a hen goes on laying eggs.

21. Injustice is relatively easy to bear; what stings is justice.

22. In the main, there are two sorts of books: those that no one reads and those that no one ought to read.

23. In the United States, doing good has come to be, like patriotism, a favorite device of persons with something to sell.

24. It is a sin to believe evil of others, but it is seldom a mistake.

25. It is hard to believe that a man is telling the truth when you know that you would lie if you were in his place.

26. It is impossible to believe that the same God who permitted His own son to die a bachelor regards celibacy as an actual sin.

27. A judge is a law student who marks his own examination papers.

28. Love is like war: easy to begin but very hard to stop.

29. Love is the delusion that one woman differs from another.

30. Love is the triumph of imagination over intelligence.

31. Man is always looking for someone to boast to; woman is always looking for a shoulder to put her head on.

32. Man weeps to think that he will die so soon; woman, that she was born so long ago.

33. Men have a much better time of it than women; for one thing, they marry later; for another thing, they die earlier.

34. The objection to Puritans is not that they try to make us think as they do, but that they try to make us do as they think.

35. The older I grow, the more I distrust the familiar doctrine that age brings wisdom.

36. On one issue at least, men and women agree: they both distrust women.

37. Opera in English is, in the main, just about as sensible as baseball in Italian.

38. The Parisians look forward to dinner as a Mississippian looks forward to his evening necking of the Scriptures.

39. The penalty for laughing in a courtroom is six months in jail; if it were not for this penalty, the jury would never hear the evidence.

40. Say what you will about the Ten Commandments, you must always come back to the pleasant fact that there are only ten of them.

41. A Sunday school is a prison in which children do penance for the evil conscience of their parents.

42. A teacher is one who, in his youth, admired teachers.

43. Theology is the effort to explain the unknowable in terms of the not worth knowing.

44. There is no record in human history of a happy philosopher.

45. 'Tis more blessed to give than to receive; for example, wedding presents.

46. The truth that survives is simply the lie that is pleasantest to believe.

47. The typical actor, at least in America, is the most upright of men; he always marries the girl.

48. Whenever a husband and wife begin to discuss their marriage, they are giving evidence at an inquest.

49. When everyone begins to believe anything it ceases to be true; for example, the notion that the homeliest girl in the party is the safest.

50. When women kiss, it always reminds me of prize fighters shaking hands.

51. Don't overestimate the decency of the human race.

52. In war the heroes always outnumber the soldiers ten to one.

53. It was as necessary to me as honey to the bee or hell to the Christians.

54. Wife: a former sweetheart.

55. A woman in love is less modest than a man; she has less to be ashamed of.

56. Women never acknowledge that they have fallen in love until the man has formally avowed his delusion and so cut off his retreat.

57. Love is based on a view of women that is impossible to those who have had any experience with them.

**MEREDITH, George**, 1828-1909, *English novelist and poet.*

1. After forty, men have married their habits, and wives are only an item in the list, and not the most important.

2. The future not being born, my friend, we will abstain from baptizing it.

3. In a dissension between a man and a wife, that one is in the right who has the most friends.

4. Kissing don't last; cookery do!

5. She poured a little social sewage into his ears.

6. Woman will be the last thing civilized by man.

**METTERNICH, Prince von,** 1773–1859, *Austrian diplomat and statesman.*

The English have better sense than any other nation—and they are fools.

**MICHELET, Jules,** 1798–1874, *French historian.*

How beautifully everything is arranged by Nature; as soon as a child enters the world, it finds a mother ready to take care of it.

**MILNE, Alan Alexander,** born 1882, *English poet, playwright, and author of juveniles.*

No doubt Jack the Ripper excused himself on the grounds that it was human nature.

**MIZNER, Addison,** 1872–1933, *American architect.*

1. Absinthe makes the heart grow fonder.
2. The poor ye have with ye always—but they are not invited.
3. Some people's genius lies in giving infinite pains.
4. Don't talk about yourself; it will be done when you leave.
5. God help those who do not help themselves!
6. They also swear who only stand and wait.
7. Where there's a will, there's a lawsuit.
8. Ignorance of the law excuses no man—from practicing it.
9. It's a strong stomach that has no turning.
10. A lie in time saves nine.
11. Matrimony is the root of all evil.
12. Misery loves company, but company does not reciprocate.
13. Never call a man a fool; borrow from him.
14. Never drink from your finger bowl—it contains only water.
15. None but the brave desert the fair.
16. A woman is never too old to yearn.
17. A woman on time is one in nine.
18. Poets are born, not paid.

**MIZNER,** Wilson, 1876–1933, *American dramatist, bon vivant, and wit.*

1. The best way to keep your friends is not to give them away.

2. The cuckoo who is on to himself is halfway out of the clock.

3. The days just prior to marriage are like a snappy introduction to a tedious book.

4. The difference between chirping out of turn and a *faux pas* depends on what kind of a bar you're in.

5. A drama critic is a person who surprises the playwright by informing him what he meant.

6. A fellow who is always declaring he's no fool usually has his suspicions.

7. The gent who wakes up and finds himself a success hasn't been asleep.

8. A good listener is not only popular everywhere, but after a while he knows something.

9. I am a stylist, and the most beautiful sentence I have ever heard is, "Have one on the house."

10. I hate careless flattery, the kind that exhausts you in your effort to believe it.

11. I know of no sentence that can induce such immediate and brazen lying as the one that begins, "Have you read——"

12. In the battle for existence, talent is the punch, and tact is the clever footwork.

13. I respect faith, but doubt is what gets you an education.

14. I've had ample contact with lawyers, and I'm convinced that the only fortune they ever leave is their own.

15. I've had several years in Hollywood and I still think the movie heroes are in the audience.

16. The man who won't loan money isn't going to have many friends —or need them.

17. Many a live wire would be a dead one except for his connections.

18. Money is the only substance which can keep a cold world from nicknaming a citizen "Hey, you!"

19. More people would go to church if they hadn't observed what sanctity had done for the dull deacons.

20. The most effective water power in the world—women's tears.

21. Most hard-boiled people are half-baked.

22. The only bird that gives the poor a real tumble is the stork.

23. The only sure thing about luck is that it will change.

24. The only time most women give their orating husbands undivided attention is when the old boys mumble in their sleep.

25. Over in Hollywood they almost made a great picture, but they caught it just in time.

26. Some of the greatest love affairs I've known have involved one actor—unassisted.

27. There is something about a closet that makes a skeleton terribly restless.

28. There's nothing so comfortable as a small bank roll; a big one is always in danger.

29. Those who welcome death have only tried it from the ears up.

30. To my embarrassment I was born in bed with a lady.

31. We all have something to fall back on, and I never knew a phony who didn't land on it eventually.

32. When a woman tells you her age, it's all right to look surprised, but don't scowl.

33. When you take stuff from one writer, it's plagiarism; but when you take it from many writers, it's research.

34. Why do women reformers almost always worry about men?

35. Women can instantly see through each other, and it's surprising how little they observe that's pleasant.

36. Be nice to people on your way up because you'll meet them on your way down.

37. If that radio announcer doesn't get off the air, I'll stop breathing it.

38. Life's a tough proposition, and the first hundred years are the hardest.

39. The worst intrusion I know is represented in the author who forgets that you are only a reader, and starts to put on a show.

**MOLEY, Raymond,** born 1886, *American journalist, editor, and political writer.*

1. He walks as if balancing the family tree on his nose.
2. A political war is one in which everyone shoots from the lip.

**MOLIÈRE,** 1622–1673, *French actor and playwright.*

1. I prefer a comfortable vice to a virtue that bores.
2. The only good thing about him is his cook, and the world visits his dinners and not him.
3. That must be wonderful; I don't understand it at all.
4. For more than forty years I have been speaking prose without knowing it.

**MONTAGU, Mary Wortley,** 1689–1762, *English society leader and letter writer.*

1. I despise the pleasure of pleasing people whom I despise.
2. If it was the fashion to go naked, the face would be hardly observed.
3. I sometimes give myself admirable advice, but I am incapable of taking it.
4. It goes far toward reconciling me to being a woman when I reflect that I am thus in no danger of marrying one.
5. When they tell me I have forsook the worship of my ancestors, I say I have had more ancestors heathen than Christian.

**MONTAGUE, Charles Edward,** 1867–1928, *British journalist, essayist, and novelist.*

War hath no fury like a noncombatant.

**MONTAIGNE, Michel Eyquem de,** 1533–1592, *French essayist.*

1. Eloquence flourished most in Rome when public affairs were in the worst condition.
2. A good marriage would be between a blind wife and a deaf husband.
3. I don't remember ever having had the itch, and yet scratching is one of nature's sweet pleasures, and so handy.

4. If the world complains that I speak too much about myself, I complain that the world doesn't think of itself at all.

5. Man is certainly stark mad: he cannot make a worm, and yet he makes gods by the dozen.

6. May God defend me from myself!

7. No one is exempt from talking nonsense; the mistake is to do it solemnly.

8. Seeing she could not make fools wise, fortune has made them lucky.

9. A doctor gets no pleasure out of the health of his friends.

10. It is easier to write a mediocre poem than to understand a good one.

## MONTESQUIEU, Baron de, 1689-1755, *French political philosopher and man of letters.*

1. An author is a fool who, not content with having bored those who have lived with him, insists on boring future generations.

2. If the triangles made a god, they would give him three sides.

3. What orators lack in depth they make up for in length.

4. When God endowed human beings with brains, He did not intend to guarantee them.

## MOORE, George, 1852-1933, *Irish novelist, art critic, and miscellaneous writer.*

1. England produced Shakespeare; the British Empire the six-shilling novel.

2. Everybody sets out to do something, and everybody does something, but no one does what he sets out to do.

3. Faith goes out through the window when beauty comes in at the door.

4. Heaven may be for the laity, but this world is certainly for the clergy.

5. If good books did good, the world would have been converted long ago.

6. If there were no husbands, who would look after our mistresses?

7. The incomparable stupidity of life teaches us to love our parents; divine philosophy teaches us to forgive them.

8. In Ireland there is so little sense of compromise that a girl has to choose between perpetual adoration and perpetual pregnancy.

9. It is only with scent and silk and artifices that we raise love from an instinct to a passion.

10. The lot of critics is to be remembered by what they failed to understand.

11. Married folk know their bedfellows; bachelors, and perhaps spinsters, are never sure of theirs.

12. My one claim to originality among Irishmen is that I have never made a speech.

13. Nothing sharpens the wits like promiscuous flirtation.

14. People say you mustn't love your friend's wife, but how are you to love your enemy's wife?

15. The poor would never be able to live at all if it weren't for the poor.

16. Remorse is beholding heaven and feeling hell.

17. Taking something from one man and making it worse is plagiarism.

18. There is nothing so consoling as to find that one's neighbor's troubles are at least as great as one's own.

19. To be able to distinguish between a badly- and well-written book is not enough; a professor of literature can do that occasionally.

20. There is always a right and a wrong way, and the wrong way always seems the more reasonable.

21. You must have women dressed, if it is only for the pleasure of imagining them as Venuses.

**MORLEY, Christopher,** born 1890, *American novelist, editor, and man of letters.*

1. By the time the youngest children have learned to keep the place tidy, the oldest grandchildren are on hand to tear it to pieces again.

2. Dancing is wonderful training for girls; it's the first way you learn to guess what a man is going to do before he does it.

3. Few girls are as well shaped as a good horse.

4. God made man merely to hear some praise of what He'd done on those five days.

5. High heels were invented by a woman who had been kissed on the forehead.

6. A human being is an ingenious assembly of portable plumbing.

7. If you have to keep reminding yourself of a thing, perhaps it isn't so.

8. I hate to see men overdressed; a man ought to look like he's put together by accident, not added up on purpose.

9. Informal's what women always say they're going to be and never are.

10. Life is a foreign language: all men mispronounce it.

11. Lots of times you have to pretend to join a parade in which you're not really interested in order to get where you're going.

12. The most important autograph in a book is your own.

13. My theology, briefly, is that the universe was dictated but not signed.

14. No man is lonely while eating spaghetti—it requires so much attention.

15. Only the sinner has a right to preach.

16. The plural of spouse is spice.

17. Prophets were twice stoned: first in anger; then, after their death, with a handsome slab in the graveyard.

18. There are certain people whom one almost feels inclined to urge to hurry up and die so that their letters can be published.

19. There is only one rule for being a good talker: learn to listen.

20. There's so much to say but your eyes keep interrupting me.

21. Truth is not a diet but a condiment.

22. The war was not expurgated for those who went through it.

23. Your mind needs an uplift as well as your bust.

**MORLEY, John,** 1838–1923, *English editor, biographer, and statesman.*

1. In politics the choice is constantly between two evils.

2. Letter-writing: that most delightful way of wasting time.

3. The proper memory for a politician is one that knows what to remember and what to forget.

4. Three things matter in a speech: who says it, how he says it, and what he says—and, of the three, the last matters the least.

5. Carlyle finally compressed his Gospel of Silence into thirty handsome octavos.

**MUMFORD, Ethel Watts,** 1878?–1940, *American novelist and humorous writer.*

1. Don't take the will for the deed; get the deed.

2. God gives us our relatives; thank God we can choose our friends.

3. Think of your ancestors and your posterity, and you will never marry.

4. In the midst of life we are in debt.

5. It is better to make friends fast than to make fast friends.

6. When folly is bliss, 'tis ignorance to be otherwise.

7. Knowledge is power, if you know it about the right person.

8. A man of courage never needs weapons, but he may need bail.

9. Oh wad some power the giftie gie us to see some people before they see us.

**MUNRO, Hector Hugh,** 1870–1916, *pen name Saki, British short-story writer and novelist.*

1. Bernard Shaw had discovered himself and gave ungrudgingly of his discovery to the world.

2. The cook was a good cook, as cooks go; and as cooks go, she went.

3. He is one of those people who would be enormously improved by death.

4. He's simply got the instinct for being unhappy highly developed.

5. I'm living so far beyond my income that we may almost be said to be living apart.

6. There's nothing in Christianity or Buddhism that quite matches the sympathetic unselfishness of an oyster.

7. Women and elephants never forget an injury.

8. She's so fond of talking of certain pictures as "growing on one" as though they were a sort of fungus.

**NAPOLEON BONAPARTE**, 1769–1821, *French general and emperor.*

1. I like convents, but I wish they wouldn't admit any women under the age of fifty.

2. Rascality has limits; stupidity has not.

3. Soldiers win battles and generals get the credit.

4. Doctors will have more lives to answer for in the next world than even we generals.

**NASBY, Petroleum V.**, 1833–1888, *pen name of David Ross Locke, American journalist and humorist.*

If there is anything in being first, man must acknowledge the supremacy of the goose, for according to Genesis the fowl was first created.

**NASH, Ogden**, born 1902, *American humorous poet.*

1. Parents were invented to make children happy by giving them something to ignore.

2. The reason for much matrimony is patrimony.

3. Why did the Lord give us so much quickness of movement unless it was to avoid responsibility?

4. A little incompatibility is the spice of life, particularly if he has income and she is pattable.

5. Marriage is the alliance of two people, one of whom never remembers birthdays and the other never forgets them.

6. Marriage is the only known example of the happy meeting of the immovable object and the irresistible force.

**NATHAN, George Jean**, born 1882, *American editor, author, and dramatic critic.*

1. Bad officials are elected by good citizens who do not vote.

2. He has ever been the tin can on his own tail.

3. He writes his plays for the ages—the ages between five and twelve.

4. Opening night: the night before the play is ready to open.

5. An optimist is a fellow who believes a housefly is looking for a way to get out.

6. What passes for woman's intuition is often nothing more than man's transparency.

**NEVINSON, Henry W.,** 1856–1941, *English newspaper correspondent and essayist.*

Chivalry: going about releasing beautiful maidens from other men's castles, and taking them to your own castle.

**NEWTON, Isaac,** 1642–1727, *English scientist and mathematician.*

O physics! Preserve me from metaphysics!

**NICHOLS, Beverley,** born 1899, *English writer.*

1. Marriage is a book of which the first chapter is written in poetry and the remaining chapters in prose.

2. When a woman is wearing shorts her charms are enlarged without being enhanced.

3. The worst thing you can possibly do to a woman is to deprive her of a grievance.

**NICOLSON, Harold,** born 1886, *English biographer and critic.*

The Irish do not want anyone to wish them well; they want everyone to wish their enemies ill.

**NIETZSCHE, Friedrich Wilhelm,** 1844–1900, *German philosopher and writer.*

1. Blessed are the forgetful, for they get the better even of their blunders.

2. A casual stroll through a lunatic asylum shows that faith does not prove anything.

3. Chastity is a virtue in some, but in many almost a vice.

4. Even concubinage has been corrupted—by marriage.

5. He who cannot lie doesn't know what truth is.

6. I do not give alms; I am not poor enough for that.

7. If a man really has strong faith he can indulge in the luxury of skepticism.

8. In the beginning was nonsense, and the nonsense was with God, and the nonsense was God.

9. I would believe only in a God that knows how to dance.

10. The last Christian died on the cross.

11. Marriage makes an end of many short follies—being one long stupidity.

12. A married philosopher is necessarily comic.

13. Neighbors praise unselfishness because they profit by it.

14. No small art is it to sleep: it is necessary to keep awake all day for that purpose.

15. One should not go into churches if one wants to breathe pure air.

16. Some die too young, and some die too old; the precept sounds strange, but die at the right time.

17. There are two things a real man likes—danger and play; and he likes woman because she is the most dangerous of playthings.

18. We are most unfair to God: we do not allow Him to sin.

19. Which is it—is man one of God's blunders or is God one of man's blunders?

20. Woman was God's second mistake.

21. The earth has a skin and that skin has diseases; one of its diseases is called man.

22. There is not enough religion in the world even to destroy the world's religions.

23. When a woman becomes a scholar there is usually something wrong with her sexual organs.

**NORRIS, Kathleen,** born 1880, *American novelist.*

Life is easier to take than you'd think; all that is necessary is to accept the impossible, do without the indispensable, and bear the intolerable.

**NYE, Edgar Wilson ("Bill"), 1850–1896, *American humorist.***

1. At a Fourth of July celebration, it is wonderful how many great men there are and how they swarm on the speaker's platform.

2. Be virtuous and you will be happy; but you will be lonesome, sometimes.

3. A bronco often becomes so attached to his master that he will lay down his life if necessary—his master's life, I mean.

4. I do not believe that it will always be popular to wear mourning for our friends, unless we feel a little doubtful about where they went.

5. I rise from bed the first thing in the morning not because I am dissatisfied with it, but because I cannot carry it with me during the day.

6. I think I like Shakespeare's expurgated poems best, and I often wish that he had confined himself entirely to that kind.

7. Kind words will never die—neither will they buy groceries.

8. Let every man who pants for fame select his own style of pant and go ahead.

9. Many public speakers are good extemporaneous listeners.

10. Men are often misunderstood; they may be rough on the exterior but they can love, oh so warmly, so truly, so deeply—and so universally.

11. No thorough metropolitan editor wants to enter upon his profession without knowing the difference between a writ of mandamus and other styles of profanity.

12. Self-made men are very apt to usurp the prerogative of the Almighty and overwork themselves.

13. Some broncos have formed the habit of bucking; they do not all buck—only those that are alive do so.

14. There are just two people entitled to refer to themselves as "we"; one is the editor and the other is the fellow with a tapeworm.

15. There must be at least 500,000,000 rats in the United States; of course, I am speaking only from memory.

16. We are both great men, but I have succeeded better in keeping it a profound secret than he has.

17. We owe it to our country to pay our taxes without murmuring; the time to get in our fine work is on the valuation.

18. Winter lingered so long in the lap of Spring that it occasioned a great deal of talk.

19. Space has no top, no bottom; in fact, it is bottomless both at the bottom and at the top.

20. Little do women realize that all a man needs under the cerulean dome of heaven is love—and board and clothes.

**O'MALLEY, Austin,** 1858–1932, *American oculist and miscellaneous writer.*

1. After thirty-five a man begins to have thoughts about women; before that age he has feelings.

2. All things come to him who waits—even justice.

3. The American government is a rule of the people, by the people, for the boss.

4. The best blood will at some time get into a fool or a mosquito.

5. The best part of a real-estate bargain is the neighbor.

6. The best throw of the dice is to throw them away.

7. Better a bald head than none at all.

8. Busy souls have no time to be busybodies.

9. Circumstantial evidence is like a blackberry, which when red or white is really green.

10. A drunkard is like a whisky bottle, all neck and belly and no head.

11. A dyspeptic is a man that can eat his cake and have it too.

12. An Englishman thinks seated; a Frenchman, standing; an American, pacing; an Irishman, afterward.

13. Exclusiveness is a characteristic of recent riches, high society, and the skunk.

14. A gentleman never heard the story before.

15. Gift is a synonym of trade.

16. God shows his contempt for wealth by the kind of person he selects to receive it.

17. A habit of debt is very injurious to the memory.

18. The half-baked sermon causes spiritual indigestion.

19. A hole is nothing at all, but you can break your neck in it.

20. If you keep your eyes so fixed on heaven that you never look at the earth, you will stumble into hell.

21. If you keep your mouth shut you will never put your foot in it.

22. In levying taxes and in shearing sheep it is well to stop when you get down to the skin.

23. An Irishman can be worried by the consciousness that there is nothing to worry about.

24. It is a foolish man that hears all he hears.

25. It is a mean thief, or a successful author, that plunders the dead.

26. It is as easy to give advice to yourself as to others, and as useless.

27. The man that leaves no will after his death had little will before his death.

28. Many social visits you think paid to yourself are paid to your bottles.

29. Marriage is a meal where the soup is better than the dessert.

30. The modern king has become a vermiform appendix: useless when quiet; when obtrusive, in danger of removal.

31. Music is another lady that talks charmingly and says nothing.

32. No man can have a reasonable opinion of women until he has long lost interest in hair restorers.

33. Often a convert is zealous not through piety, but because of the novelty of his experience.

34. The perjurer's mother told white lies.

35. The person that always says just what he thinks at last gets just what he deserves.

36. A politician is like quicksilver; if you try to put your finger on him, you will find nothing under it.

37. Practical prayer is harder on the soles of your shoes than on the knees of your trousers.

38. The reason there are so many imbeciles among imprisoned criminals is that an imbecile is so foolish even a detective can detect him.

39. Revenge is often like biting a dog because the dog bit you.

40. Show me a genuine case of platonic friendship, and I shall show you two old or homely faces.

41. The smaller the head, the bigger the dream.

42. Some men are like a clock on a roof; they are useful only to the neighbors.

43. Some men can live up to their loftiest ideals without ever going higher than a basement.

44. The statesman shears the sheep, the politician skins them.

45. There are ten church members by inheritance for one by conviction.

46. There should be more in American liberty than the privilege we enjoy of insulting the President with impunity.

47. The three most important events of human life are equally devoid of reason: birth, marriage, and death.

48. Those that think it permissible to tell white lies soon grow color-blind.

49. Those who live in stone houses should not throw glass.

50. Ugliness is a point of view: an ulcer is wonderful to a pathologist.

51. We smile at the women who are eagerly following the fashions in dress whilst we are as eagerly following the fashions in thought.

52. When there is no will, there is no way for the lawyers.

53. Why is the word "tongue" feminine in Greek, Latin, Italian, Spanish, French, and German?

54. The worst misfortune that can happen to an ordinary man is to have an extraordinary father.

OSLER, William, 1849-1919, *Canadian physician, writer, and teacher of medicine.*

1. The natural man has only two primal passions—to get and to beget.

2. The desire to take medicine is perhaps the greatest feature which distinguishes man from animals.

3. There are only two sorts of doctors: those who practice with their brains, and those who practice with their tongues.

**OSTENSO, Martha,** born 1900, *Norwegian-American novelist.*

Edith was a little country bounded on the north, south, east, and west by Edith.

**OVID,** 43 B.C.–A.D. 17?, *Roman poet.*

1. Chaste is she whom no one has asked.
2. If Jupiter hurled his thunderbolt as often as men sinned, he would soon be out of thunderbolts.
3. Let the man who does not wish to be idle fall in love.

**PAIN, Barry,** 1865–1928, *English humorist and parodist.*

1. Buy visiting cards for the cat; she knows a lot more cats than we know people.
2. Don't answer back if you're out to make money, but do if you're out for enjoyment.

**PAINE, Thomas,** 1737–1809, *American political philosopher, revolutionist, and author.*

It would have approached nearer to the idea of miracle if Jonah had swallowed the whale.

**PALMERSTON, Lord,** 1784–1865, *English statesman.*

1. The best thing for the inside of a man is the outside of a horse.
2. Dirt is not dirt, but only matter in the wrong place.

**PARKER, Dorothy,** born 1893, *American wit, poet, and short-story writer.*

1. Brevity is the soul of lingerie.
2. A girl's best friend is her mutter.
3. Men seldom make passes at girls who wear glasses.
4. The only "ism" Hollywood believes in is plagiarism.
5. She ran the whole gamut of the emotions from A to B.

**PARKHURST, Charles H.**, 1842–1933, *American clergyman and reformer.*

The man who lives by himself and for himself is apt to be corrupted by the company he keeps.

**PASCAL, Blaise,** 1623–1662, *French scientist, mathematician, and philosopher.*

1. If all men knew what each said of the other, there would not be four friends in the world.

2. The last thing we decide in writing a book is what to put first.

3. Had Cleopatra's nose been shorter, the whole face of the world would have been different.

4. I have made this a rather long letter because I haven't had time to make it shorter.

5. Those we call the ancients were really new in everything.

6. To be a real philosopher one must be able to laugh at philosophy.

**PEACOCK, Thomas Love,** 1785–1866, *English poet and novelist.*

1. I never failed to convince an audience that the best thing they could do was to go away.

2. There are two reasons for drinking: one is, when you are thirsty, to cure it; the other, when you are not thirsty, to prevent it.

**PEPYS, Samuel,** 1633–1703, *English diarist.*

1. I went out to see him hanged, drawn, and quartered, which was done, he looking as cheerful as any man could do in that condition.

2. My wife, poor wretch, is troubled with her lonely life.

3. The silk suit cost me much money, and I pray God to make me able to pay for it.

4. Strange to say what delight we married people have to see these poor fools decoyed into our condition.

**PHELPS, William Lyon,** 1865–1943, *American educator and literary critic.*

1. At a certain age some people's minds close up; they live on their intellectual fat.

2. A cold is both positive and negative; sometimes the Eyes have it and sometimes the Nose.

3. I divide all readers into two classes: those who read to remember and those who read to forget.

4. If I were running the world I would have it rain only between 2 and 5 A.M.—anyone who was out then ought to get wet.

5. This is the final test of a gentleman: his respect for those who can be of no possible service to him.

6. Nature makes boys and girls lovely to look upon so they can be tolerated until they acquire some sense.

**PHILLIPS, Wendell, 1811–1884,** *American reformer and orator.*

You can always get the truth from an American statesman after he has turned seventy, or given up all hope of the Presidency.

**PINERO, Arthur Wing, 1855–1934,** *English dramatist.*

1. A financier is a pawnbroker with imagination.

2. How many "coming men" has one known! Where on earth do they all go to?

3. If there were many more like her, the stock of halos would give out.

4. Married men are viler than bachelors.

5. A married woman's as old as her husband makes her feel.

**PITT, William, 1759–1806,** *English statesman and prime minister.*

1. It was a saying of Lord Chatham that the parks were the lungs of London.

2. Don't tell me of a man's being able to talk sense; everyone can talk sense—can he talk nonsense?

3. Poverty of course is no disgrace, but it is damned annoying.

**PLATO, 427?–347 B.C.,** *Greek philosopher, pupil of Socrates, and teacher of Aristotle.*

1. The Athenians do not mind a man being clever, as long as he keeps it to himself.

2. A boy is, of all wild beasts, the most difficult to manage.

3. Man is a two-legged animal without feathers.

4. O ye Gods, grant us what is good whether we pray for it or not, but keep evil from us even though we pray for it.

5. Poets utter great and wise things which they do not themselves understand.

6. Wise men talk because they have something to say; fools, because they have to say something.

## PLUTARCH, A.D. 46?–120?, *Greek biographer.*

It is indeed desirable to be well descended, but the glory belongs to our ancestors.

## POE, Edgar Allan, 1809–1849, *American poet, editor, and story writer.*

1. The dearth of genius in America is owing to the continual teasing of mosquitoes.

2. I have great faith in fools; self-confidence my friends call it.

3. The people have nothing to do with the laws but to obey them.

4. Of puns it has been said that they who most dislike them are least able to utter them.

## POLLOCK, Channing, 1880–1946, *American critic, dramatist, novelist, and lecturer.*

1. A critic is a legless man who teaches running.

2. He admits that there are two sides to every question—his own and the wrong side.

3. No man in the world has more courage than the man who can stop after eating one peanut.

4. She wore a silk jersey dress that held fast going around curves.

## POPE, Alexander, 1688–1744, *English poet.*

1. Blessed is he who expects nothing for he shall never be disappointed.

2. A family is but too often a commonwealth of malignants.

3. Some people will never learn anything, for this reason, because they understand everything too soon.

4. Histories are more full of examples of the fidelity of dogs than of friends.

5. I am dying, sir, of a hundred good symptoms.

**PRENTICE, George D.,** 1802–1870, *American journalist and humorist.*

1. About the only person we ever heard of that wasn't spoiled by being lionized was a Jew named Daniel.

2. A bare assertion is not necessarily the naked truth.

3. Be gentle in old age; peevishness is worse in second childhood than in first.

4. Be sure not to tell a first falsehood, and you needn't fear being detected in any subsequent ones.

5. A dentist at work in his vocation always looks down in the mouth.

6. The difference between us and our neighbor is that we don't tell half of what we know while he doesn't know half of what he tells.

7. Farmers ought to learn to make better fences; why not establish a fencing school for their benefit?

8. The Great Author of All made everything out of nothing, but many a human author makes nothing out of everything.

9. If a woman could talk out of the two sides of her mouth at the same time, a great deal would be said on both sides.

10. If you want a man to do fair work for you, let him have fair play.

11. In these days the greater part of whitewashing is done with ink.

12. It is a very rare thing to find a man preferring his neighbor's son or daughter to his own, but not his neighbor's wife.

13. It is our will to speak the plain truth and, what is better, our wont.

14. A man bitten by a dog, no matter whether the animal is mad or not, is apt to get mad himself.

15. A man's shoes get tight by imbibing water, but he doesn't.

16. Many a man keeps on drinking till he hasn't a coat to either his back or his stomach.

17. Many a writer seems to think he is never profound except when he can't understand his own meaning.

18. Men should not think too much of themselves, and yet a man should always be careful not to forget himself.

19. Much smoking kills live men and cures dead swine.

20. One of the very best of all earthly possessions is self-possession.

21. One swallow doesn't make a summer but too many swallows make a fall.

22. A pin has as much head as some authors, and a good deal more point.

23. Some members of Congress would best promote the country's peace by holding their own.

24. Some old women and men grow bitter with age; the more their teeth drop out, the more biting they get.

25. Some people use one half their ingenuity to get into debt, and the other half to avoid paying it.

26. Some persons can be everywhere at home; others can sit musingly at home and be everywhere.

27. Some things are much better eschewed than chewed; tobacco is one of them.

28. There are two classes of persons whose word is as good as their bond: those whose word is never broken, and those whose bond is good for nothing.

29. There are two periods when Congress does no business: one is before the holidays, and the other after.

30. To keep your friends, treat them kindly; to kill them, treat them often.

31. We are in favor of tolerance, but it is a very difficult thing to tolerate the intolerant and impossible to tolerate the intolerable.

32. We have heard of men celebrating their country's battles who in war were celebrated for keeping out of them.

33. When a young man complains that a young lady has no heart, it is a pretty certain sign that she has his.

34. Why can't the captain of a vessel keep a memorandum of the weight of his anchor, instead of weighing it every time he leaves port?

35. What man wants: all he can get; what woman wants: all she can't get.

**PRIESTLEY, John Boynton,** born 1894, *English novelist, dramatist, and critic.*

A loving wife will do anything for her husband except stop criticizing and trying to improve him.

**PULITZER, Joseph,** 1847–1911, *American journalist.*

What is everybody's business is nobody's business—except the journalist's.

**QUARLES, Francis,** 1592–1644, *English poet.*

1. Friendship will not continue to the end which is begun for an end.
2. Physicians of all men are most happy; what good success they have, the world proclaimeth, and what faults they commit, the earth covereth.

**QUILLEN, Robert,** born 1887, *American journalist and columnist.*

1. Another good reducing exercise consists in placing both hands against the table edge and pushing back.
2. Character is made by what you stand for; reputation, by what you fall for.
3. A hick town is one where there is no place to go where you shouldn't be.
4. There is some co-operation between wild creatures; the stork and the wolf usually work the same neighborhood.

**RABELAIS, François,** 1495?–1553, *French humorist and satirist.*

1. He was subject to a kind of disease which at that time they called lack of money.
2. If you wish to avoid seeing a fool you must first break your mirror.

3. I never sleep comfortably except when I am at a sermon.

4. I owe much; I have nothing; the rest I leave to the poor.

5. Keep running after a dog, and he will never bite you.

6. When I drink, I think; and when I think, I drink.

7. God forbid that I should be out of debt, as if, indeed, I could not be trusted.

**RASCOE, Burton,** born 1892, *American writer, editor, and anthologist.*

1. In national affairs a million is only a drop in the budget.

2. What no wife of a writer can ever understand is that a writer is working when he's staring out the window.

**RASPE, Rudolph Erich,** 1737–1794, *German mineralogist and creator of "Baron Munchausen."*

If anyone doubts my veracity, I can only say that I pity his lack of faith.

**READE, Charles,** 1814–1884, *English novelist and dramatist.*

We go on fancying that each man is thinking of us, but he is not; he is like us: he is thinking of himself.

**RENAN, Joseph Ernest,** 1823–1890, *French philologist, philosopher, and historian.*

1. The ignorance of French society gives one a rough sense of the infinite.

2. O Lord, if there is a Lord, save my soul, if I have a soul.

**RENARD, Jules,** 1864–1910, *French novelist and dramatist.*

A cold in the head causes less suffering than an idea.

**REPPLIER, Agnes,** born 1858, *American author and essayist.*

The diseases of the present have little in common with the diseases of the past save that we die of them.

**RICHELIEU, Duke of,** 1585–1642, *French cardinal and statesman.*

If you give me six lines written by the most honest man, I will find something in them to hang him.

**RICHTER, Jean Paul,** 1847–1937, *British art critic and historian.*

1. Spring makes everything young again except man.

2. A variety of nothing is better than a monotony of something.

**RINEHART, Mary Roberts,** born 1876, *American novelist and playwright.*

He soft-soaped her until she couldn't see for the suds.

**RIVAROL, Comte de,** 1753–1801, *French journalist and epigrammatist.*

1. Friendship among women is only a suspension of hostilities.

2. It is an immense advantage to have done nothing, but one should not abuse it.

3. The personal pronoun "I" should be the coat of arms of some individuals.

**ROBINSON, Edwin Arlington,** 1869–1935, *American poet.*

Friends: people who borrow my books and set wet glasses on them.

**ROCHE, James Jeffrey,** 1847–1908, *American journalist, poet, and author.*

1. Be not concerned if thou findest thyself in possession of unexpected wealth; Allah will provide an unexpected use for it.

2. Pay as you go, but not if you intend going for good.

3. Some men borrow books; some men steal books; and others beg presentation copies from the author.

4. To be constant in love to one is good; to be constant to many is great.

**ROCHESTER, Lord,** 1647–1680, *English poet.*

1. Before I got married I had six theories about bringing up children; now I have six children, and no theories.

2. He never says a foolish thing nor ever does a wise one.

**ROGERS, Will,** 1879–1935, *American humorist, motion-picture actor, and lecturer.*

1. All I know is what I read in the papers.

2. Congressional investigations are for the benefit of photographers.

3. Everybody is ignorant, only on different subjects.

4. Everything is funny, as long as it is happening to somebody else.

5. Gentlemen, you have just been listening to that Chinese sage, On Too Long.

6. The good old horse-and-buggy days: then you lived until you died and not until you were just run over.

7. A holding company is a thing where you hand an accomplice the goods while the policeman searches you.

8. I don't make jokes; I just watch the government and report the facts.

9. I never expected to see the day when girls would get sunburned in the places they now do.

10. In Hollywood the woods are full of people that learned to write but evidently can't read; if they could read their stuff, they'd stop writing.

11. Maybe *ain't* ain't so correct, but I notice that lots of folks who ain't using *ain't*, ain't eating.

12. My folks didn't come over on the *Mayflower*, but they were there to meet the boat.

13. No party is as bad as its leaders.

14. One third of the people in the United States promote while the other two thirds provide.

15. Our foreign dealings are an open book—generally a checkbook.

16. Our country has plenty of good five-cent cigars, but the trouble is they charge fifteen cents for them.

17. The Republicans have their splits right after election, and Democrats have theirs just before an election.

18. Spinning a rope's a lot of fun—providing your neck ain't in it.

19. There is no more independence in politics than there is in jail.

20. Ukulele: a so-called musical instrument which, when listened to, you cannot tell whether one is playing on it or just monkeying with it.

21. The United States never lost a war or won a conference.

22. What the country needs is dirtier fingernails and cleaner minds.

23. With Congress, every time they make a joke it's a law; and every time they make a law it's a joke.

24. Wrigley was the first man to discover that American jaws must wag; so why not give them something to wag against?

25. America is a nation that conceives many odd inventions for getting somewhere but can think of nothing to do when it gets there.

26. The nation is prosperous on the whole, but how much prosperity is there in a hole?

27. I never lack material for my humor column when Congress is in session.

28. The income tax has made more liars out of the American people than gold has.

29. The only time people dislike gossip is when you gossip about them.

30. So live that you wouldn't be ashamed to sell the family parrot to the town gossip.

**ROMBERG**, Sigmund, born 1887, *American composer*.

A love song is just a caress set to music.

**ROOSEVELT**, Franklin Delano, 1882–1945, *President of the United States*.

1. The ablest man I ever met is the man you think you are.

2. When you get to the end of your rope, tie a knot and hang on.

3. It got to a point where I had to get a haircut or a violin.

4. A conservative is a man with two perfectly good legs who has never learned to walk.

5. A radical is a man with both feet firmly planted in the air.

6. A reactionary is a somnambulist walking backward.

**ROOSEVELT**, Theodore, 1858–1919, *President of the United States*.

1. I am only an average man but, by George, I work harder at it than the average man.

2. I suppose I overdo it, but when I'm mad at a man I want to climb right up his chest.

3. I think there is only one quality worse than hardness of heart and that is softness of head.

4. I took the Canal Zone and let Congress debate, and while the debate goes on the canal does too.

5. A man who has never gone to school may steal from a freight car; but if he has a university education, he may steal the whole railroad.

6. The most successful politician is he who says what everybody is thinking most often and in the loudest voice.

**ROSSINI, Gioacchino Antonio,** 1792–1868, *Italian operatic composer.*

1. Give me a laundry list and I'll set it to music.

2. How wonderful opera would be if there were no singers.

3. Wagner has beautiful moments but awful quarter hours.

**ROSTAND, Edmond,** 1868–1918, *French poet and playwright.*

To offend is my pleasure; I love to be hated.

**ROUSSEAU, Jean Jacques,** 1712–1778, *French philosopher and author.*

1. Happiness: a good bank account, a good cook, and a good digestion.

2. There is a period of life when we go backwards as we advance.

3. To write a love letter we must begin without knowing what we intend to say, and end without knowing what we have written.

**ROWLAND, Helen,** born 1876, *American humorous columnist and author.*

1. A bachelor gets tangled up with a lot of women in order to avoid getting tied up to one.

2. A bachelor never quite gets over the idea that he is a thing of beauty and a boy forever.

3. A Bachelor of Arts is one who makes love to a lot of women, and yet has the art to remain a bachelor.

4. Before marriage, a man will lie awake all night thinking about something you said; after marriage, he'll fall asleep before you finish saying it.

5. Every man wants a woman to appeal to his better side, his nobler instincts and his higher nature—and another woman to help him forget them.

6. The follies which a man regrets most in his life are those which he didn't commit when he had the opportunity.

7. A fool and her money are soon courted.

8. From the day on which she weighs 140, the chief excitement of a woman's life consists in spotting women who are fatter than she is.

9. A good woman is known by what she does; a good man by what he doesn't.

10. Grass widow: the angel a man loved, the human being he married, and the devil he divorced.

11. Half a love is better than none.

12. The hardest task of a girl's life is to prove to a man that his intentions are serious.

13. The honeymoon is not over until we cease to stifle our sighs and begin to stifle our yawns.

14. A husband is what is left of the lover after the nerve has been extracted.

15. In olden times sacrifices were made at the altar—a custom which is still continued.

16. In the spring a young man's fancy lightly turns—and turns—and turns.

17. It is easier to keep half a dozen lovers guessing than to keep one lover after he has stopped guessing.

18. It's as hard to get a man to stay home after you've married him as it was to get him to go home before you married him.

19. It takes one woman twenty years to make a man of her son, and another woman twenty minutes to make a fool of him.

20. Love is woman's eternal spring and man's eternal fall.

21. Love, the quest; marriage, the conquest; divorce, the inquest.

22. A man loses his illusions first, his teeth second, and his follies last.

23. A man marries one woman to escape from many others, and then chases many others to forget he's married to one.

24. A man never knows how to say good-by; a woman never knows when to say it.

25. A man's ideal woman is the one he passes with a worshipful bow—when he's on his way to call on the other woman.

26. A man snatches the first kiss, pleads for the second, demands the third, takes the fourth, accepts the fifth—and endures all the rest.

27. A man will joyfully pay a lawyer five hundred dollars for untying the knot that he begrudged a clergyman fifty dollars for tying.

28. Marriage: a souvenir of love.

29. Marriage is the miracle that transforms a kiss from a pleasure into a duty, and a life from a luxury into a necessity.

30. Matrimony is a bargain, and somebody has to get the worst of the bargain.

31. Never trust a husband too far, nor a bachelor too near.

32. Nobody is as sophisticated as a boy of nineteen who is just recovering from a baby-grand passion.

33. No man can understand why a woman should prefer a good reputation to a good time.

34. Nowadays most women grow old gracefully; most men, disgracefully.

35. One man's folly is another man's wife.

36. The only original thing about some men is original sin.

37. The softer a man's head, the louder his socks.

38. Soft, sweet things with a lot of fancy dressing—that's what a little boy loves to eat and a grown man prefers to marry.

39. Some men feel that the only thing they owe the woman who marries them is a grudge.

40. Some men think that being married to a woman means merely seeing her in the mornings instead of in the evenings.

41. Some widowers are bereaved; others, relieved.

42. Telling lies is a fault in a boy, an art in a lover, an accomplishment in a bachelor, and second nature in a married woman.

43. There are more ways of killing a man's love than by strangling it to death, but that's the usual way.

44. To a woman the first kiss is just the end of the beginning; to a man it is the beginning of the end.

45. Wedding: the point at which a man stops toasting a woman and begins roasting her.

46. When a girl marries she exchanges the attentions of many men for the inattention of one.

47. When a man makes a woman his wife, it's the highest compliment he can pay her, and it's usually the last.

48. When it comes to making love, a girl can always listen so much faster than a man can talk.

49. When mother-in-law comes in at the door, love flies out at the window.

50. When you see a married couple coming down the street, the one who is two or three steps ahead is the one that's mad.

51. When you see what some girls marry, you realize how they must hate to work for a living.

52. A woman marries the first time for love, the second time for companionship, the third time for support, and the rest of the time just from habit.

53. It isn't tying himself to one woman that a man dreads when he thinks of marrying; it's separating himself from all the others.

54. Woman: the peg on which the wit hangs his jest, the preacher his text, the cynic his grouch, and the sinner his justification.

55. A woman's last resort is henna; a man's, Gehenna.

**RUNYON, Damon,** 1884–1946, *American journalist and short-story writer.*

1. Much as he is opposed to lawbreaking, he is not bigoted about it.

2. The race is not always to the swift, nor the battle to the strong— but that's the way to bet.

**RUSKIN**, John, 1819–1900, *English art critic, social reformer, and miscellaneous writer.*

1. An artist should be fit for the best society and keep out of it.
2. He thinks by infection, catching an opinion like a cold.
3. There is hardly anything in the world that some man cannot make a little worse and sell a little cheaper.
4. When a man is wrapped up in himself he makes a pretty small package.
5. You knock a man into the ditch, and then you tell him to remain content in the position in which Providence has placed him.
6. The first of all English games is making money.

**RUSSELL**, Bertrand, born 1872, *English philosopher, mathematician, and writer.*

1. Christian humility is preached by the clergy, but practiced only by the lower classes.
2. Even when the experts all agree, they may well be mistaken.
3. Few people can be happy unless they hate some other person, nation, or creed.
4. The fundamental defect of fathers is that they want their children to be a credit to them.
5. In America law and custom alike are based upon the dreams of spinsters.
6. Most people would die sooner than think; in fact, they do so.
7. The trouble with the world is that the stupid are cocksure and the intelligent full of doubt.
8. We have two kinds of morality side by side: one which we preach but do not practice, and another which we practice but seldom preach.
9. Even in civilized mankind faint traces of a monogamic instinct can sometimes be perceived.

**SAINT-GAUDENS**, Augustus, 1848–1907, *American sculptor.*

What garlic is to salad, insanity is to art.

**SALTUS, Edgar,** 1855–1921, *American author.*

1. It is better to have loved your wife than never to have loved at all.
2. Divorce is like matrimony: a fellow has got to go through it three or four times before he knows how.
3. Society would be delightful were all women married and all men single.

**SANDBURG, Carl,** born 1878, *American poet and biographer.*

1. I won't take my religion from any man who never works except with his mouth.
2. Slang is language that takes off its coat, spits on its hands, and goes to work.

**SANTAYANA, George,** born 1863, *American poet, philosopher, and essayist.*

1. An artist may visit a museum, but only a pedant can live there.
2. Broad-mindedness is the result of flattening high-mindedness out.
3. Declarations of Independence make nobody really independent.
4. The Difficult is that which can be done immediately; the Impossible that which takes a little longer.
5. Fanaticism consists in redoubling your effort when you have forgotten your aim.
6. It is a great advantage for a system of philosophy to be substantially true.
7. Life is not a spectacle or a feast; it is a predicament.
8. There is no cure for birth or death save to enjoy the interval.
9. Those who cannot remember the past are condemned to repeat it.

**SARGENT, John Singer,** 1856–1925, *American portrait painter.*

Every time I paint a portrait I lose a friend.

**SCHLEGEL, August Wilhelm von,** 1767–1845, *German editor, translator, and man of letters.*

The historian is a prophet looking backwards.

**SCHOPENHAUER, Arthur,** 1788–1860, *German philosopher.*

1. Reading is thinking with someone else's head instead of one's own.

2. The first forty years of life give us the text; the next thirty supply the commentary.

3. It is difficult to keep quiet if you have nothing to do.

**SCHUMANN, Robert,** 1810–1856, *German composer.*

In order to compose, all you need to do is remember a tune that nobody else has thought of.

**SCOTT, Sir Walter,** 1771–1832, *Scotch novelist, poet, historian, and biographer.*

1. It requires no small talents to be a decided bore.

2. Many of our cares are but a morbid way of looking at our privileges.

3. The most effectual way of conferring a favor is condescending to accept one.

4. Please return this book; I find that though many of my friends are poor arithmeticians, they are nearly all good bookkeepers.

5. When a man hasn't a good reason for doing a thing, he has a good reason for letting it alone.

**SELDEN, John,** 1584–1654, *English jurist, scholar, and statesman.*

Preachers say, do as I say, not as I do.

**SÉVIGNÉ, Marquise de,** 1626–1696, *French lady of fashion and letter writer.*

1. Fortune is always on the side of the biggest battalions.

2. Religious people spend so much time with their confessors because they like to talk about themselves.

3. He lacked only a few vices to be perfect.

**SHAKESPEARE, William,** 1564–1616, *English poet and dramatist.*

1. A barber's chair fits all buttocks.

2. Better a witty fool than a foolish wit.

3. Commit the oldest sins the newest kind of ways.

4. Everyone can master a grief but he that has it.

5. The first thing we do, let's kill all the lawyers.

6. God has given you one face, and you make yourself another.

7. God made him, and therefore let him pass for a man.

8. Gratiano speaks an infinite deal of nothing, more than any man in all Venice.

9. He draweth out the thread of his verbosity finer than the staple of his argument.

10. He is winding the watch of his wit; by and by it will strike.

11. He that dies this year is quit for the next.

12. I am Sir Oracle, and when I ope my lips let no dog bark.

13. I can easier teach twenty what were good to be done than be one of the twenty to follow mine own teaching.

14. I do desire we may be better strangers.

15. I have no other but a woman's reason; I think him so because I think him so.

16. I had rather have a fool to make me merry than experience to make me sad.

17. In converting Jews to Christians, you raise the price of pork.

18. I thank God I am as honest as any man living that is an old man and no honester than I.

19. I will praise any man that will praise me.

20. Maids want nothing but husbands, and when they have them, they want everything.

21. Many a good hanging prevents a bad marriage.

22. A miser grows rich by seeming poor; an extravagant man grows poor by seeming rich.

23. O that he were here to write me down an ass.

24. "So-so" is good, very good, very excellent maxim; and yet it is not; it is but so-so.

25. There's not a note of mine that's worth the noting.

26. There was never yet philosopher that could endure the toothache patiently.

27. Two women placed together make cold weather.

28. Unbidden guests are often welcomest when they are gone.

29. Vanity keeps persons in favor with themselves who are out of favor with all others.

30. Were kisses all the joy in bed, one woman would another wed.

31. When I said I would die a bachelor, I did not think I would live till I were married.

32. When I tell him he hates flatterers, he says he does, being then the most flattered.

33. When my love swears that she is made of truth, I do believe her though I know she lies.

34. You are one of those that will not serve God if the devil bid you.

35. A young man married is a man that's marred.

**SHAW, George Bernard,** born 1856, *British dramatist, critic, novelist, social reformer, and wit.*

1. All my life, affection has been showered upon me, and every forward step I have made has been taken in spite of it.

2. Assassination is the extreme form of censorship.

3. An asylum for the sane would be empty in America.

4. Baseball has the great advantage over cricket of being sooner ended.

5. Beauty is all very well at sight, but who can look at it when it has been in the house three days?

6. The best reformers the world has ever seen are those who commence on themselves.

7. The British churchgoer prefers a severe preacher because he thinks a few home truths will do his neighbors no harm.

8. Cannons are not trade; they are enterprise.

9. Censorship ends in logical completeness when nobody is allowed to read any books except the books nobody can read.

10. The chief objection to playing wind instruments is that it prolongs the life of the player.

11. The churches must learn humility as well as teach it.

12. Common people do not pray; they only beg.

13. Decency is indecency's conspiracy of silence.

14. Democracy substitutes election by the incompetent many for appointment by the corrupt few.

15. The devil can quote Shakespeare for his own purpose.

16. Do not do unto others as you would they should do unto you; their tastes may not be the same.

17. England and America are two countries separated by the same language.

18. An Englishman does everything on principle: he fights you on patriotic principles; he robs you on business principles; he enslaves you on imperial principles.

19. Englishmen never will be slaves; they are free to do whatever the Government and public opinion allow them to do.

20. An Englishman thinks he is moral when he is only uncomfortable.

21. Every man over forty is a scoundrel.

22. Everything happens to everybody sooner or later if there is time enough.

23. Except during the nine months before he draws his first breath, no man manages his affairs as well as a tree does.

24. Few people think more than two or three times a year; I have made an international reputation for myself by thinking once or twice a week.

25. The fickleness of the women I love is only equaled by the infernal constancy of the women who love me.

26. First love is only a little foolishness and a lot of curiosity.

27. The formation of a young lady's mind and character usually consists in telling her lies.

28. Gambling promises the poor what property performs for the rich—something for nothing.

29. A gentleman is a gentleman the world over; loafers differ.

30. The golden rule is that there are no golden rules.

31. The great advantage of a hotel is that it's a refuge from home life.

32. Greek scholars are privileged men; few of them know Greek, and most of them know nothing else.

33. Hamlet's experiences simply could not have happened to a plumber.

34. He's a devout believer in the department of witchcraft called medical science.

35. He's a man of great common sense and good taste—meaning thereby a man without originality or moral courage.

36. He who can, does; he who cannot, teaches.

37. He who would reform himself must first reform society.

38. Human beings are the only animals of which I am thoroughly and cravenly afraid.

39. The ideal love affair is one conducted by post.

40. I dislike feeling at home when I'm abroad.

41. I enjoy convalescence; it is the part that makes the illness worth while.

42. If a great man could make us understand him we should hang him.

43. If all economists were laid end to end, they would not reach a conclusion.

44. If ever I utter an oath again may my soul be blasted to eternal damnation.

45. If history repeats itself, and the unexpected always happens, how incapable must man be of learning from experience!

46. If you are a bore, strive to be a rascal also so that you may not discredit virtue.

47. I have never thought much of the courage of a lion-tamer; inside the cage he is, at least, safe from other men.

48. I'm only a beer teetotaler, not a champagne teetotaler; I don't like beer.

49. Imprisonment, as it exists today, is a worse crime than any of those committed by its victims.

50. In heaven an angel is nobody in particular.

51. In literature the ambition of the novice is to acquire the literary language; the struggle of the adept is to get rid of it.

52. I often quote myself; it adds spice to my conversation.

53. I strive automatically to bring the world into harmony with my own nature.

54. It is a woman's business to get married as soon as possible, and a man's to keep unmarried as long as he can.

55. Kings are not born; they are made by universal hallucination.

56. Lack of money is the root of all evil.

57. Ladies and gentlemen are permitted to have friends in the kennel but not in the kitchen.

58. A learned man is an idler who kills time by study.

59. Leave it to the coward to make a religion of his cowardice by preaching humility.

60. The liar's punishment is not in the least that he is not believed, but that he cannot believe anyone else.

61. A lifetime of happiness! No man alive could bear it; it would be hell on earth.

62. Love is a gross exaggeration of the difference between one person and everybody else.

63. A man without an address is a vagabond; a man with two addresses is a libertine.

64. Marriage is all very well, but it isn't romance; there's nothing wrong in it.

65. Marriage is popular because it combines the maximum of temptation with the maximum of opportunity.

66. A married man can do anything he likes if his wife doesn't mind; a widower can't be too careful.

67. Martyrdom is the only way in which a man can become famous without ability.

68. Men have to do some awfully mean things to keep up their respectability.

69. Men like conventions because men made them.

70. A miracle is an event which creates faith; that is the purpose and nature of miracles.

71. The mistake was in not forbidding the serpent; then Adam would have eaten the serpent.

72. The more things a man is ashamed of, the more respectable he is.

73. The most anxious man in a prison is the warden.

74. My specialty is being right when other people are wrong.

75. My way of joking is to tell the truth; it's the funniest joke in the world.

76. Nothing soothes me more after a long and maddening course of pianoforte recitals than to sit and have my teeth drilled.

77. Obscenity can be found in every book except the telephone directory.

78. The 100 per cent American is 99 per cent an idiot.

79. The only way a woman can provide for herself decently is to be good to some man that can afford to be good to her.

80. The other evening, feeling rather in want of a headache, I bethought me that I had not been to a music hall for a long time.

81. Patriotism is your conviction that this country is superior to all other countries because you were born in it.

82. A perpetual holiday is a good working definition of hell.

83. A pessimist thinks everybody as nasty as himself, and hates them for it.

84. Put an Irishman on the spit, and you can always get another Irishman to turn him.

85. Rich men without convictions are more dangerous in modern society than poor women without chastity.

86. Science is always wrong: it never solves a problem without creating ten more.

87. The secret of being miserable is to have leisure to bother about whether you are happy or not.

88. Self-denial is not a virtue; it is only the effect of prudence on rascality.

89. Success covers a multitude of blunders.

90. Take care to get what you like, or you will end by liking what you get.

91. There are fools everywhere, even in asylums.

92. There are no secrets better kept than the secrets that everybody guesses.

93. There are not competent people enough in the world to go round; somebody must get the incompetent lawyers and doctors.

94. There are only two classes in good society in England: the equestrian classes and the neurotic classes.

95. Youth is a wonderful thing; what a crime to waste it on children.

96. There is no love sincerer than the love of food.

97. There is no satisfaction in hanging a man who does not object to it.

98. There is not much harm in a lion; he has no ideals, no religion, no politics, no chivalry, no gentility.

99. There is only one religion, though there are a hundred versions of it.

100. There may be some doubt as to who are the best people to have charge of children, but there can be no doubt that parents are the worst.

101. The things most people want to know about are usually none of their business.

102. The truth is the one thing that nobody will believe.

103. Virtue is insufficient temptation.

104. We are told that when Jehovah created the world he saw that it was good; what would he say now?

105. What God hath joined together no man shall ever put asunder; God will take care of that.

106. What is the matter with the poor is poverty; what is the matter with the rich is uselessness.

107. What man is capable of the insane self-conceit of believing that an eternity of himself would be tolerable even to himself?

108. What really flatters a man is that you think him worth flattering.

109. When a man wants to murder a tiger he calls it sport; when a tiger wants to murder him, he calls it ferocity.

110. When a stupid man is doing something he is ashamed of, he always declares that it is his duty.

111. When we want to read of the deeds that are done for love, whither do we turn? To the murder column.

112. When you read a biography remember that the truth is never fit for publication.

113. Why was I born with such contemporaries?

114. With the exception of capitalism, there is nothing so revolting as revolution.

115. The worst cliques are those which consist of one man.

116. The writer who aims at producing the platitudes which are "not for an age but for all time" has his reward in being unreadable in all ages.

117. You don't expect me to know what to say about a play when I don't know who the author is, do you?

118. You must not suppose, because I am a man of letters, that I never tried to earn an honest living.

119. No sooner had Jesus knocked over the dragon of superstition than Paul boldly set it on its legs again in the name of Jesus.

120. Reading made Don Quixote a gentleman, but believing what he read made him mad.

121. The test of a man or woman's breeding is how they behave in a quarrel.

122. You'll never have a quiet world till you knock the patriotism out of the human race.

123. A man never tells you anything until you contradict him.

**SHELLEY, Percy Bysshe,** 1792–1822, *English poet.*

Hell is a city very much like London.

**SHERIDAN, Philip Henry,** 1831–1888, *American general.*

If I owned Texas and Hell, I'd rent out Texas and live in Hell.

**SHERIDAN, Richard Brinsley,** 1751–1816, *Irish dramatist.*

1. A fluent tongue is the only thing a mother doesn't like her daughter to resemble her in.

2. He is indebted to his memory for his jests and to his imagination for his facts.

3. If it is abuse, why, one is always sure to hear of it from one damned good-natured friend or another.

4. I think the interpreter is the hardest to be understood of the two.

5. Our ancestors are very good kind of folks, but they are the last people I should choose to have a visiting acquaintance with.

6. 'Tis safest in matrimony to begin with a little aversion.

7. The quarrel is a very pretty quarrel as it stands; we should only spoil it by trying to explain it.

**SHERMAN, William Tecumseh,** 1820–1891, *American general.*

1. Grant stood by me when I was crazy, and I stood by him when he was drunk, and now we stand by each other.

2. Vox populi, vox humbug.

3. If forced to choose between the penitentiary and the White House for four years, I would say the penitentiary, thank you.

**SIBELIUS, Jean,** born 1865, *Finnish composer.*

Pay no attention to what the critics say; there has never been set up a statue in honor of a critic.

**SIENKIEWICZ, Henryk,** 1846–1916, *Polish novelist and short-story writer.*

The greater the philosopher, the harder it is for him to answer the questions of the average man.

**SIMONDS, Frank H.,** 1878–1936, *American journalist and war correspondent.*

There is but one way for a newspaperman to look at a politician, and that is down.

**SINCLAIR, Upton,** born 1878, *American novelist and social reformer.*

It is difficult to get a man to understand something when his salary depends upon his not understanding it.

**SITWELL, Osbert,** born 1892, *English poet, playwright, and novelist.*

I am most fond of talking and thinking; that is to say, talking first and thinking afterward.

**SKINNER, Cornelia Otis,** born 1901, *American actress and author.*

1. Mosquitoes were using my ankles for filling stations.
2. One learns in life to keep silent and draw one's own confusions.
3. She was permanently waved both as to hair and figure.

**SMITH, Adam,** 1723–1790, *Scottish political economist.*

Man is an animal that makes bargains; no other animal does this— no dog exchanges bones with another.

**SMITH, Logan Pearsall,** 1865–1946, *English essayist and critic.*

1. All my life, as down an abyss without a bottom, I have been pouring vanloads of information into that vacancy of oblivion I call my mind.
2. All reformers, however strict their conscience, live in houses just as big as they can pay for.
3. The denunciation of the young is a necessary part of the hygiene of older people, and greatly assists the circulation of their blood.
4. Don't laugh at a youth for his affectations; he is only trying on one face after another to find his own.
5. Hearts that are delicate and kind, and tongues that are neither— these make the finest company in the world.
6. How I should like to distil my disesteem of my contemporaries into prose so perfect that all of them would have to read it!
7. If you want to be thought a liar always tell the truth.
8. I hate having new books forced upon me, but how I love cram-throating other people with them.
9. I might give my life for my friend, but he had better not ask me to do up a parcel.

10. An improper mind is a perpetual feast.
11. Isn't it odd that flowers are the reproductive organs of the plants they grow on?
12. It is just as well to be a little giddy-pated, if you are to feel at home on this turning earth.
13. It is the wretchedness of being rich that you have to live with rich people.
14. One can be bored until boredom becomes a mystical experience.
15. Thank heavens! The sun has gone in, and I don't have to go out and enjoy it.
16. Those who set out to serve both God and Mammon soon discover that there is no God.
17. We are told by moralists with the plainest faces that immorality will spoil our looks.
18. What music is more enchanting than the voices of young people when you can't hear what they say?
19. When they come downstairs from their ivory towers, idealists are apt to walk straight into the gutter.

**SMITH**, Sydney, 1771–1845, *English clergyman, essayist, and wit.*

1. As the French say, there are three sexes—men, women, and clergymen.
2. Benevolence is a natural instinct of the human mind; when A sees B in distress, his conscience always urges him to entreat C to help him.
3. The best way of answering a bad argument is to let it go on.
4. Correspondences are like small-clothes before the invention of suspenders; it is impossible to keep them up.
5. Daniel Webster struck me much like a steam engine in trousers.
6. The first receipt to farm well is to be rich.
7. The further he went west, the more convinced he felt that the wise men came from the east.
8. He deserves to be preached to death by wild curates.
9. He has no command over his understanding; it is always getting between his legs and tripping him up.

10. He has not body enough to cover his mind decently; his intellect is improperly exposed.

11. He has returned from Italy a greater bore than ever; he bores on architecture, painting, statuary, and music.

12. He is remarkably well, considering that he has been remarkably well for so many years.

13. How can a bishop marry? How can he flirt? The most he can say is: "I will see you in the vestry after service."

14. I am convinced digestion is the great secret of life.

15. I am just going to pray for you at St. Paul's, but with no very lively hope of success.

16. I hate a woman who seems to be hermetically sealed in the lower regions.

17. I have been looking for a person who disliked gray all my life; let us swear eternal friendship.

18. I have gout, asthma, and seven other maladies, but am otherwise very well.

19. I have no relish for the country; it is a kind of healthy grave.

20. I have the most perfect confidence in your indiscretion.

21. I heard him speak disrespectfully of the equator.

22. I like him and his wife; he is so ladylike, and she's such a perfect gentleman.

23. I must believe in the Apostolic Succession, there being no other way of accounting for the descent of the Bishop of Exeter from Judas Iscariot.

24. In composing, as a general rule, run your pen through every other word you have written; you have no idea what vigor it will give your style.

25. I never read a book before reviewing it; it prejudices one so.

26. It was so hot here that I found there was nothing left for it but to take off my flesh and sit in my bones.

27. It would be an entertaining change in human affairs to determine everything by minorities; they are almost always in the right.

28. Macaulay has occasional flashes of silence that make his conversation perfectly delightful.

29. Marriage resembles a pair of shears, so joined that they cannot be separated; often moving in opposite directions, yet always punishing anyone who comes between them.

30. The most solemn and terrible duty of a bishop is the entertainment of the clergy.

31. My idea of heaven is eating *pâtés de foie gras* to the sound of trumpets.

32. No furniture is so charming as books, even if you never open them or read a single word.

33. No man should write on Christianity unless he is prepared to go the whole *lamb*.

34. The observances of the church concerning feasts and fasts are tolerably well kept since the rich keep the feasts and the poor the fasts.

35. Poverty is no disgrace to a man, but it is confoundedly inconvenient.

36. The preterpluperfect tense has always occasioned him much uneasiness though he has appeared to the world cheerful and serene.

37. A sparrow fluttering about the church is an antagonist which the most profound theologian in Europe is wholly unable to overcome.

38. There is not the least use in preaching to anyone unless you chance to catch them ill.

39. What a mystery is the folly and stupidity of the good!

40. What a pity it is that we have no amusements in England but vice and religion.

41. When a man is a fool, in England we only trust him with the immortal concerns of human beings.

42. Whenever I enter a village, straightway I find an ass.

43. When I am in the pulpit, I have the pleasure of seeing my audience nod approbation while they sleep.

44. When I hear any man talk of an unalterable law, I am convinced that he is an unalterable fool.

45. When I take a gun in hand, the safest place for a pheasant is just opposite the muzzle.

46. The whole of my life has passed like a razor—in hot water or a scrape.

47. You and I are exceptions to the laws of nature; you have risen by your gravity, and I have sunk by my levity.

48. I think breakfast so pleasant because no one is conceited before one o'clock.

49. My handwriting looks as if a swarm of ants, escaping from an ink bottle, had walked over a sheet of paper without wiping their legs.

**SOCRATES,** 470–339 B.C., *Greek philosopher.*

1. As to marriage or celibacy, let a man take which course he will, he will be sure to repent.

2. By all means marry; if you get a good wife, you'll become happy; if you get a bad one, you'll become a philosopher.

3. Call no man unhappy until he is married.

4. Once made equal to man, woman becomes his superior.

**SOUSA,** John Philip, 1854–1932, *American bandmaster and composer.*

Jazz will endure just as long as people hear it through their feet instead of their brains.

**SPENCER,** Herbert, 1820–1903, *English philosopher.*

1. A jury is a group of twelve people of average ignorance.

2. Marriage: a ceremony in which rings are put on the finger of the lady and through the nose of the gentleman.

3. The saying that beauty is but skin-deep is but a skin-deep saying.

4. To play billiards well is a sign of an ill-spent youth.

5. The ultimate result of shielding men from the effects of folly is to fill the world with fools.

**SPURGEON,** Charles Haddon, 1834–1892, *English preacher.*

1. Alteration is not always improvement, as the pigeon said when it got out of the net and into the pie.

2. Feel for others—in your pocket.

3. Train your child in the way you now know you should have gone yourself.

4. Some ministers would make good martyrs: they are so dry they would burn well.

**STAËL, Madame de,** 1766–1817, *French social leader and writer.*

1. I'm glad I'm not a man, for if I were I'd be obliged to marry a woman.

2. The more I see of men, the more I like dogs.

**STEELE, Richard,** 1672–1729, *British essayist and playwright.*

1. Ceremony is the invention of wise men to keep fools at a distance.

2. Good breeding is an expedient to make fools and wise men equals.

3. What's the first excellence in a lawyer? Tautology. What the second? Tautology. What the third? Tautology.

4. A woman seldom writes her mind but in her postscript.

**STEINBECK, John,** born 1902, *American novelist.*

Coney Island: where the surf is one third water and two thirds people.

**STENDHAL,** 1783–1842, *pen name of Marie Henri Beyle, French novelist, critic, and biographer.*

1. All religions are founded on the fear of the many and the cleverness of the few.

2. Life is too short, and the time we waste in yawning never can be regained.

3. The only excuse for God is that he doesn't exist.

4. The shepherd always tries to persuade the sheep that their interests and his own are the same.

**STEPHENS, James,** born 1882, *Irish poet and novelist.*

1. Sleep is an excellent way of listening to an opera.

2. Women are wiser than men because they know less and understand more.

**STERNE, Laurence,** 1713–1768, *English novelist and clergyman.*

1. Had God thought that sin would enter Eden, He would have created a parson also.

2. Men tire themselves in pursuit of rest.

3. Of all the cants which are canted in this canting world, though the cant of hypocrites may be the worst, the cant of criticism is the most tormenting.

4. There are worse occupations in this world than feeling a woman's pulse.

5. 'Tis known by the name of perseverance in a good cause, and obstinacy in a bad one.

6. Women are timid, and 'tis well they are—else there would be no dealing with them.

**STEVENSON, Robert Louis,** 1850–1894, *Scottish novelist, essayist, and poet.*

1. Every man has a sane spot somewhere.

2. Everyone lives by selling something.

3. Give me the young man who has brains enough to make a fool of himself.

4. He sows hurry and reaps indigestion.

5. If your morals make you dreary, depend on it they are wrong.

6. If we take matrimony at its lowest, we regard it as a sort of friendship recognized by the police.

7. I've a grand memory for forgetting.

8. Marriage is one long conversation, chequered by disputes.

9. Politics is perhaps the only profession for which no preparation is thought necessary.

10. There is nothing more certain than that age and youth are right, except perhaps that both are wrong.

11. Vanity dies hard; in some obstinate cases it outlives the man.

**STRACHEY, Lionel,** 1864–1927, *British writer, translator, and humorist.*

1. Any woman in the world, even a nun, would rather lose her virtue than her reputation.

2. A brilliant epigram is a solemn platitude gone to a masquerade ball.

3. Statistics are mendacious truths.

4. To be patriotic, hate all nations but your own; to be religious, all sects but your own; to be moral, all pretenses but your own.

5. When humor is meant to be taken seriously, it's no joke.

6. Who says marriage is a failure? It's nothing of the kind—provided you let it alone.

**STRUNSKY, Simeon,** 1879–1948, *American editor, essayist, and author.*

The thing which in the subway is called congestion is highly esteemed in the night spots as intimacy.

**SWIFT, Jonathan,** 1667–1745, *English satirist and social reformer.*

1. Argument is the worst sort of conversation.

2. Better belly burst than good liquor be lost.

3. Coming! Ay, so is Christmas.

4. Complaint is the largest tribute heaven receives and the sincerest part of our devotion.

5. A dead wife under the table is the best goods in a man's house.

6. Every man desires to live long, but no man would be old.

7. Faith, that's as well said as if I had said it myself.

8. Fine words! I wonder where you stole 'em.

9. Fish should swim thrice: first it should swim in the sea, then it should swim in butter, and at last, it should swim in good claret.

10. Good God! What a genius I had when I wrote that book.

11. The greatest advantage I know of being thought a wit by the world is that it gives one the greater freedom of playing the fool.

12. Happiness is the perpetual possession of being well deceived.

13. I'm as old as my tongue and a little older than my teeth.

14. He was an ingenious man that first found out eating and drinking.

15. How is it possible to expect mankind to take advice when they will not so much as take warning?

16. If a man makes me keep my distance, the comfort is he keeps his at the same time.

17. If Heaven had looked upon riches to be a valuable thing, it would not have given them to such a scoundrel.

18. I must complain the cards are ill shuffled till I have a good hand.

19. It is a miserable thing to live in suspense; it is the life of a spider.

20. I never knew any man in my life who could not bear another's misfortune perfectly like a Christian.

21. Last week I saw a woman flayed, and you will hardly believe how much it altered her person for the worse.

22. Lord, I wonder what fool it was that first invented kissing.

23. May you live all the days of your life.

24. A nice man is a man of nasty ideas.

25. No man will take counsel, but every man will take money; therefore, money is better than counsel.

26. "Now we are even," quoth Stephen, when he gave his wife six blows for one.

27. Promises and piecrust are made to be broken.

28. Punning is a talent which no man affects to despise but he that is without it.

29. Satire is a sort of glass wherein beholders do generally discover everybody's face but their own.

30. She wears her clothes as if they were thrown on her with a pitchfork.

31. Taverns are places where madness is sold by the bottle.

32. There are few wild beasts more to be dreaded than a talking man having nothing to say.

33. There is nothing in this world constant but inconstancy.

34. Thou hast a head, and so has a pin.

35. 'Tis very warm weather when one's in bed.

36. The two maxims of any great man at court are—always to keep his countenance and never to keep his word.

37. We are so fond of one another because our ailments are the same.

38. What they do in heaven, we are ignorant of; what they do not, we are told expressly: they neither marry nor are given in marriage.

39. When men grow virtuous in their old age, they only make a sacrifice to God of the devil's leavings.

40. When you have done a fault, be always pert and insolent, and behave yourself as if you were the injured person.

41. Augustus, meeting an ass with a lucky name, foretold himself good fortune; I meet many asses but none of them have lucky names.

42. Censure is the tax a man pays to the public for being eminent.

43. I always like to begin a journey on Sundays because I shall have the prayers of the church to preserve all that travel by land or by water.

44. It is useless for us to attempt to reason a man out of a thing he has never been reasoned into.

45. It is with narrow-souled people as with narrow-necked bottles: the less they have in them, the more noise they make in pouring it out.

46. The latter part of a wise man's life is taken up in curing the follies, prejudices, and false opinions he had contracted in the former.

47. The longer we live the more we should be convinced that it is reasonable to love God and despise man.

48. A man of business may talk of philosophy, a man who has none may practice it.

49. The reason why so few marriages are happy is because young ladies spend their time in making nets, not in making cages.

50. Two women seldom grow intimate but at the expense of a third person.

51. Venus, a beautiful good-natured lady, was the goddess of love; Juno, a terrible shrew, the goddess of marriage; and they were always mortal enemies.

52. A very little wit is valued in a woman, as we are pleased with a few words spoken plain by a parrot.

53. We have just enough religion to make us hate but not enough to make us love one another.

54. When a true genius appears in the world you may know him by this sign, that the dunces are all in confederacy against him.

55. Wit in conversation is, in the midwives' phrase, a quick conception and an easy delivery.

56. Elephants are always drawn smaller in life, but a flea always larger.

57. What religion is he of? Why, he is an Anythingarian.


**TAFT, William Howard,** 1857–1930, *President of the United States and Chief Justice of U. S. Supreme Court.*

Some men are graduated from college *cum laude,* some are graduated *summa cum laude,* and some are graduated *mirabile dictu.*

**TALLEYRAND, Charles Maurice de,** 1754–1838, *French statesman and diplomat.*

1. A court is an assembly of noble and distinguished beggars.

2. Don't trust first impulses—they are always good.

3. He thinks he is deaf because he no longer hears himself talked about.

4. If you wish to appear agreeable in society, you must consent to be taught many things which you know already.

5. In order to avoid being called a flirt, she always yielded easily.

6. It is worse than a crime, it is a blunder.

7. Never speak ill of yourself; your friends will always say enough on that subject.

8. Only a man who has loved a woman of genius can appreciate what happiness there is in loving a fool.

9. She is intolerable, but that is her only fault.

10. What I have been taught, I have forgotten; what I know, I have guessed.

**TARKINGTON, Booth,** 1869-1946, *American novelist and playwright.*

1. An ideal wife is any woman who has an ideal husband.
2. There are two things that will be believed of any man whatsoever, and one of them is that he has taken to drink.
3. The only good in pretending is the fun we get out of fooling ourselves that we fool somebody.

**TENNYSON, Alfred,** 1809-1892, *English poet.*

1. Charm us, orator, till the lion look no larger than the cat.
2. The curate—he was fatter than his cure.

**TERENCE,** 190?-159? B.C., *Roman playwright.*

1. She never was really charming till she died.
2. There is nothing that can't be made worse by telling.

**THACKERAY, William Makepeace,** 1811-1863, *English novelist.*

1. A clever, ugly man every now and then is successful with the ladies, but a handsome fool is irresistible.
2. He that hath ears to hear, let him stuff them with cotton.
3. If a man's character is to be abused, there's nobody like a relative to do the business.
4. 'Tis strange what a man may do, and a woman yet think him an angel.
5. To love and win is the best thing; to love and lose, the next best.
6. When I walk with you I feel as if I had a flower in my buttonhole.

**THOMAS, Albert Ellsworth,** born 1872, *American playwright.*

It takes a major operation to extract money from a minor poet.

**THOREAU, Henry David,** 1817-1862, *American author and naturalist.*

1. Any fool can make a rule, and every fool will mind it.
2. Be not simply good; be good for something.
3. Beware of all enterprises that require new clothes.

4. The boy gathers materials for a temple, and then when he is thirty concludes to build a woodshed.

5. City life: millions of people being lonesome together.

6. Every generation laughs at the old fashions, but follows religiously the new.

7. If I repent of anything, it is very likely to be my good behavior.

8. If words were invented to conceal thought, newspapers are a great improvement on a bad invention.

9. I have three chairs in my house: one for solitude, two for friendship, three for company.

10. It is an interesting question how far men would retain their relative rank if they were divested of their clothes.

11. It is not worth while to go round the world to count the cats in Zanzibar.

12. It makes but little difference whether you are committed to a farm or a county jail.

13. A man is rich in proportion to the number of things which he can afford to let alone.

14. The mass of men lead lives of quiet desperation.

15. My dwelling was small, and I could hardly entertain an echo in it.

16. Nothing makes the earth seem so spacious as to have friends at a distance; they make the latitudes and longitudes.

17. Not that the story need be long, but it will take a long while to make it short.

18. The rarest quality in an epitaph is truth.

19. Some circumstantial evidence is very strong, as when you find a trout in the milk.

20. I cannot easily buy a blankbook to write thoughts in; they are commonly ruled for dollars and cents.

21. I have received no more than one or two letters in my life that were worth the postage.

22. There are nowadays professors of philosophy, but not philosophers.

23. What is commonly called friendship is only a little more honor among rogues.

24. What men call good fellowship is commonly but the virtue of pigs in a litter which lie close together to keep each other warm.

**THURBER, James,** born 1894, *American humorous writer and artist.*

1. Early to rise and early to bed makes a male healthy and wealthy and dead.

2. He fell down a great deal during his boyhood because of a trick he had of walking into himself.

3. Well, if I called the wrong number, why did you answer the phone?

4. While he was not dumber than an ox he was not any smarter.

**TOLSTOI, Lev Nikolaevich,** 1828–1910, *Russian novelist, social reformer, and mystic.*

1. All happy families are alike, but each unhappy family is unhappy in its own way.

2. He never chooses an opinion; he just wears whatever happens to be in style.

3. He will do almost anything for the poor, except get off their backs.

**TOSCANINI, Arturo,** born 1867, *Italian operatic and symphonic conductor.*

I kissed my first woman and smoked my first cigarette on the same day; I have never had time for tobacco since.

**TREE, Herbert Beerbohm,** 1853–1917, *English actor and theatrical manager.*

A man never knows what a fool he is until he hears himself imitated by one.

**TROLLOPE, Anthony,** 1815–1882, *English novelist.*

The best right a woman has is the right to a husband.

**TWAIN, Mark,** 1835–1910, *pen name of Samuel Langhorne Clemens, American humorous writer and wit.*

1. Adam and Eve had many advantages, but the principal one was that they escaped teething.

2. Adam was human; he didn't want the apple for the apple's sake; he wanted it because it was forbidden.

3. All religions issue Bibles against Satan, and say the most injurious things against him, but we never hear his side.

4. All that I care to know is that a man is a human being—that is enough for me; he can't be any worse.

5. All you need in this life is ignorance and confidence, and then success is sure.

6. Always do right; this will gratify some people and astonish the rest.

7. Animals talk to each other; I never knew but one man who could understand them—I knew he could because he told me so himself.

8. April 1 is the day upon which we are reminded of what we are on the other 364.

9. A banker is a fellow who lends you his umbrella when the sun is shining and wants it back the minute it begins to rain.

10. Barring that natural expression of villainy which we all have, the man looked honest enough.

11. Be good and you will be lonesome.

12. Be virtuous and you will be eccentric.

13. By trying we can easily learn to endure adversity—another man's I mean.

14. The chief dish was the renowned fish called pompano, delicious as the less criminal forms of sin.

15. A classic is something that everybody wants to have read and nobody wants to read.

16. The Creator made Italy from designs by Michelangelo.

17. The difference between the right word and the almost right word is the difference between lightning and the lightning bug.

18. The efficiency of our criminal jury system is only marred by the difficulty of finding twelve men every day who don't know anything and can't read.

19. The emperor sent his troops to the field with immense enthusiasm; he will lead them in person—when they return.

20. The English are mentioned in the Bible: Blessed are the meek, for they shall inherit the earth.

21. Everybody was sorry she died; but I reckoned with her disposition—she was having a better time in the graveyard.

22. Familiarity breeds contempt—and children.

23. Few things are harder to put up with than the annoyance of a good example.

24. The first half of life consists of the capacity to enjoy without the chance; the last half consists of the chance without the capacity.

25. Fleas can be taught nearly anything that a Congressman can.

26. Get your facts first, and then you can distort them as much as you please.

27. Good breeding consists in concealing how much we think of ourselves and how little we think of the other person.

28. A good memory and a tongue tied in the middle is a combination which gives immortality to conversation.

29. Hain't we got all the fools in town on our side, and ain't that a big enough majority in any town?

30. Have a place for everything and keep the thing somewhere else; this is not advice, it is merely custom.

31. Heaven goes by favor; if it went by merit, you would stay out and your dog would go in.

32. He charged nothing for his preaching, and it was worth it, too.

33. He has been a doctor a year now and has had two patients—no, three, I think—yes, it was three; I attended their funerals.

34. He liked to like people, therefore people liked him.

35. He was a very inferior farmer when he first began, and he is now fast rising from affluence to poverty.

36. His money is twice tainted: 'taint yours and 'taint mine.

37. The holy passion of friendship is of so sweet and steady and loyal and enduring a nature that it will last through a whole lifetime, if not asked to lend money.

38. Honest poverty is a gem that even a king might be proud to call his own, but I wish to sell out.

39. The human race consists of the dangerously insane and such as are not.

40. Hurry up and come to visit me before we get too old to hear each other swear.

41. I am an old man and have known a great many troubles, but most of them never happened.

42. I can live for two months on a good compliment.

43. I can't do no literary work the rest of this year because I'm meditating another lawsuit and looking around for a defendant.

44. I could never learn to like her—except on a raft at sea with no other provisions in sight.

45. I don't give a damn for a man that can spell a word only one way.

46. If you don't like the weather in New England, just wait a few minutes.

47. If you tell the truth, you don't have to remember anything.

48. If you wish to lower yourself in a person's favor, one good way is to tell his story over again, the way *you* heard it.

49. If you pick up a starving dog and make him prosperous, he will not bite you; that is the principal difference between a dog and a man.

50. Ignorant people think it's the noise which fighting cats make that is so aggravating, but it ain't so; it's the sickening grammar they use.

51. I have been an author for twenty-two years and an ass for fifty-five.

52. I have never let my schooling interfere with my education.

53. I like criticism, but it must be my way.

54. In all matters of opinion, our adversaries are insane.

55. In all my travels the thing that has impressed me the most is the universal brotherhood of man—what there is of it.

56. Information seems to stew out of me naturally, like the precious otter of roses out of an otter.

57. In our country we have those three unspeakably precious things: freedom of speech, freedom of conscience, and the prudence never to practice either.

58. In statesmanship, get the formalities right; never mind about the moralities.

59. In the first place God made idiots; this was for practice; then he made school boards.

60. It could probably be shown by facts and figures that there is no distinctly native American criminal class except Congress.

61. It is a mistake that there is no bath that will cure people's manners, but drowning would help.

62. It is a difference of opinion that makes horse races.

63. It is inferior for coffee, but it is pretty fair tea.

64. It is more trouble to make a maxim than it is to do right.

65. It is not best that we use our morals weekdays; it gets them out of repair for Sundays.

66. It seems such a pity that Noah and his party did not miss the boat.

67. It used to be a good hotel, but that proves nothing—I used to be a good boy.

68. It used to take me all vacation to grow a new hide in place of the one they flogged off me during school term.

69. It usually takes me more than three weeks to prepare a good impromptu speech.

70. It was wonderful to find America, but it would have been more wonderful to miss it.

71. It would have been foolish to stand upon our dignity in a place where there was hardly room to stand upon our feet.

72. I've never heard a blue jay use bad grammar, but very seldom; and when they do, they are as ashamed as a human.

73. Let us be thankful for the fools; but for them the rest of us could not succeed.

74. Let us endeavor so to live that when we come to die even the undertaker will be sorry.

75. Let us not be too particular; it is better to have old secondhand diamonds than none at all.

76. A man is accepted into a church for what he believes and he is turned out for what he knows.

77. Man is the only animal that blushes—or needs to.

78. Man was made at the end of the week's work when God was tired.

79. The man who can't tell a lie thinks he is the best judge of one.

80. The man who is a pessimist before forty-eight knows too much; the man who is an optimist after forty-eight knows too little.

81. The moral sense enables one to perceive morality—and avoid it; the immoral sense enables one to perceive immorality—and enjoy it.

82. More than one cigar at a time is excessive smoking.

83. Most writers regard truth as their most valuable possession, and therefore are most economical in its use.

84. Never run after your own hat—others will be delighted to do it; why spoil their fun.

85. Noise proves nothing; often a hen who has merely laid an egg cackles as if she had laid an asteroid.

86. Nothing helps scenery like ham and eggs.

87. Nothing so needs reforming as other people's habits.

88. The older we grow the greater becomes our wonder at how much ignorance one can contain without bursting one's clothes.

89. One of the striking differences between a cat and a lie is that a cat has only nine lives.

90. Only presidents, editors, and people with tapeworms have the right to use the editorial "we."

91. The only way to keep your health is to eat what you don't want, drink what you don't like, and do what you'd rather not.

92. "On with the dance, let joy be unconfined" is my motto, whether there's any dance to dance or any joy to unconfine.

93. Our Heavenly Father invented man because he was disappointed in the monkey.

94. Principles have no real force except when one is well fed.

95. Put all your eggs in one basket, and—watch the basket.

96. Reader, suppose you were an idiot; and suppose you were a member of Congress; but I repeat myself.

97. Repartee is something we think of twenty-four hours too late.

98. The reports of my death are greatly exaggerated.

99. The secret source of humor is not joy but sorrow; there is no humor in heaven.

100. Soap and education are not as sudden as a massacre, but they are more deadly in the long run.

101. Some of the commonest English words are not in use with us —such as 'ousemaid, 'ospital, 'otel, 'istorian.

102. There are many humorous things in the world: among them the white man's notion that he is less savage than the other savages.

103. There are many scapegoats for our sins, but the most popular is Providence.

104. There are no people who are quite so vulgar as the over-refined ones.

105. There are several good protections against temptation, but the surest is cowardice.

106. There are two times in a man's life when he should not speculate: when he can't afford it, and when he can.

107. There is a lot to say in her favor, but the other is more interesting.

108. There is no end to the laws, and no beginning to the execution of them.

109. There is no use in your walking five miles to fish when you can depend on being just as unsuccessful near home.

110. There isn't a Parallel of Latitude but thinks it would have been the Equator if it had had its rights.

111. There's always something about your success that displeases even your best friends.

112. There ain't no way to find out why a snorer can't hear himself snore.

113. They spell it Vinci and pronounce it Vinchy; foreigners always spell better than they pronounce.

114. Thrusting my nose firmly between his teeth, I threw him heavily to the ground on top of me.

115. To be good is noble, but to teach others how to be good is nobler—and less trouble.

116. To cease smoking is the easiest thing I ever did; I ought to know because I've done it a thousand times.

117. To create man was a fine and original idea; but to add the sheep was a tautology.

118. To eat is human; to digest, divine.

119. Training is everything: the peach was once a bitter almond; cauliflower is nothing but cabbage with a college education.

120. Truth is stranger than fiction; fiction is obliged to stick to possibilities, truth isn't.

121. Truth is stranger than fiction—to some people.

122. Virtue has never been as respectable as money.

123. Wagner's music is better than it sounds.

124. Water, taken in moderation, cannot hurt anybody.

125. We do not deal much in facts when we are contemplating ourselves.

126. We owe a deep debt of gratitude to Adam, the first great benefactor of the human race: he brought death into the world.

127. What a good thing Adam had—when he said a good thing, he knew nobody had said it before.

128. What a man misses mostly in heaven is company.

129. Whatever a man's age, he can reduce it several years by putting a bright-colored flower in his buttonhole.

130. What is the difference between a taxidermist and a tax collector? The taxidermist takes only your skin.

131. When a man's dog turns against him it is time for a wife to pack her trunk and go home to mama.

132. When angry, count four; when very angry, swear.

133. When in doubt, tell the truth.

134. When I reflect upon the number of disagreeable people who I know have gone to a better world, I am moved to lead a different life.

135. When I speak my native tongue in its utmost purity in England, an Englishman can't understand me at all.

136. When some men discharge an obligation you can hear the report for miles around.

137. When you cannot get a compliment in any other way, pay yourself one.

138. Why is it that we rejoice at a birth and grieve at a funeral? Is it because we are not the person concerned?

139. A wise man does not waste so good a commodity as lying for naught.

140. Woman is unrivaled as a wet nurse.

141. Wrinkles should merely indicate where smiles have been.

142. It has always been my rule never to smoke when asleep, and never to refrain when awake.

143. Part of the secret of success in life is to eat what you like and let the food fight it out inside.

144. Twenty-four years ago I was strangely handsome; in San Francisco in the rainy season I was often mistaken for fair weather.

**TYRRELL, George,** 1861–1909, *Irish theologian.*

The *reductio ad absurdum* is God's favorite argument.

**UNDSET, Sigrid,** born 1882, *Norwegian novelist.*

He was not made for climbing the tree of knowledge.

**VOLTAIRE,** 1694–1778, *pen name of François Marie Arouet, French political philosopher, historian, satirist, dramatist, essayist, and novelist.*

1. Animals have these advantages over man: they have no theologians to instruct them, their funerals cost them nothing, and no one starts lawsuits over their wills.

2. The art of government consists in taking as much money as possible from one class of citizens to give to the other.

3. The art of medicine consists of amusing the patient while nature cures the disease.

4. A clergyman is one who feels himself called upon to live without working at the expense of the rascals who work to live.

5. Common sense is not so common.

6. Divorce dates from just about the same time as marriage; I think that marriage is a few weeks older.

7. Doctors pour drugs of which they know little, to cure diseases of which they know less, into human beings of whom they know nothing.

8. England has forty-two religions and only two sauces.

9. Every species of mankind is good except the bore species.

10. The fate of a nation has often depended upon the good or bad digestion of a prime minister.

11. God created woman only to tame man.

12. Heaven made virtue; man, its appearance.

13. The Holy Roman Empire was neither holy, nor Roman, nor an empire.

14. The husband who desires to surprise is often very much surprised himself.

15. Ideas are like beards: men do not have them until they grow up.

16. If God did not exist, it would be necessary to invent Him.

17. I know I am among civilized men because they are fighting so savagely.

18. Illusion is the first of all pleasures.

19. The infinitely little have pride infinitely great.

20. In the great game of human life one begins by being a dupe and ends by being a rogue.

21. I was never ruined but twice: once when I lost a lawsuit, and once when I won one.

22. Marriage is the only adventure open to the cowardly.

23. The multitude of books is making us ignorant.

24. My life's dream has been a perpetual nightmare.

25. My prayer to God is a very short one: "O Lord, make my enemies most ridiculous!" God has granted it.

26. Originality is nothing but judicious imitation.

27. The punishment of criminals should be of use: when a man is hanged he is good for nothing.

28. Satire lies about literary men while they live, and eulogy lies about them when they die.

29. The secret of being a bore is to tell everything.

30. The superfluous: a very necessary thing.

31. To forgive our enemies their virtues—that is a greater miracle.

32. We use ideas merely to justify our evil, and speech merely to conceal our ideas.

33. When he who hears doesn't know what he who speaks means, and when he who speaks doesn't know what he himself means —that is philosophy.

34. When it is a question of money, everybody is of the same religion.

35. A woman can keep one secret—the secret of her age.

**VORSE, Mary Heaton,** born 1880?, *American short-story writer, author, and social reformer.*

The art of writing is the art of applying the seat of the pants to the seat of the chair.

**WADE, Harry V.,** born 1894, *American newspaperman and comic columnist, creator of "Senator Soaper."*

1. Aziz Ezzet, a gentleman of importance in Egypt, says his name can be pronounced by opening a soda bottle slowly.

2. Gypsy Rose Lee, the strip-tease artist, has arrived in Hollywood with twelve empty trunks.

3. The ideal voice for radio may be defined as having no substance, no sex, no owner, and a message of importance to every housewife.

4. Paragraphing is one of the lower forms of cunning, like a way with women.

5. Though General Sherman lived on into the peace, he never said what he thought of it.

6. Youth today must be strong, unafraid, and a better taxpayer than its father.

**WALKER, James J.**, 1881–1946, *American politician.*

1. If you're there before it's over, you're on time.

2. A reformer is a man who rides through a sewer in a glass-bottomed boat.

**WALKER, Stanley**, born 1898, *American journalist and author.*

He was an author whose works were so little known as to be almost confidential.

**WALLACE, Edgar**, 1875–1932, *English novelist and playwright.*

There is so much nastiness in modern literature that I like to write stories which contain nothing worse than a little innocent murdering.

**WALPOLE, Horace**, 1717–1797, *English author, letter writer, and antiquarian.*

1. I never knew but one woman who would not take gold—and she took diamonds.

2. I never understand anything until I have written about it.

3. Spring has set in with its usual severity.

4. The way to endure summer in England is to have it framed and glazed in a comfortable room.

5. We are now so badly degenerated that three Frenchmen can evidently beat one Englishman.

6. The wisest prophets make sure of the event first.

7. Art and life ought to be hurriedly remarried and brought to live together.

8. In my youth I thought of writing a satire on mankind, but now in my age I think I should write an apology for them.

9. There are playthings for all ages; the playthings of old people is to talk of the playthings of their youth.

10. The newspapers have given the rage of going to Paris a good name: they call it the French disease.

**WALTON, Izaak,** 1593–1683, *English author and biographer.*

1. Every misery I miss is a new blessing.

2. That which is everybody's business is nobody's business.

**WARD, Artemus,** 1834–1867, *pen name of Charles Farrar Browne, American humorist.*

1. Alas, she married another; they frequently do; I hope she is happy—because I am.

2. By a sudden and adroit movement I placed my left eye against his fist.

3. Did you ever have the measles, and if so, how many?

4. The female woman is one of the greatest institutions of which this land can boast.

5. The ground flew up and hit me in the head.

6. I am not a politician, and my other habits are good.

7. I am saddest when I sing; so are those who hear me; they are sadder even than I am.

8. I have already given two cousins to the war, and I stand ready to sacrifice my wife's brother.

9. I now bid you a welcome adieu.

10. I prefer temperance hotels, although they sell worse liquor than any other kind of hotels.

11. It is a pity that Chawcer, who had geneyus, was so unedicated; he's the wuss speller I know of.

12. I wish there was windows to my soul, so that you could see some of my feelings.

13. Let us all be happy and live within our means, even if we have to borrow the money to do it with.

14. One of the principal features of my entertainment is that it contains so many things that don't have anything to do with it.

15. There's a good deal of human nature in man.

16. They drink with impunity, or anybody who invites them.

17. Thrice is he armed that hath his quarrel just—and four times he who gets his fist in fust.

18. I have no politics—nary a one.

19. The Mormon's religion is singular, and his wives are plural.

20. Shakespeare endorses polygamy: he speaks of the Merry Wives of Windsor; how many wives did Mr. Windsor have?

21. Why care for grammar as long as we are good?

22. Why is this thus? What is the reason of this thusness?

**WARNER, Charles Dudley,** 1829-1900, *American editor and essayist.*

1. Blessed be agriculture—if one does not have too much of it.

2. Everybody talks about the weather but nobody does anything about it.

3. Nothing can move a man who is paid by the hour; how sweet the flight of time seems to his calm mind.

4. One of the best things in the world to be is a boy; it requires no experience, but needs some practice to be a good one.

5. The thing generally raised on city land is taxes.

6. What a man needs in gardening is a cast-iron back, with a hinge in it.

7. There is but one pleasure in life equal to that of being called on to make an after-dinner speech, and that is not being called on to make one.

**WELLES, Orson,** born 1915, *American actor, director, and producer of motion pictures, radio, and stage.*

1. I don't say we all ought to misbehave, but we ought to look as if we could.

2. Now we sit through Shakespeare in order to recognize the quotations.

3. When you're down and out, something always turns up—and it's usually the noses of your friends.

**WELLS, Carolyn,** 187-?-1942, *American humorous and voluminous writer.*

1. Actions lie louder than words.
2. At times there is nothing so unnatural as nature.
3. A blunder at the right moment is better than cleverness at the wrong time.
4. Charity uncovers a multitude of sins.
5. Circumstances alter faces.
6. A critic is a necessary evil, and criticism is an evil necessity.
7. A cynic is a man who looks at the world with a monocle in his mind's eye.
8. Dead men sell no tales.
9. Epigrams cover a multitude of sins.
10. Every dogma must have its day.
11. A guilty conscience is the mother of invention.
12. He who loves and runs away may live to love another day.
13. It's a wise child that owes his own father.
14. Man's importunity is woman's opportunity.
15. Of two evils choose the prettier.
16. One man's fish is another man's *poisson.*
17. The wages of sin is alimony.
18. We should live and learn; but by the time we've learned, it's too late to live.

**WELLS, Herbert George,** 1866-1946, *English novelist, short-story writer, historian, and sociologist.*

1. Every time Europe looks across the Atlantic to see the American eagle, it observes only the rear end of an ostrich.
2. His studies were pursued but never effectually overtaken.
3. Moral indignation: jealousy with a halo.
4. She had a lot of fat that did not fit.

5. What on earth would a man do with himself if something did not stand in his way?

**WEST, Rebecca,** born 1892, *English novelist and critic.*

He is every other inch a gentleman.

**WESTCOTT, Edward Noyes,** 1846–1898, *American banker and novelist.*

A reasonable amount of fleas is good for a dog; it keeps him from brooding over being a dog.

**WHATELY, Richard,** 1787–1863, *English prelate, logician, theologian, and author.*

1. Honesty is the best policy, but he who is governed by that maxim is not an honest man.

2. It is a folly to expect men to do all that they may reasonably be expected to do.

3. Never argue at the dinner table, for the one who is not hungry always gets the best of the argument.

4. Party spirit enlists a man's virtues in the cause of his vices.

**WHEATLEY, Henry Benjamin,** 1838–1917, *English bibliographer and scholar.*

We usually call our blunders mistakes, and our friends style our mistakes blunders.

**WHISTLER, James McNeill,** 1834–1903, *American painter and etcher.*

1. An artist's career always begins tomorrow.

2. I am not arguing with you—I am telling you.

3. I'm lonesome; they are all dying; I have hardly a warm personal enemy left.

**WHITE, William Allen,** 1868–1944, *American journalist and author.*

My advice to the women's clubs of America is to raise more hell and fewer dahlias.

**WHITMAN, Walt,** 1819-1892, *American poet.*

1. The Americans, like the English, probably make love worse than any other race.
2. Damn all expurgated books; the dirtiest book of all is the expurgated book.
3. I am as bad as the worst but, thank God, I am as good as the best.
4. I find no sweeter fat than sticks to my own bones.

**WILDE, Oscar,** 1856-1900, *British wit, poet, and dramatist.*

1. The advantage of the emotions is that they lead us astray.
2. After a good dinner, one can forgive anybody, even one's own relatives.
3. Alas, I am dying beyond my means.
4. All charming people are spoiled; it is the secret of their attraction.
5. All women become like their mothers—that is their tragedy; no man does—that's his.
6. Ambition is the last refuge of the failure.
7. Anybody can be good in the country; there are no temptations there.
8. Anybody can make history; only a great man can write it.
9. Anyone can sympathize with the sufferings of a friend, but it requires a very fine nature to sympathize with a friend's success.
10. Arguments are extremely vulgar, for everybody in good society holds exactly the same opinions.
11. Arguments are to be avoided; they are always vulgar and often convincing.
12. As long as a woman can look ten years younger than her own daughter, she is perfectly satisfied.
13. As soon as people are old enough to know better, they don't know anything at all.
14. Bad manners make a journalist.
15. Being natural is simply a pose.

16. Bernard Shaw is an excellent man; he has not an enemy in the world, and none of his friends like him.

17. The best way to make children is to make them happy.

18. A bishop keeps on saying at the age of eighty what he was told to say when he was a boy of eighteen.

19. The Book of Life begins with a man and a woman in a garden, and it ends with Revelations.

20. Books of poetry by young writers are usually promissory notes that are never met.

21. The books that the world calls immoral are books that show the world its own shame.

22. By persistently remaining single, a man converts himself into a permanent public temptation.

23. Caricature is the tribute that mediocrity pays to genius.

24. Charity creates a multitude of sins.

25. Children begin by loving their parents; as they grow older they judge them; sometimes they forgive them.

26. Conscience makes egotists of us all.

27. Consistency is the last refuge of the unimaginative.

28. Crying is the refuge of plain women, but the ruin of pretty ones.

29. A cynic is a man who knows the price of everything and the value of nothing.

30. Democracy means simply the bludgeoning of the people, by the people, for the people.

31. The difference between literature and journalism is that journalism is unreadable and literature is unread.

32. Don't be misled into the paths of virtue.

33. Duty is what one expects from others.

34. English actors act quite well, but they act best between the lines.

35. The English country gentleman galloping after a fox—the unspeakable in full pursuit of the uneatable.

36. The English have a miraculous power of turning wine into water.

37. The English public takes no interest in a work of art until it is told that the work in question is immoral.

38. Everybody who is incapable of learning has taken to teaching.
39. Everyone should keep someone else's diary.
40. Experience is simply the name we give our mistakes.
41. Fashion is a form of ugliness so intolerable that we have to alter it every six months.
42. Fashion is that by which the fantastic becomes for a moment universal.
43. Fashion is what one wears oneself: what is unfashionable is what other people wear.
44. Fathers should be neither seen nor heard; that is the only proper basis for family life.
45. Few parents nowadays pay any regard to what their children say to them; the old-fashioned respect for the young is fast dying out.
46. The first duty in life is to be as artificial as possible; what the second duty is, no one has yet discovered.
47. Frank Harris is invited to all the great houses in England—once.
48. Genius is born, not paid.
49. A gentleman is one who never hurts anyone's feelings unintentionally.
50. George Moore wrote brilliant English until he discovered grammar.
51. The good end happily, the bad unhappily—that is what fiction means.
52. He doesn't act on the stage—he behaves.
53. He had the sort of face that, once seen, is never remembered.
54. He hasn't a single redeeming vice.
55. He is old enough to know worse.
56. He knew the precise psychological moment when to say nothing.
57. Henry James writes fiction as if it were a painful duty.
58. Her capacity for family affection is extraordinary; when her third husband died, her hair turned quite gold from grief.
59. He was always late on principle, his principle being that punctuality is the thief of time.

60. I beg your pardon, I didn't recognize you—I've changed a lot.

61. I can believe anything—provided it is incredible.

62. I can resist everything except temptation.

63. I choose my friends for their good looks, my acquaintances for their good characters, and my enemies for their good intellects.

64. I do not approve of anything which tampers with natural ignorance.

65. I do not play cricket because it requires me to assume such indecent postures.

66. If a woman wants to hold a man she has only to appeal to what is worst in him.

67. If one hears bad music it is one's duty to drown it in conversation.

68. If one tells the truth, one is sure sooner or later to be found out.

69. If the lower orders don't set us a good example, what on earth is the use of them?

70. Ignorance is like a delicate exotic fruit: touch it, and the bloom is gone.

71. I like men who have a future and women who have a past.

72. I like Wagner's music better than anybody's; it is so loud, one can talk the whole time without other people hearing what one says.

73. I must decline your invitation owing to a subsequent engagement.

74. In America, the President reigns for four years, and journalism governs forever and ever.

75. In America, the young are always ready to give to those who are older than themselves the full benefits of their inexperience.

76. I never put off till tomorrow what I can possibly do the day after.

77. In examinations the foolish ask questions that the wise cannot answer.

78. In love, one always begins by deceiving oneself, and one always ends by deceiving others; that is what the world calls a romance.

79. In married life, three is company and two none.

80. Insincerity is merely a method by which we can multiply our personalities.

81. In the old days men had the rack; now they have the press.

82. In this world there are only two tragedies: one is not getting what one wants, and the other is getting it.

83. It is always a silly thing to give advice, but to give good advice is absolutely fatal.

84. It is a terrible thing for a man to find out suddenly that all his life he has been speaking nothing but the truth.

85. It is dangerous to be sincere unless you are also stupid.

86. It is only an auctioneer who should admire all schools of art.

87. It is only by not paying one's bills that one can hope to live in the memory of the commercial classes.

88. It is perfectly monstrous the way people go about nowadays saying things against one, behind one's back, that are absolutely and entirely true.

89. Land gives one position, and prevents one from keeping it up.

90. Laughter is not a bad beginning for a friendship, and it is the best ending for one.

91. Life is far too important a thing ever to talk seriously about.

92. The London season is entirely matrimonial; people are either hunting for husbands or hiding from them.

93. The longer I live the more keenly I feel that whatever was good enough for our fathers is not good enough for us.

94. A man can be happy with any woman as long as he does not love her.

95. A man cannot be too careful in the choice of his enemies.

96. Man is a rational animal who always loses his temper when he is called upon to act in accordance with the dictates of reason.

97. A man who desires to get married should know either everything or nothing.

98. A man who moralizes is usually a hypocrite, and a woman who moralizes is invariably plain.

99. A map of the world that does not include Utopia is not worth glancing at.

100. Marriage is the one subject on which all women agree and all men disagree.

101. Memory is the diary that we all carry about with us.

102. Men always want to be a woman's first love; women have a more subtle instinct: what they like is to be a man's last romance.

103. Men become old but they never become good.

104. Men marry because they are tired, women because they are curious; both are disappointed.

105. Meredith is a prose Browning, and so is Browning; he used poetry as a medium for writing in prose.

106. Misfortunes one can endure, they come from the outside; but to suffer for one's faults—ah! there is the sting of life.

107. Modern journalism justifies its own existence by the great Darwinian principle of the survival of the vulgarest.

108. Morality is simply the attitude we adopt towards people whom we personally dislike.

109. More women grow old nowadays through the faithfulness of their admirers than through anything else.

110. Murder is always a mistake; one should never do anything that one cannot talk about after dinner.

111. My own business always bores me to death; I prefer other people's.

112. Never buy a thing you don't want merely because it is dear.

113. No man should have a secret from his wife; she invariably finds it out.

114. Nothing spoils a romance so much as a sense of humor in the woman.

115. Nothing succeeds like excess.

116. Nowadays all the married men live like bachelors, and all the bachelors live like married men.

117. Nowadays to be intelligible is to be found out.

118. No woman should ever be quite accurate about her age—it looks so calculating.

119. Of course, America had often been discovered before Columbus, but it had always been hushed up.

120. The old believe everything, the middle-aged suspect everything, the young know everything.

121. On an occasion of this kind it becomes more than a moral duty to speak one's mind; it becomes a pleasure.

122. One can always recognize women who trust their husbands; they look so thoroughly unhappy.

123. One can survive everything nowadays except death.

124. One half of the world does not believe in God, and the other half does not believe in me.

125. One man's poetry is another man's poison.

126. One should always be in love; that is the reason one should never marry.

127. One should always play fairly when one has the winning cards.

128. One should never make one's debut with a scandal; one should reserve that to give interest to one's old age.

129. One should never trust a woman who tells one her real age; a woman who would tell one that would tell one anything.

130. One should not be too severe on English novels; they are the only relaxation of the intellectually unemployed.

131. One's real life is so often the life that one does not lead.

132. The only difference between a caprice and a lifelong passion is that the caprice lasts a little longer.

133. The only difference between the saint and the sinner is that every saint has a past and every sinner has a future.

134. The only form of lying that is absolutely beyond reproach is lying for its own sake.

135. The only really humanizing influence in prison is the influence of the prisoners.

136. The only thing to do with good advice is to pass it on; it is never of any use to oneself.

137. The only way a woman can ever reform a man is by boring him so completely that he loses all possible interest in life.

138. The only way to behave to a woman is to make love to her if she is pretty and to someone else if she is plain.

139. The only way to get rid of a temptation is to yield to it.

140. A poet can survive everything but a misprint.

141. Prayer must never be answered; if it is, it ceases to be prayer and becomes a correspondence.

142. The proper basis for marriage is a mutual misunderstanding.

143. The public is wonderfully tolerant—it forgives everything except genius.

144. Questions are never indiscreet; answers sometimes are.

145. The real tragedy of the poor is that they can afford nothing but self-denial.

146. A really well-made buttonhole is the only link between art and nature.

147. Relations are simply a tedious pack of people who haven't got the remotest knowledge of how to live nor the smallest instinct about when to die.

148. She has the remains of really remarkable ugliness.

149. She is a peacock in everything but beauty.

150. She looks like the de luxe edition of a wicked French novel meant especially for the English market.

151. She who hesitates is won.

152. She wore far too much rouge last night and not quite enough clothes; that is always a sign of despair in a woman.

153. Society produces rogues, and education makes one rogue cleverer than another.

154. Simple pleasures are the last refuge of the complex.

155. There are moments when art attains almost to the dignity of manual labor.

156. There are only five women in London worth talking to, and two of these can't be admitted into decent society.

157. There are terrible temptations which it requires strength and courage to yield to.

158. There are two ways of disliking art: one is to dislike it; the other, to like it rationally.

159. There is only one class in the community that thinks more about money than the rich, and that is the poor.

160. There is only one thing in the world worse than being talked about, and that is not being talked about.

161. There's nothing in the world like the devotion of a married woman; it's a thing no married man knows anything about.

162. Thirty-five is a very attractive age; London society is full of women who have of their own free choice remained thirty-five for years.

163. Those who are faithless know the pleasures of love; it is the faithful who know love's tragedies.

164. Those who see any difference between soul and body have neither.

165. To expect the unexpected shows a thoroughly modern intellect.

166. To lose one parent may be regarded as a misfortune; to lose both looks like carelessness.

167. To love oneself is the beginning of a lifelong romance.

168. Truly religious people are resigned to everything, even to mediocre poetry.

169. Twenty years of romance make a woman look like a ruin, but twenty years of marriage make her something like a public building.

170. Vulgarity is simply the conduct of others.

171. We have really everything in common with America nowadays except, of course, language.

172. We live in an age when unnecessary things are our only necessities.

173. A well-tied tie is the first serious step in life.

174. We think we are generous because we credit our neighbor with the possession of those virtues that are likely to benefit us.

175. When a woman marries again it is because she detested her first husband; when a man marries again it is because he adored his first wife.

176. Whenever a man does a thoroughly stupid thing, it is always from the noblest motives.

177. Whenever cannibals are on the brink of starvation, Heaven in its infinite mercy sends them a nice plump missionary.

178. Whenever one has anything unpleasant to say, one should always be quite candid.

179. When I was young I used to think that money was the most important thing in life; now that I am old, I know it is.

180. When people agree with me I always feel that I must be wrong.

181. When the gods wish to punish us they answer our prayers.

182. Whistler, with all his faults, was never guilty of writing a line of poetry.

183. Wicked women bother one; good women bore one; that is the only difference between them.

184. With an evening coat and a white tie, anybody, even a stockbroker, can gain a reputation for being civilized.

185. Woman begins by resisting a man's advances and ends by blocking his retreat.

186. A woman with a past has no future.

187. Women are meant to be loved, not to be understood.

188. Women have a much better time than men in this world; there are far more things forbidden to them.

189. Women have a wonderful instinct about things; they can discover anything except the obvious.

190. Women love us for our defects; if we have enough of them they will forgive us everything, even our superior intellects.

191. Women's styles may change but their designs remain the same.

192. Women treat us just as humanity treats its gods; they worship us and are always bothering us to do something for them.

193. The world is a stage, but the play is badly cast.

194. The world is divided into two classes: those who believe the incredible, and those who do the improbable.

195. The world reads too much to be wise and thinks too much to be beautiful.

196. You know what a woman's curiosity is—almost as great as a man's.

197. Young men want to be faithful and are not; old men want to be faithless and cannot.

198. You should study the Peerage; it is the best thing in fiction the English have ever done.

199. The youth of America is their oldest tradition; it has been going on now for three hundred years.

200. Clever people never listen and stupid people never talk.

201. Divorces are made in heaven.

202. The fatality of good resolutions is that they are always too late.

203. Flowers are as common in the country as people are in London.

204. The happiness of a married man depends on the people he has not married.

205. If one could only teach the English how to talk and the Irish how to listen, society would be quite civilized.

206. If one plays good music, people don't listen; if one plays bad music, people don't talk.

207. Modern women understand everything except their husbands.

208. More than half of modern culture depends on what one shouldn't read.

209. Nothing looks so like innocence as an indiscretion.

210. The one charm of marriage is that it makes a life of deception absolutely necessary for both parties.

211. Philanthropy is the refuge of people who wish to annoy their fellow creatures.

212. The reason we are so pleased to find out other people's secrets is that it distracts public attention from our own.

213. There is hardly a person in the House of Commons worth painting, though many of them would be better for a little whitewashing.

214. Women as a sex are sphinxes without secrets.

215. Women have been so highly educated that nothing should surprise them except happy marriages.

216. The public have an insatiable curiosity to know everything—except what is worth knowing.

**WILDER, Thornton,** born 1897, *American novelist and playwright.*

She's going to make some man a good wife someday, provided he comes down off the movie screen and asks her.

**WILSON, Woodrow,** 1856–1924, *President of the United States.*

1. A conservative is a man who just sits and thinks, mostly sits.

2. Every man who takes office in Washington either grows or swells.

3. Gossip: sociologists on a mean and petty scale.

4. He is more apt to contribute heat than light to a discussion.

5. Some Americans need hyphens in their name because only part of them has come over.

6. All the extraordinary men I have ever known were chiefly extraordinary in their own estimation.

**WODEHOUSE, Pelham Grenville,** born 1881, *English humorous novelist.*

1. The butler entered the room, a solemn procession of one.

2. The girl had as many curves as a scenic railway.

3. I could see that, if not actually disgruntled, he was far from being gruntled.

4. It was one of those parties where you cough twice before you speak and then decide not to say it after all.

5. She looked as if she had been poured into her clothes and had forgotten to say "when."

6. She turned him down like a bedspread.

7. Why don't you get a haircut; you look like a chrysanthemum.

**WOOLLCOTT, Alexander,** 1887–1943, *American journalist, dramatic critic, anthologist, author, and wit.*

1. All the things I really like to do are either immoral, illegal, or fattening.

2. The audience strummed their catarrhs.

3. The English have an extraordinary ability for flying into a great calm.

4. Everything I know about her is merely daresay.

5. His huff arrived and he departed in it.

6. I must get out of these wet clothes and into a dry martini.

7. Many of us spend half our time wishing for things we could have if we didn't spend half our time wishing.

8. The scenery in the play was beautiful, but the actors got in front of it.

9. There's nothing wrong with Oscar Levant—nothing that a miracle couldn't cure.

**WOTTON, Henry,** 1568–1639, *English diplomat and poet.*

1. An ambassador is an honest man sent to lie abroad for the good of his country.

2. Hanging is the worst use man can be put to.

3. Next to no wife and children, your own wife and children are best pastime; another's wife and your children worse; your wife and another's children worst.

4. Tell the truth, and so puzzle and confound your adversaries.

**WYCHERLEY, William,** 1640?–1716, *English dramatist.*

1. Go to your business, pleasure, whilst I go to my pleasure, business.

2. He's a fool that marries; but he's a greater that does not marry a fool.

3. Next to the pleasure of making a new mistress is that of being rid of an old one.

4. She is as implacable an adversary as a wife suing for alimony.

**WYLIE, Philip,** born 1902, *American editor, columnist, and author.*

We're about to enter the age of flight before we've even developed a chair that a man can sit on comfortably.

**YBARRA, Thomas Russell,** born 1880, *American biographer and writer.*

He owned and operated a ferocious temper.

**YEATS-BROWN, Francis,** 1886–1944, *British army officer and author.*

To me the charm of an encyclopedia is that it knows—and I needn't.

**ZANGWILL, Israel,** 1864–1926, *English novelist and dramatist.*

1. The way Bernard Shaw believes in himself is very refreshing in these atheistic days when so many believe in no God at all.
2. Dead men hear no tales; posthumous fame is an Irish bull.
3. Editors are constantly on the watch to discover new talents in old names.
4. Scratch the Christian and you find the pagan—spoiled.
5. A man likes his wife to be just clever enough to comprehend his cleverness, and just stupid enough to admire it.
6. The only true love is love at first sight; second sight dispels it.

**ZOLA, Émile,** 1840–1902, *French novelist.*

1. If I cannot overwhelm with my quality, I will overwhelm with my quantity.
2. Perfection is such a nuisance that I often regret having cured myself of using tobacco.

# Index

All *numbers* in this index refer to quotations, *not* to pages. Since authors are arranged alphabetically in the dictionary, there is no need to give page numbers here.

*Entries* in this index generally consist of a key word, author's name, and quotation number. (**ACTION.** Congreve 8.) This example indicates that the key word "ACTION" is referred to in the eighth quotation under Congreve.

When two or more authors have the same last name, their initials are added to distinguish them. (**ACTION.** Mann, H. 1.) In this example the reference is to Horace Mann to tell him apart from Thomas Mann who is indexed as Mann, T.

When a key word or subject is followed by several authors, these are separated by semicolons. (**ACTION.** Congreve 8; Johnson 43; Maurois 3; Scott 5.)

When an author is followed by numbers which are separated by commas, these numbers refer to different quotations by him on the same subject. (**ACTION.** Chesterton 16, 17; Lamb 3, 5, 17; La Rochefoucauld 57, 62.)

When there is only one unnumbered quotation by an author in the dictionary, his name is not followed by any number in this index. (**ACTION.** Landor; Selden.)

This index contains compound key words and phrases not found in other indexes because comic quotations often turn on comparisons. (**BEGINNING & END. BEST & WORST. BORROW vs. LEND.**)

Certain subjects are cited too frequently in the dictionary to warrant inclusion in this index. These excluded subjects are HUSBAND, LOVE, MAN, MARRIAGE, MONEY, WIFE, and WOMAN.

ACCEPT vs. REJECT. Jackson 1; Twain 76.

ACCIDENT. Marquis 3; Morley, C. 8; Rogers 6.

ACCOMPLISH. Barrie 1; Dumas, père 4; Howe 1; Moore 2; Rowland 42; Santayana 4.

ACCURATE. Kipling 16; Wilde 118.

ACHE. See HEADACHE, PAIN, TOOTHACHE.

ACTING. Barrymore 3; Beerbohm 2; Wilde 52. See also ACTOR, THEATER.

ACTION. Bagehot 9; Chesterton 16, 17; Congreve 8; Hubbard, E. 34; Johnson 43; Lamb 3, 5, 17; Landor; La Rochefoucauld 57, 62; Macaulay, T. B. 1; Mann, H. 1; Maurois 3; Mencken 13, 34; Rowland 9; Scott 5; Selden; Twain 91; Wells, C. 1; Wilde 194. See also BEHAVIOR.

ACTOR. Benchley 6; Cervantes 5; Chekhov 5; Field 1; Hazlitt 1; Herford 1; Johnson 34; Mencken 47; Mizner, W. 26; Wilde 34; Woollcott 8. See also ACTING, THEATER, TRAGEDY.

ADAM. Billings 1; Boucicault; Delavigne; Dewar 4; Kipling 17; Shaw 71; Twain 2, 126, 127.

ADAM & EVE. Bierce 53; Sterne 1; Twain 1. See also EVE.

ADMIRATION. Agate 1; Bierce 4; Howe 29; Johnson 2; Lamartine; La Rochefoucauld 46; Mencken 42; Wilde 86, 109; Zangwill 4.

ADULTERY. Byron 17; Cervantes 7; Jackson 8; Mencken 1. See also FAITHFUL vs. UNFAITHFUL.

ADVANTAGE. France 13; Herold 4, 38; Hubbard, Kin 107; Jerome 5; Jerrold 16; Johnson 36; La Bruyère 2; Maurois 2; Rivarol 2; Santayana 6; Shaw 4, 31; Swift 11; Twain 1; Wilde 1, 75, 174. See also FAVOR, PRIVILEGE.

ADVENTURE. Baer 8; Chesterton 1; Voltaire 22.

ADVERSITY. Hubbard, Kin 42; Johnson 2; Twain 13. See also MISERY, MISFORTUNE.

ADVERTISING. Allen, F. 1; Cobb 2; Hubbard, E. 14; Jefferson 3.

ADVICE. Addison 6; Bailey, P. J.; Billings 2, 128; Churchill 1; Collins 5; Howe 17; Hubbard, Kin 4; La Rochefoucauld 21, 50; Masson 3; Montagu 3; O'Malley 26; Shakespeare 13; Swift 15, 25; Wilde 83, 136.

AFFECTATION. Billings 91; La Rochefoucauld 48; Smith, L. P. 4; Wilde 15. See also HYPOCRISY.

AFFORD. Ade 7; Twain 106; Wilde 145.

AGE. Dunne 9; Emerson 3; Frost 6, 17; Gilbert 8; Howe 20, 28; Mencken 35; Mizner, A. 16; Mizner, W. 32; Nathan 3; O'Malley 1; Pinero 5; Prentice 24; Twain 129; Voltaire 35; Wilde 13, 109, 118, 129, 162. See also LONGEVITY, MIDDLE AGE, OLD, OLD AGE, YOUTH vs. AGE.

AGREE. Billings 26, 96; Congreve 1; Disraeli 16; Farquhar 2; Hubbard, Kin 8, 22; Johnson 23; La Rochefoucauld 61; Lloyd George; Mencken 36; Russell 2; Wilde 180. See also HARMONY.

AGREEABLE. Bagehot 2; Chamfort 9; Hubbard, Kin 69; Lavater 1; Little 13. See also PLEASANT, PLEASE.

AIM. Jerrold 30; Santayana 5.

AIR. Lytton 1; Mizner, W. 37; Nietzsche 15.

ALIKE. Lippman; Lowell, J. R. 8; Stendhal 4; Swift 37; Tolstoi 1; Wilde 10.

ALIMONY. Baer 1; Barrymore 16; Herford 3; Herold 39; Wells, C. 17; Wycherley 4. See also DIVORCE.

ALONE. See LONELY.

AMATEUR vs. PROFESSIONAL. Allen, F. 12; Huxley, A. 8; Shaw 51.

AMBIGUITY. Franklin 5; Hope 5; Lincoln 6; Molière 3; Plato 5; Prentice 17; Sheridan, R. B. 4; Voltaire 33. See also MEANING.

AMBITION. Herford 45; Moore 2; Thoreau 4; Wilde 6.

AMERICA. Barrymore 1; Coolidge 1, 4; Hughes, C. E. 1; Marshall; Maurois 2; Poe 1; Rogers 21, 25; Russell 5;

Shaw 3, 17; Twain 70; Wells, H. G. 1; Wilde 74, 75, 119, 199. *See also* CALIFORNIA, FLORIDA, NEW ENGLAND, NEW YORK.

**AMERICAN.** Chesterton 42; Guedalla 4; Howe 22; Johnson 9; Maugham 1; Maurois 4; O'Malley 3, 12, 46; Shaw 78; Whitman 1; Wilson 5.

**AMUSE.** Disraeli 21; Howe 45; Lytton 8; Smith, S. 40. *See also* ENTERTAIN, FUN, FUNNY, LAUGH.

**ANCESTOR.** Agar; Bierce 28; Butler, S. 15; Dumas, père 5; Holmes 10; Hugo 4; Ingersoll 7; Lincoln 5; Lytton 10; Montagu 5; Mumford 3; Plutarch; Sheridan, R. B. 5. *See also* GENEALOGY.

**ANGEL.** Billings 67; Little 5; Rowland 10; Shaw 50; Thackeray 4. *See also* HALO, HEAVEN.

**ANGER.** Franklin 3; Howe 46; Martial 5; Roosevelt, T. 2; Rowland 39, 50; Twain 132; Woollcott 5. *See also* INDIGNATION, TEMPER.

**ANIMAL.** Bierce 33; Billings 43; Broun 1; Butler, S. 1, 44; Coleridge 4; Dewar 7; Eliot 1; Herford 4; Hubbard, Kin 98; La Fontaine 3, 4; Maeterlinck 1; Mencken 12; Shaw 38; Twain 7, 17, 56. *See also* MAN vs. ANIMAL, PET, TAXIDERMY, ZOO. *Also individual animals such as* ANT, ASS, BEAR, BEDBUG, BEE, BIRD, *et cetera.*

**ANSWER.** Adams, H. 2; Byron 9; Pain 2; Wilde 141. *See also* QUESTION & ANSWER, REPARTEE.

**ANT.** Franklin 32.

**APOLOGY.** Bierce 46; Holmes 2; Walpole 8. *See also* REGRET.

**APOSTLE.** Mann, H. 1; Smith, S. 23.

**APPEAL.** Rowland 5; Wilde 66.

**APPEARANCE.** Ade 15; Barrymore 7; Burgess 3; Butler, S. 51, 60; Cobb 3; Dali; Frederick the Great 3; Herold 73; Hubbard, Kin 36, 47; Irving 3; Jowett 5; La Rochefoucauld 20, 37, 41; Nichols 2; Pepys 1; Shakespeare 22; Smith, L. P. 17; Swift 21; Twain 10; Voltaire 12; Welles 1; Wilde 12, 63, 150, 169; Wodehouse

7. *See also* BEAUTY, ILLUSION, UGLY.

**APPETITE.** Bailey, J. M. 1; Chamfort 16. *See also* FOOD.

**APPLAUSE.** Bierce 5; Colton 12.

**APPLE.** Byron 11; Jerrold 6; Twain 2.

**ARCHITECT.** Bierce 6.

**ARGUMENT.** Barrymore 8; Beaumarchais; Billings 103; Brandeis; Cato 3; Chesterton 19; Cicero 1; Disraeli 7; Goldsmith 3; Hubbard, E. 16; Johnson 45; Lowell, J. R. 7; Shakespeare 9; Smith, S. 3; Stevenson 8; Swift 1; Tyrrell; Whately 3; Whistler 2; Wilde 10, 11. *See also* DEBATE, DISCUSSION, OPPONENT, QUARREL.

**ARISTOCRACY.** Colby 1; Heine 10. *See also* CLASS.

**ARITHMETIC.** Scott 4.

**ARMY.** Adams, F. P. 13; Arp; Berle 5; Sévigné 1. *See also* GENERAL, SOLDIER, WAR.

**ART.** Benton; Chekhov 6; Chesterton 4; Dali; Disraeli 25; Fadiman 3; Fontenelle 1; Gide; Huxley, A. 9; Kipling 7; Rowland 3, 42; Saint Gaudens; Walpole 7; Wilde 37, 86, 146, 155, 158. *See also* DANCING, MUSIC, PAINTING, POETRY, STATUE.

**ARTIST.** Butler, S. 5, 49; Gide; Herold 10; Ruskin 1; Santayana 1; Whistler.

**ASS.** Colman (younger); Dickens 10; Eliot 2; Heine 6, 10; Mencken 12; Shakespeare 23; Smith, S. 42; Swift 41; Twain 51. *See also* FOOL, MULE.

**ASYLUM.** Butler, S. 65; Shaw 3, 91. *See also* MENTAL INSTITUTION.

**ATHEIST.** Broun 2; Buchan; Darrow 4; Zangwill 1. *See also* BELIEF, GOD.

**ATTENTION.** Chase, I. 2; Collins 8; Mizner, W. 24; Morley, C. 14; Rowland 46; Wilde 212. *See also* LISTEN.

**ATTRACTION.** Thackeray 1; Wilde 4. *See also* CHARM.

**AUCTIONEER.** Billings 52; Wilde 86.

**AUDIENCE.** Barrymore 3; Macaulay, T. B. 4; Mizner, W. 15; Peacock 1; Woollcott 2.

**AUSTRALIA.** Jerrold 1.

**AUTHOR.** Addison 2; Disraeli 1; Holmes 18; Mizner, W. 39; Montesquieu 1; Nathan 3; O'Malley 25; Prentice 8, 22; Shaw 117, 118; Twain 51; Walker, S. *See also* BOOK, WRITER.

**AUTOGRAPH.** Allen, F. 23; Morley, C. 12.

**AUTOMOBILE.** Hoffenstein 2; Hubbard, Kin 50, 108; Maurois 2.

**AVERAGE.** Roosevelt, T. 1; Spencer 1.

**BABY.** Billings 87; Dickens 6; Herold 78; Howe 15; Hubbard, Kin 130; Jerrold 35; Loomis 1; Mencken 2. *See also* CHILDREN, PREGNANCY, TWINS.

**BACHELOR.** Butler, S. 27; Chamfort 1; Colman (elder); Dunne 12; Herold 35, 47; Lucas 2; Mencken 4, 26; Moore 11; Pinero 4; Rowland 1, 2, 3, 42; Shakespeare 31; Shaw 54; Wilde 22, 116. *See also* CELIBACY.

**BACKWARD.** Huxley, A. 4; Kierkegaard; Rousseau 2; Schlegel. *See also* RETREAT.

**BAD.** Franklin 18; Johnson 11; Rogers 13. *See also* EVIL, GOOD vs. BAD.

**BALD.** Herold 70; O'Malley 7, 32. *See also* HAIR.

**BANK.** Frost 1; Twain 9. *See also* INTEREST.

**BAPTISM.** Butler, S. 72; Ingersoll 9; Meredith 2.

**BARGAIN.** France 15; Howe 43; Jackson 11; Rowland 30; Smith, A. *See also* BUY, SELL.

**BASEBALL.** Baer 12; Mencken 37; Shaw 4.

**BATH.** Burgess 4; Twain 61. *See also* WASH, WATER.

**BATHING SUIT.** Rogers 9.

**BATTLE.** Hugo 8; Runyon 2. *See also* FIGHT, WAR.

**BEACH.** Jerrold 22; Steinbeck.

**BEAR.** Macaulay, T. B. 4.

**BEAUTY.** Barrymore 14; Billings 5; Chesterfield 12; Emerson 38; Fielding 1; Goldberg 3; Haldane 1; Heine 12; Hubbard, Kin 74, 116; Joubert 4;

Little 1; Mencken 6; Mizner, A. 15; Moore 3; Pascal 3; Phelps 6; Rowland 2, 34; Shaw 5; Spencer 3; Twain 144; Wells, C. 15; Wilde 149, 195. *See also* APPEARANCE, COSMETICS.

**BEAUTY vs. UGLY.** La Bruyère 8; Thackeray 1; Wilde 28, 138.

**BED.** Ade 2; Baudelaire 1; Billings 7; Davis; Huxley, A. 7; Inge 5; Johnson 41; Mizner, W. 30; Nye 5; Shakespeare 30; Swift 35; Wodehouse 6. *See also* SLEEP.

**BEDBUG.** Billings 7.

**BEDFELLOW.** Lamb 14; Moore 11.

**BEE.** Bangs 6; Hubbard, Kin 5; Lincoln 17.

**BEER.** Shaw 48. *See also* DRINK.

**BEFORE & AFTER.** Franklin 24; O'Malley 1, 27; Rogers 17; Rowland 4, 18.

**BEG.** Shaw 12, 63; Talleyrand 1. *See also* CHARITY.

**BEGIN.** Butler, S. 55; Hubbard, E. 1; Whistler 1. *See also* INTRODUCTION.

**BEGINNING & END.** Bourget; Cobb 7; Dumas, père 5; Gourmont 6; Howe 40; Hubbard, Kin 49; La Bruyère 1; Mencken 28; Quarles 1; Rowland 44, 45; Twain 108; Voltaire 20; Wilde 19, 90, 185. *See also* END.

**BEHAVIOR.** Ade 5; Billings 43; Herold 45; Hubbard, Kin 113; Mizner, W. 36; Shaw 16; Thoreau 7; Welles 1; Wilde 52, 170. *See also* ACTION, AFFECTATION, GOLDEN RULE, MANNERS, POLITE.

**BELIEF.** Ade 6; Butler, S. 43; Chesterton 25; Fischer 3; Fontenelle 2; Gay 2; Goldberg 5; Herold 64; Irving 1; Jackson 5; Marquis 6; Mencken 16, 25, 46; Mizner, W. 10; Nietzsche 9; Shakespeare 33; Shaw 34, 60, 85, 102, 120; Tarkington 2; Twain 76; Wilde 61, 120, 124, 194; Zangwill 1. *See also* ATHEIST, FAITH, IDEA, MARTYR, OPINION, PRINCIPLE, RELIGION, THEOLOGY, TRUTH, WORSHIP.

**BEST & WORST.** Adams, F. P. 17; Bailey, P. J.; Shaw 100; Whitman 3.

**BET.** Runyon 2. *See also* GAMBLING.

BIBLE. Barrymore 5; Butler, S. 4; Chesterton 5; Dumas, fils 4; Ellis 1; Mann, H. 1; Mencken 38; Nietzsche 8; Twain 3, 20; Wilde 19.

BIERCE, Ambrose. Fadiman 1.

BIGAMY. Herford 3. See also POLYGAMY.

BILL. Masson 19; Wilde 87.

BILLIARDS. Spencer 4.

BIOGRAPHY. Arbuthnot 2; Butler, S. 30; Carlyle 7; Guedalla 2; Maurois 3; Shaw 112. See also LIFE.

BIRD. Baer 16; Fischer 2; Hubbard, Kin 19; Prentice 21; Smith, S. 37, 45; Twain 72.

BIRTH. Allen, F. 9; Allen, G. 1; Billings 10; Butler, S. 15, 25, 74; Congreve 2; Emerson 10; Hubbard, Kin 134; Inge 9; Mencken 32; Michelet; Mizner, A. 18; Mizner, W. 30; O'Malley 47; Osler 1; Santayana 8; Shaw 81, 113; Swift 55; Wilde 48. See also PREGNANCY, STORK.

BIRTH & DEATH. Mencken 32; Twain 138. See also LIFE & DEATH.

BIRTHDAY. Frost 6; Lamb 26; Nash 5.

BITE. Billings 70; Little 4; O'Malley 39; Prentice 14, 24; Rabelais 5; Twain 49. See also DOG.

BLAME. Colton 12; Dumas, père 6. See also FAULT.

BLESSING. Mathews 2; Walton 1. See also PRAYER.

BLIND. Billings 65; Farquhar 3; Herford 43; Masson 11; Montaigne 2.

BLISS. Billings 47; Mumford 6. See also ENJOY, HAPPY.

BLONDE. Baer 21; Herold 18.

BLOOD. Burgess 6; O'Malley 4; Smith, L. P. 3.

BLUNDER. Bailey, J. M. 2; Billings 83, 119; Cowley; Mizner, W. 4; Nietzsche 1, 19; Shaw 89; Talleyrand 6; Wells, C. 3; Wheatley. See also ERROR, MISTAKE.

BOARD. Hubbard, Kin 48; Nye 20. See also FOOD.

BOAST. Emerson 5, 37; Helps 2; Johnson 26; Mencken 31. See also PRIDE.

BOAT. Prentice 34; Rogers 12; Twain 66; Walker, J. 2.

BODY. Baer 7; Bierce 18; Boucicault; Butler, S. 8, 13; Franklin 36; Haldane 1; Halsey 1; Howe 26; Leacock 2; Smith, L. P. 11. See also OPERATION. Also individual parts of the body such as BOSOM, HAND, HEAD, et cetera.

BODY & MIND. La Rochefoucauld 29; Smith, S. 10.

BODY & SOUL. O'Malley 8; Wilde 164.

BONE. Barrie 8; Frost 11; Little 10; Smith, S. 26; Whitman 4. See also BODY.

BOOK. Adams, F. P. 2; Bierce 50; Butler, S. 33, 53; Byron 16; Chamfort 12, 17; Chesterton 24, 41; Colton 6; Darrow 11; Dickens 16; Disraeli 1, 2, 24; Einstein 1; France 10, 19; Gibbon 2; Goldsmith 2; Gourmont 4; Heine 4; Hubbard, Kin 3, 16; Huxley, A. 1; Karr 4; Lamb 1; Levant 3; Lincoln 1; Macaulay, R.; Masson 16; Mencken 5, 22; Mizner, W. 3; Moore 5, 19; Morley, C. 12; Morley, J. 5; Nichols 1; Pascal 2; Roche 3; Rogers 15; Scott 4; Shaw 9, 77; Smith, L. P. 8; Smith, S. 25, 32; Swift 10; Twain 15; Voltaire 23; Whitman 2; Wilde 21, 150. See also BIOGRAPHY, CRITIC, DIARY, DICTIONARY, ENCYCLOPEDIA, LIBRARY, LITERATURE, MANUSCRIPT, NOVEL, TEXT, WRITING.

BOOK BORROWING. Lamb 1; Robinson; Roche 3; Scott 4.

BORE. Bierce 8; Brillat-Savarin; Byron 12; Emerson 9; Holmes 1, 3; Howells, W. D.; Landon 1; La Rochefoucauld 47, 54; Little 12; Molière 1; Montesquieu 1; Scott 1; Shaw 46; Smith, L. P. 14; Smith, S. 11; Swift 32; Voltaire 9, 29; Wilde 111, 137, 183. See also DULL, YAWN.

BORROW. Billings 63; Churchill 3; Franklin 21; Hubbard, Kin 61; Lamb 1; Mizner, A. 13; Ward 13. See also BOOK BORROWING.

**BORROW vs. LEND.** Bierce 3; Billings 21; France 10; Lamb 6.

**BOSOM.** Johnson 34; Morley, C. 23.

**BOSS.** Frost 4; O'Malley 3.

**BOTHER.** Hubbard, Kin 89; Smith, S. 35; Wilde 183, 192. *See also* TROUBLE.

**BOTTLE.** Baudelaire 3; Bierce 22; Herold 76; O'Malley 10, 28; Swift 31; Wade 1. *See also* LIQUOR.

**BOY.** Baer 33; Bierce 23; Howe 13; Hubbard, Kin 6, 25, 105; Leacock 7; Lytton 6; Plato 2; Rowland 2, 42; Twain 67; Warner 4. *See also* CHILDREN.

**BRAINS.** Bierce 9; Billings 48; Chesterfield 13; Dawes; Frost 3; Hecht 2; Masson 10; Montesquieu 4; Osler 3; Sousa; Stevenson 3. *See also* INTELLIGENCE, MIND.

**BRAVE.** Butler, S. 7; Chesterton 43; Emerson 16; Franklin 46; Hubbard, Kin 74; Karr 1; Mizner, A. 15; Mumford 8; Shaw 35, 47.

**BREAD.** Billings 35, 45; Fischer 4; Howe 75.

**BREAK.** Marquand; Masefield; Swift 27.

**BREAKFAST.** Billings 86; Butler, S. 19; Hubbard, Kin 66; Smith, S. 48. *See also* EAT.

**BREATHE.** Mizner, W. 37.

**BREEDING.** Shaw 121; Steele 2; Twain 22, 27. *See also* MANNERS.

**BREVITY.** Butler, S. 10; Parker 1. *See also* SHORT.

**BRIBE.** Cameron; Herford 43; Mencken 14.

**BRIDE.** Addison 6; Mencken 19. *See also* WEDDING.

**BROADWAY.** Chesterton 46.

**BROKER.** Balzac 5; Wilde 184.

**BROOKLYN.** Herford 16.

**BROTHER.** Billings 38, 66; Hubbard, Kin 20.

**BROWNING, Robert.** Wilde 105.

**BURY.** Lichtenberg 5; Martial 7, 8. *See also* FUNERAL, UNDERTAKER.

**BUSINESS.** Augustine 2; Bierce 27; Billings 56, 109; Coolidge 1; Dickens 5; Disraeli 12; Dumas, fils 2; Howe 40; Hubbard, Kin 49; Irving 4; Pulitzer; Shaw 8, 18; Swift 48; Thoreau 3; Walton 2; Wilde 87, 111. *See also* MANAGEMENT, WORK.

**BUSINESS vs. PLEASURE.** Dickens 2; Wycherley 1.

**BUSY.** Hubbard, Kin 5; Lytton 9; Marquis 14; O'Malley 8.

**BUTLER.** Maugham 1; Wodehouse 1. *See also* SERVANT.

**BUTTONHOLE.** Thackeray 6; Twain 129; Wilde 146.

**BUY.** Hubbard, Kin 46; Lewis 2; Wilde 112. *See also* BROKER, SHOPPING.

**CABBAGE.** Bierce 10; Twain 119.

**CAESAR, Julius.** Hume.

**CALIFORNIA.** Allen, F. 3.

**CALM.** Emerson 20; Woollcott 3. *See also* QUIET, SILENCE.

**CAMEL.** Bierce 12.

**CAN.** Galsworthy 2; Hubbard, E. 26; Nathan 2.

**CAPITAL PUNISHMENT.** Chamfort 5; Karr 2. *See also* HANGING, KILL.

**CAPITALISM.** Dunne 2; Shaw 114.

**CAPTAIN.** Prentice 34.

**CAR.** *See* AUTOMOBILE.

**CARDS.** Dunne 15, 22; Field 1; Herold 27, 41; Lamb 8; Swift 18; Wilde 127.

**CAREFUL.** Howe 5; Shaw 66; Wilde 95. *See also* DISCRETION.

**CARESS.** Chase, I. 2; Romberg. *See also* KISS.

**CARLYLE, Thomas.** Morley, J. 5.

**CASTLE.** Lytton 1; Nevinson.

**CAT.** Eliot 7; Herford 4; Kingsley 3; Lichtenberg 4; Pain 1; Tennyson 1; Thoreau 11; Twain 50, 89.

**CATHOLIC.** Inge 5.

**CAUSE.** Peacock 2; Ward 22. *See also* REASON.

**CELEBRATE.** Jerrold 13; Prentice 32.

**CELIBACY.** Franklin 31; Johnson 20; Mencken 26; Socrates 1; Swift 38. *See also* BACHELOR, SPINSTER.

**CEMETERY.** Beecher, H. W. 2; Brisbane; Hubbard, E. 13; Hubbard, Kin 33; Twain 21. *See also* BURY, GRAVE.

**CENSORSHIP.** Butler, S. 26; Lindsey; Masson 6; Shaw 2, 9. *See also* EXPURGATE.

**CEREMONY.** Butler, S. 35, 72; Lamb 5; Steele 1; Twain 58.

**CHAIR.** Gilbert 4; Shakespeare 1; Thoreau 9; Vorse; Wylie.

**CHAMPAGNE.** Kipling 5; Shaw 48. *See also* DRINK.

**CHANGE.** Burbank 2; Herford 6; Lowell, J. R. 4; Mizner, W. 23; Spurgeon 1; Twain 26, 46; Wilde 60. *See also* EXCHANGE.

**CHANGE vs. CONSTANCY.** Swift 33; Wilde 191.

**CHARACTER.** Bierce 33; Billings 111; Heine 7; Herold 42; Hubbard, E. 21; Quillen 2; Shaw 27. *See also* REPUTATION.

**CHARITY.** Dickens 23; Herford 5; Hubbard, E. 1; Masson 11; Nietzsche 6; Wells, C. 4; Wilde 24. *See also* BEG, HELP, PHILANTHROPIST.

**CHARM.** Balzac 11; Barrie 7; Butler, S. 59; Herford 27; Nichols 2; Terence 1; Wilde 4. *See also* ATTRACTION, PLEASE.

**CHASTITY.** Augustine 1; Billings 15; Congreve 5; Gourmont 9; Nietzsche 3; Ovid 1; Shaw 85. *See also* MODESTY, VIRTUE.

**CHEAP.** Hubbard, Kin 19, 35; Ruskin 3. *See also* COST.

**CHEAT.** Bierce 39; Billings 88; Eliot 5; France 15; Hubbard, Kin 57; Leacock 5. *See also* DECEIT, TRICK.

**CHEWING GUM.** Rogers 24.

**CHEWING TOBACCO.** Allen, F. 24; Prentice 27.

**CHICKEN.** Baer 23; Fischer 5.

**CHILD TRAINING.** Franklin 40; Inge 10; Plato 2; Rochester 1; Spurgeon 3.

**CHILDREN.** Banning; Benchley 4; Billings 124; Chamfort 1; Disraeli 1; Fielding 10; Franklin 48; Goethe 1, 7; Herold 65; Holmes 21; Howe 8; Hubbard, Kin 114; Joubert 1; Masson 8; Morley, C. 1; Prentice 3; Rochester 1; Shaw 95; Twain 22; Wilde 17, 166; Wotton 3. *See also* BABY, BOY, DAUGHTER, FAMILY, INFANT PRODIGY, PARENTS & CHILDREN, SON.

**CHINA.** Buck; Rogers 5.

**CHIP.** Holmes 18.

**CHIVALRY.** Byron 17; Nevinson; Shaw 98.

**CHOOSE.** Bierce 36; France 18; Geraldy 2; James, W. 3; Morley, J. 1; Wells, C. 15; Wilde 63, 95.

**CHRIST.** Butler, S. 16, 56; Herold 35; Lindsey; Mencken 3; Nietzsche 10.

**CHRISTIAN.** Bierce 12; Broun 2; Emerson 12; Mencken 3; Montagu 5; Nietzsche 10; Shakespeare 17; Zangwill 4.

**CHRISTIANITY.** Chesterton 6; Dunne 5; Ellis 7; Gourmont 2; Munro 6; Shaw 119; Smith, S. 33. *See also* RELIGION.

**CHRISTMAS.** Hubbard, Kin 26; Swift 3.

**CHURCH.** Allen, F. 22; Darrow 1; Erskine; Herold 78; Inge 4; Ingersoll 2; Mencken 7, 26; Mizner, W. 19; Nietzsche 15; O'Malley 45; Shaw 7, 11; Twain 76. *See also* WORSHIP.

**CIGAR.** Adams, F. P. 2; Frost 5; Kipling 15; Little 17; Lytton 2; Rogers 16; Twain 82. *See also* SMOKING.

**CIGARETTE.** Allen, F. 24; Fishbein; Hubbard, Kin 134. *See also* SMOKING.

**CIRCUMSTANTIAL EVIDENCE.** Eliot 7; O'Malley 9; Thoreau 19. *See also* CRIME.

**CIRCUS.** Allen, F. 13; Hubbard, Kin 25.

**CITY.** Colton 3; Herold 16; Thoreau 5. *See also* BROOKLYN, HOLLYWOOD, LONDON, NEW YORK, PARIS, ROME, TOWN.

**CITY vs. COUNTRY.** Jerrold 3; Marquis 4. *See also* COUNTRY.

**CIVIL SERVICE.** Hubbard, Kin 10, 39. *See also* GOVERNMENT, OFFICIAL.

**CIVILIZATION.** Emerson 8; Hubbard, E. 26. *See also* CULTURE.

**CIVILIZE.** Hugo 4; Ingersoll 8; Meredith 6; Voltaire 17; Wilde 184.

**CLASS.** Jackson 13; Shaw 94; Voltaire 2; Wilde 69, 194. *See also* ARISTOCRACY, GENTLEMAN, RANK.

**CLEAN.** Barrymore 4; Burbank 2; Butler, S. 12; Chesterton 15; Franklin 4; Herford 6; Ingersoll 1; Rogers 22. *See also* NEAT, WASH.

**CLERGY.** Bierce 13; Billings 13; Chamfort 20; Inge 1; Jerrold 33; Jowett 2; Landon 2; Mencken 3, 8; Mizner, W. 19; Moore 4; Rowland 27; Russell 1; Sandburg 1; Smith, S. 1, 8, 13, 30, 41; Sterne 1; Tennyson 2; Voltaire 4; Wilde 18. *See also* PREACHER.

**CLEVER.** Chesterton 9; Disraeli 9; Hubbard, E. 28; Hurst 2; Kipling 7, 12; La Rochefoucauld 15, 65; Plato 1; Stendhal 1; Wells, C. 3. *See also* CUNNING, INTELLIGENT.

**CLIMB.** Jerrold 31; Roosevelt, T. 2; Undset.

**CLOCK.** Mizner, W. 2; O'Malley 42. *See also* TIME, WATCH.

**CLOTHES.** Addison 6; Allen, F. 15; Bailey, J. M. 3; Barrie 11; Beerbohm 2; Bierce 7; Billings 130; Chamfort 19; Cobb 17; Dewar 6; France 12; Hecht 2; Heine 2; Herford 15; Herold 54, 61; Howe 26; Hubbard, Kin 78, 80; Ibsen 2; Jerrold 6, 27; Lin Yutang; Marquis 2; Moore 21; Morley, C. 8; Nichols 2; Nye 20; O'Malley 51; Parker 1; Pepys 3; Pollock 4; Rogers 9; Rowland 38; Smith, S. 4; Swift 30; Thoreau 3; Twain 88; Wilde 152, 173, 184; Wodehouse 5; Woollcott 6. *See also* FASHION, STYLE. *Also articles of clothing like* BATHING SUIT, COAT, DIAPER, *et cetera.*

**COAT.** Lowell, J. R. 7; Prentice 16.

**COCK.** Aldington; Eliot 4. *See also* HEN.

**COCKROACH.** Allen, G. 2.

**COFFEE.** Lincoln 7; Twain 63.

**COLD.** Chamfort 20; Hubbard, Kin 4; Phelps 2; Renard; Ruskin 2; Shakespeare 27. *See also* ICE.

**COLLEGE.** Burgess 7; Haliburton 1; Hubbard, E. 31; Masson 5; Roosevelt, T. 5; Twain 119. *See also* EDUCATION, UNIVERSITY.

**COLLEGE GRADUATE.** Hutchins 1; Taft.

**COLOR.** Field 5; Kipling 11; Luce; O'Malley 9, 48.

**COLUMBUS, Christopher.** Wilde 119.

**COMEDY.** Byron 1; Cervantes 5; Chesterton 11. *See also* HUMOR, THEATER, WIT.

**COMFORT.** Lamb 22; Marquis 15; Mizner, W. 28; Molière 1; Wylie. *See also* LUXURY.

**COMMON.** Twain 22; Voltaire 5; Wilde 203.

**COMMON SENSE.** Shaw 35; Voltaire 5. *See also* INTELLIGENCE, HORSE SENSE, SENSE.

**COMPANION.** Chesterton 7; Rowland 52. *See also* FRIENDSHIP.

**COMPANY.** Halifax 2; Herford 38; Johnson 8, 12, 17; La Rochefoucauld 47; Mizner, A. 12; Parkhurst; Smith, L. P. 5; Thoreau 9; Twain 128; Wilde 79. *See also* GUEST, VISIT.

**COMPETITION.** Ade 1; Allen, F. 12; Billings 17; Dewar 2; Emerson 2.

**COMPLAINT.** Burke 2; Gilbert 3; Karr 3; Herold 47; Hubbard, Kin 8; La Rochefoucauld 2; Nichols 3; Swift 4. *See also* FAULT, GROUCH.

**COMPLIMENT.** Hubbard, Kin 97, 101; Kipling 10; Rowland 47; Twain 42, 137. *See also* FLATTERY, PRAISE.

**COMPOSITION.** Butler, S. 75; Schumann; Smith, S. 24. *See also* MUSIC, WRITING.

**CONCEIT.** Billings 78; Disraeli 4; Eliot 9; La Rochefoucauld 1; Masson 21; Mizner, W. 26; Smith, S. 48; Wilson 2. *See also* EGOTISM, VANITY.

**CONCLUSION.** Butler, S. 40; Shaw 43. *See also* END.

**CONDUCT.** *See* ACTION, BEHAVIOR.

**CONFERENCE.** Allen, F. 4; Rogers 21.

**CONFESSION.** Billings 12, 133; Dewar 1; Hay, I.; Huneker 6; La Rochefoucauld 49, 52; Sévigné 2. *See also* SIN.

CONFIDENCE. Poe 2; Smith, S. 20; Twain 5; Walker, S. *See also* TRUST.

CONFUSION. Allen, F. 1; Skinner 2; Twain 30.

CONGRESS. Masson 17; Prentice 23, 29; Rogers 2, 23, 27; Roosevelt, T. 1; Twain 25, 60, 96. *See also* ELECTION, PARLIAMENT, REPRESENTATIVE, STATESMAN.

CONQUEST. Jerrold 40; Lenclos 2; Rowland 21. *See also* COURTSHIP.

CONSCIENCE. Madariaga; Mencken 9, 41; Twain 57; Wells, C. 11; Wilde 26. *See also* RIGHT vs. WRONG.

CONSERVATIVE. Emerson 25; Hubbard, E. 2; Jerrold 4; Roosevelt, F. D. 4; Wilson 1. *See also* LIBERAL vs. CONSERVATIVE, POLITICS.

CONSTANT. Congreve 7; Roche 4; Smith, S. 44; Swift 33. *See also* CHANGE vs. CONSTANCY.

CONSTITUTION. Darrow 10; Dunne 10; Hughes, C. E. 2.

CONTEMPT. Montagu 1; O'Malley 16.

CONTENT. Jackson 2, 9; Ruskin 5. *See also* PLEASE, SATISFACTION.

CONVENT. Haliburton 4; Napoleon 1; Strachey 1.

CONVERSATION. Ade 3; Disraeli 8; Emerson 2, 23; Franklin 16; Goethe 4; Hazlitt 11; Herold 11; Hope 3; Hubbard, Kin 12; La Bruyère 5; La Rochefoucauld 1; Shaw 52; Smith, S. 28; Stevenson 8; Swift 1; Twain 28; Wilde 67. *See also* INTERRUPTION, SPEECH, TALK, TALK vs. LISTEN, TELEPHONE.

CONVERT. Moore 5; O'Malley 33; Shakespeare 17. *See also* MISSIONARY, RELIGION.

COOK. Butler, S. 13, 41; Frost 16; Galsworthy 2; Hood 3; Jerrold 9; Meredith 4; Mizner, W. 21; Molière 2; Munro 2; Rousseau 1. *See also* FOOD.

CORRESPONDENCE. Morley, J. 2; Smith, S. 4; Wilde 141. *See also* LETTER, WRITING.

COSMETICS. Chamfort 5; Hubbard, Kin 116; Shakespeare 6; Wilde 152. *See also* BEAUTY, FACE.

COST. Emerson 3, 28; Gibbs, P.; Hubbard, Kin 30, 123; Masson 1; Wilde 29. *See also* CHEAP, EXPENSE, VALUE, WORTH.

COST OF LIVING. Darrow 1; Hubbard, Kin 45, 93. *See also* INFLATION.

COUGH. Lamb 14; Wodehouse 4.

COUNT. Emerson 3; Johnson 10; Twain 132.

COUNTRY. Baer 32, 33; Burgess 6; Chesterton 29; Ostenso; Smith, S. 19; Wilde 7, 203; Wotton 1. *See also* CITY vs. COUNTRY.

COURAGE. *See* BRAVE.

COURT. Dunne 10; Irving 4; Mencken 39; Swift 36; Talleyrand 1; Twain 43. *See also* JUDGE, JUSTICE.

COURTSHIP. Bagehot 7; Hubbard, Kin 7; Masson 19, 20; Mizner, W. 3; Rowland 7. *See also* CONQUEST, ROMANCE.

COW. Billings 58, 87; Emerson 29; Franklin 15; Mencken 11. *See also* MILK.

COWARD. Bierce 15; Hubbard, E. 2; Shaw 59; Twain 105; Voltaire 22. *See also* FEAR.

CREATION. Billings 67; Browne 3; Hubbard, E. 17; Hugo 3; Jackson 15; Jerrold 8; Luther 1; Montesquieu 4; Morley, C. 4; Nasby; Shaw 104; Twain 59, 78, 93, 117; Voltaire 11.

CREDIT. Billings 15; Dickens 4; Franklin 6; Howe 41; Howell; Russell 4.

CRICKET. Shaw 4; Wilde 65.

CRIME. Benchley 2; Bierce 50; Butler, S. 9; Chamfort 7; Hubbard, Kin 84; La Rochefoucauld 31; Runyon 1; Shaw 49; Talleyrand 6. *See also* CIRCUMSTANTIAL EVIDENCE, PRISON, WRONG.

CRIMINAL. O'Malley 38; Twain 60; Voltaire 27.

CRITIC. Byron 3; Disraeli 25; Helps 1; Holmes 18; Huneker 2; Joubert 1; Mizner, W. 5; Moore 10; Pollock 1; Sibelius; Wells, C. 6. *See also* FAULT, JUDGMENT.

**CRITICISM.** Billings 96; Disraeli 11; Eliot 1; Franklin 28; Howe 7; Hubbard, E. 32; Hubbard, Kin 121; Johnson 3; Pascal 1; Priestley; Shaw 117; Smith, S. 25; Sterne 3; Swift 21, 42; Talleyrand 7; Twain 53. *See also* FAULT, JUDGMENT.

**CROCODILE.** Butler, S. 62.

**CROP.** Billings 46; Stevenson 4. *See also* FARM.

**CROW.** Eliot 4.

**CROWD.** Barnum 1; Hubbard, Kin 88; Strunsky.

**CRY.** Baer 2, 25; Cervantes 6; Eliot 10; Franklin 34; Haliburton 2; Lytton 2; Wilde 28. *See also* EYES, TEARS.

**CULTURE.** Ade 22; Butler, S. 45; Emerson 4; Wilde 208. *See also* CIVILIZATION, EDUCATION, HIGHBROW.

**CUNNING.** La Fontaine 4; Wade 4. *See also* CLEVER, DECEIT.

**CURE.** Browne 2; Herford 44; Herold 13; Hubbard, Kin 107, 135; Lamb 2; Peacock 2; Prentice 19; Santayana 8; Tennyson 2; Voltaire 3; Woollcott 9; Zola 2. *See also* HEALTH, NURSE.

**CURIOSITY.** Shaw 26; Wilde 104, 196, 216.

**CURVE.** Lardner 5; Pollock 4; Wodehouse 2.

**CUSTOM.** Russell 5; Shaw 69; Twain 30; Wilde 199. *See also* HABIT.

**CYNIC.** Beecher, H. W. 1; Bierce 16; Hurst 2; Mencken 10; Rowland 54; Wells, C. 7; Wilde 29.

**DANCING.** Hubbard, Kin 37; Lincoln 10; Morley, C. 2; Nietzsche 9; Twain 92.

**DANDRUFF.** Baer 10; Howe 11.

**DANGER.** Huxley, T. H. 1; Krutch; La Rochefoucauld 30; Marquis 1; Mizner, W. 28; Nietzsche 17; Shaw 85; Twain 39; Wilde 85. *See also* HARM.

**DARK.** Masson 9.

**DAUGHTER.** Balzac 8; Goethe 3; Hubbard, Kin 90, 115; Prentice 12. *See also* CHILDREN, MOTHER vs. DAUGHTER.

**DAY.** Billings 20; Burdette 3; Goldberg 5; Herold 61; Hubbard, Kin 128; Marquis 12; Twain 8, 65; Wells, C. 10. *See also* EVENING, HOLIDAY, MORNING, TIME.

**DEAF.** Montaigne 2; Talleyrand 3.

**DEATH.** Alexander; Arbuthnot 2; Bradley 1; Browne 2; Butler, S. 37; Byron 1; Chapman 2; Chesterfield 1; Coleridge 4; Darrow 6; Dickens 7; Emerson 31; Franklin 44; Goncourt; Herford 34; Herold 46; Hubbard, E. 3; Hubbard, Kin 67; Little 6; Macaulay, R.; Maeterlinck 1; Mann, T.; Martial 3; Mencken 32; Mizner, W. 29; Munro 3; Napoleon 4; Nietzsche 16; O'Malley 25, 47; Pope 5; Repplier; Rowland 43; Russell 6; Santayana 8; Shakespeare 11; Terence 1; Twain 21, 98, 126; Wilde 3, 123; Zangwill 2. *See also* BIRTH & DEATH, CAPITAL PUNISHMENT, DROWN, HANGING, LIFE & DEATH, MARTYR, MURDER, SUICIDE.

**DEBATE.** Joubert 2; Roosevelt, T. 4. *See also* ARGUMENT, DISCUSSION, OPPONENT.

**DEBT.** Billings 16, 33, 85, 122; Franklin 6; Howell; Ingersoll 5; Mumford 4; O'Malley 17; Pepys 3; Prentice 25; Rabelais 7; Rowland 39; Wells, C. 13. *See also* BILL.

**DECEIT.** Barnum 2; Behn 2; Billings 28, 109; Johnson 37; La Rochefoucauld 13, 25, 55; Swift 12; Tarkington 3; Wilde 78, 210. *See also* CHEAT, LIE, TRICK.

**DECOMPOSE.** Butler, S. 75; Herold 29.

**DEFEND.** Jerrold 26; Kingsley 1; La Fontaine 3.

**DEFINITION.** France 11; Shaw 82. *See also* DICTIONARY, EXPLANATION, MEANING.

**DELIRIUM.** Carlyle 4.

**DELUSION.** Bierce 49; Mencken 29, 56.

**DEMOCRACY.** Cabell 2; Emerson 6; Jackson 4; Lowell, J. R. 2; Mencken 1, 12; Shaw 14; Wilde 30.

DEMOCRATIC PARTY. Dunne 3; Greeley 1; Hubbard, Kin 133; Rogers 17. See also POLITICAL PARTY.

DENTIST. Bierce 17; Prentice 5. See also TEETH.

DEPARTURE. Bailey, J. M. 5; Hubbard, Kin 31; Mizner, A. 4; Munro 2; Peacock 1; Roche 2; Rowland 24; Shakespeare 28; Ward 9; Woollcott 5. See also EXIT.

DEPRESSION. See COST OF LIVING, INFLATION.

DESERTION. Hays 1; Jerrold 20; Mizner, A. 15.

DESERVE. Hubbard, Kin 95; O'Malley 35.

DESIGN. Morley, C. 8; Wilde 191. See also INTENTION, MODEL.

DESIRE. Hegel 1; Marquis 11; Mizner, A. 25; Prentice 35; Shakespeare 20; Wilde 82. See also WISH.

DEVIL. Arnould 2; Billings 17, 33; Butler, S. 16; Eliot 8; Hubbard, Kin 40; Landon 2; Rowland 10; Shaw 15; Twain 3. See also GOD vs. DEVIL.

DIAMOND. Twain 75; Walpole 1. See also JEWELRY.

DIAPER. Herold 29.

DIARY. Wilde 39, 101.

DICE. O'Malley 6. See also GAMBLING.

DICTIONARY. Butler, S. 70; Gourmont 2. See also DEFINITION.

DIET. Baer 4; Fischer 5. See also EAT, FOOD.

DIFFERENCE. Addison 4; Frost 5; Mencken 29; Shaw 62; Twain 11, 49, 62, 89; Wilde 100, 164.

DIGESTION. Billings 48; Butler, S. 13; Masson 20; Rousseau 1; Smith, S. 14; Twain 118, 143; Voltaire 10. See also DYSPEPSIA, EAT, FOOD, INDIGESTION.

DIGNITY. Bennett, A. 7; Chesterton 45; Herold 29; Twain 71; Wilde 155. See also PRIDE.

DINNER. Bagehot 6; Byron 11; Chamfort 13, 16; Colton 7; Emerson 25; Hubbard, Kin 48, 137; Johnson 18, 19; Mencken 38; Molière 2; Whately 3; Wilde 2, 110. See also EAT, FOOD.

DIOGENES. Burton 1.

DIPLOMACY. Cavour; Claudel; Dawes; Frost 6; Goldberg 1; Hay, J.; Herford 10; Rogers 15; Wotton 1. See also INTERNATIONAL.

DIRECTION. Brush 2; Guedalla 2; Leacock 1; Ostenso; Smith, S. 7.

DIRT. Lamb 8; Palmerston 2; Rogers 22.

DISAPPOINT. Bierce 37; Disraeli 3; Pope 1; Wilde 104.

DISCOVER. Fischer 1; Lamb 3; Munro 1; Twain 70; Wilde 119, 189.

DISCRETION. La Fontaine 4; Lincoln 18.

DISCUSSION. Bierce 19; Wilde 110, 160; Wilson 4. See also ARGUMENT, DEBATE.

DISEASE. Billings 8; Browne 2; Ellis 1; Fielding 2; Fischer 4; Hubbard, Kin 100, 113; Johnson 22; Nietzsche 21; O'Malley 50; Rabelais 1; Repplier; Smith, S. 18; Swift 37; Voltaire 3, 7; Walpole 10. See also DRUGS, MEDICINE, SICK.

DISLIKE. Rowland 39; Sheridan, R. B. 6; Twain 44, 91; Wilde 108, 158. See also HATE.

DISPLEASE. La Rochefoucauld 12; Twain 111; Wodehouse 3.

DISTANCE. Cocteau 4; Galsworthy 4; Hubbard, Kin 11; Rowland 31; Swift 16; Thoreau 16.

DISTRUST. Mencken 36; Wilde 129. See also SUSPICION.

DIVORCE. Barrymore 11; Butler, S. 35; Hays 1; Herford 3; Levant 4; Little 8; Rowland 10, 21, 27; Saltus 2; Shaw 105; Voltaire 6; Wilde 201. See also ALIMONY.

DOCTOR. Alexander; Billings 107; Bryce; Chamfort 20; Diderot; Dunne 5; Fielding 2; Fischer 4; Fishbein; Franklin 8, 11, 41; Herold 12, 13; Hubbard, Kin 107; Martial 2; Montaigne 9; Napoleon 4; Osler 3; Quarles 2; Shaw 93; Sterne 4; Twain 33; Voltaire 7. See also DISEASE, OPERATION, PATIENT, SICK.

DOG. Balzac 13; Billings 18, 19, 69, 70, 89, 93; Capek; Franklin 42; Howe 2; Huxley, A. 5; Jackson 6; Jerrold 5;

Johnson 43; Lamartine; O'Malley 39; Pope 4; Prentice 14; Rabelais 5; Shakespeare 12; Shaw 57; Smith, A.; Staël 2; Twain 31, 49, 131; Westcott. *See also* BITE.

**DOGMATISM.** Broun 5; Guedalla 1; Jerrold 5; Marquis 9; Wells, C. 10. *See also* OPINION, POSITIVE, SURE.

**DOOR.** Moore 3; Rolland 49.

**DOUBT.** Carlyle 3; Mizner, W. 13; Twain 133. *See also* SKEPTICISM.

**DREAM.** Adams, F. P. 5; Allen, F. 5; Fadiman 2; O'Malley 41; Russell 5; Voltaire 24. *See also* SLEEP.

**DRESS.** *See* CLOTHES.

**DRINK.** Benchley 2; Blackie; Cervantes 4; Coleridge 3; Herford 38; Holmes 16; Housman; Jerome 6; Jerrold 19; Mizner, A. 14; Mizner, W. 9; Peacock 2; Prentice 16, 21; Rabelais 6; Swift 14; Tarkington 2; Twain 9; Ward 16; Woollcott 6. *See also* BOTTLE, COFFEE, DRUNKARD, LIQUOR, TAVERN, TEA.

**DROWN.** Baer 19; Ferber; Twain 61.

**DRUGS.** Barrymore 1; Fischer 2; Voltaire 7. *See also* DISEASE, DOCTOR, MEDICINE, POISON, SICK.

**DRUGSTORE.** Dunne 9; Herold 69.

**DRUNKARD.** Chesterton 8; Franklin 41; O'Malley 10. *See also* DRINK.

**DUCK.** Jerrold 12.

**DULL.** Addison 2; Beecher, H. W. 8; Foote; France 5; Galton; Johnson 7; Mizner, W. 19; Stevenson 5; Thurber 1. *See also* BORE, PLATITUDE, STUPID.

**DUTY.** Joubert 4, 5; Rowland 29; Shaw 110; Twain 136; Wilde 33, 46, 57, 121. *See also* RIGHT.

**DYSPEPSIA.** Ingersoll 6; O'Malley 11. *See also* INDIGESTION.

**EAGLE.** Dunne 1; Wells, H. G. 1.

**EAR.** Cato 3; Lichtenberg 3; Meredith 5; Thackeray 2. *See also* HEAR.

**EARLY.** Ade 2; Mencken 33. *See also* PUNCTUAL.

**EARN.** Agate 2; Herold 39; Hubbard, Kin 110; Jackson 13; Marquis 10. *See also* PAY.

**EARTH.** Adams, F. P. 4; Byron 7; Hubbard, Kin 52; Jerrold 13; Nietzsche 21; O'Malley 20; Smith, L. P. 12; Twain 20. *See also* EQUATOR, LONGITUDE & LATITUDE, WORLD.

**EAT.** Allen, F. 5; Bennett, A. 9; Brillat-Savarin; Butler, S. 44; Ford 1; Hubbard, Kin 64, 134; Inge 13; Ingersoll 11; O'Malley 11; Rogers 11; Rowland 38; Smith, S. 31; Swift 14; Twain 91, 94, 118, 142. *See also* BREAKFAST, DIET, DIGESTION, DINNER, FEAST, FOOD, GLUTTON, LUNCH, SUPPER.

**ECHO.** Allen, F. 10; Bierce 5; Marquis 13; Thoreau 15. *See also* REPEAT.

**ECONOMICS.** Hubbard, Kin 83; Leacock 3; Shaw 43.

**ECONOMY.** Billings 63; Dumas, père 2; Hope 1; Hubbard, Kin 19; Leacock 3. *See also* SAVE, STINGY.

**EDITOR.** Emerson 6; Hubbard, E. 6; Nye 11, 14; Twain 90; Zangwill 3. *See also* NEWSPAPER, WRITER.

**EDUCATION.** Bierce 20; Burgess 7; Butler, S. 17; Halifax 3; Holmes 4; Jefferson 2; Matthews; Mizner, W. 13; Talleyrand 10; Twain 52, 100; Wilde 153, 215. *See also* COLLEGE, COLLEGE GRADUATE, CULTURE, TEACH.

**EGG.** Billings 78; Butler, S. 23; Harris 2; Herford 45; Mencken 20; Twain 85, 95. *See also* HEN.

**EGOTISM.** Bierce 21; Billings 119; Disraeli 20; Emerson 5, 35; France 20; Hazlitt 5; Holmes 2; Levant 3; Masson 4; Montaigne 4; Munro 1; Ostenso; Prentice 18; Reade; Rivarol 3; Roosevelt, F. D. 1; Ruskin 4; Shaw 107; Swift 10; Talleyrand 3; Whitman 4; Wilde 26; Wilson 6. *See also* CONCEIT, SELF, VANITY.

**EGYPT.** Wade 1.

**ELECTION.** Dunne 10; Hubbard, Kin 13, 94; Rogers 17; Shaw 14. *See also* CONGRESS, VOTE.

**ELECTRIC FAN.** Herford 45; Herold 14.

**ELEPHANT.** Billings 55; Hubbard, Kin 127; Lincoln 18; Munro 7.

**ELOPE.** Ade 9; Howe 6. *See also* ESCAPE, FLIGHT.

**EMBARRASS.** La Bruyère 1; Mizner, W. 30.

**EMOTION.** Cobb 12; Dewar 8; Parker 5; Wilde 1. *See also* FEELING, PASSION.

**EMPTY.** Baer 3; Shaw 3.

**ENCYCLOPEDIA.** Lamb 11; Yeats-Brown. *See also* INFORMATION, KNOWLEDGE.

**END.** Baer 15; Balzac 7; Johnson 5; Shaw 4, 9, 43, 90; Wilde 51. *See also* BEGINNING & END, CONCLUSION, LIMIT.

**ENEMY.** Arp; Bierce 54; Billings 68; Brougham; Chesterton 5; Dunne 8; Franklin 26; Heine 8; Hubbard, E. 14; Huneker 4; Jerrold 16; La Rochefoucauld 24; Nicolson; Voltaire 25; Whistler 3; Wilde 95. *See also* FRIEND vs. ENEMY, OPPONENT.

**ENFORCEMENT.** Coolidge 3; Twain 108.

**ENGAGEMENT.** Bailey, J. M. 7; Wilde 73.

**ENGINEER.** Ade 10; Bailey, J. M. 4.

**ENGLAND.** Byron 4; Jerrold 2, 13; Johnson 29; Moore 1; Shaw 17, 94; Smith, S. 40, 41; Voltaire 8; Walpole 4.

**ENGLISHMAN.** Agate 1; Guedalla 5; Heine 1; Inge 3, 7; Johnson 40; Macaulay, T. B. 6; Maugham 1; Metternich; O'Malley 12; Shaw 18, 19, 20; Twain 20, 135; Walpole 5; Wilde 36, 37, 198, 205; Woollcott 3.

**ENJOY.** Butler, S. 1; Madariaga; Pain 2; Santayana 8; Smith, L. P. 15; Twain 24. *See also* BLISS, HAPPY, PLEASURE.

**ENTERTAIN.** Howe 35; Hubbard, Kin 85, 102; Strunsky. *See also* AMUSE.

**EPIGRAM.** Levant 1; Martial 6; Mathews 1; Strachey 2; Wells, C. 9. *See also* WIT.

**EPITAPH.** Byron 3; Cobb 2; Dewar 2; Dunne 17; Eldridge 5; Johnson 13; Jowett 4; Thoreau 18. *See also* TOMBSTONE.

**EQUALITY.** Barrie 4; Chesterton 40; France 9; Martial 9; Socrates 4.

**EQUATOR.** Smith, S. 21; Twain 110. *See also* LONGITUDE & LATITUDE.

**ERROR.** Bierce 19, 51; Burke 4; Lamb 25; Wilde 140. *See also* BLUNDER, MISTAKE.

**ESCAPE.** Ade 24; Baudelaire 4; Rowland 23. *See also* ELOPE, FLIGHT.

**ESTATE.** Brougham; Franklin 29; Howe 25, 33. *See also* PROPERTY.

**EUROPE.** Louis XIV 2; Wells, H. G. 1.

**EVE.** Billings 28; Byron 11; Heine 2; Jerrold 6. *See also* ADAM & EVE.

**EVENING.** Hubbard, Kin 7; Lamb 22; Rowland 40. *See also* DAY, NIGHT.

**EVIL.** Balzac 1; Beecher, H. W. 1; Bierce 36; Bradley 3; Broun 6; Chesterton 47; Conrad 1; Fielding 8; La Rochefoucauld 56; Mencken 24; Mizner, A. 11; Morley, J. 1; Shaw 56; Twain 4; Voltaire 32; Wells, C. 6, 15. *See also* BAD, DEVIL, GOOD vs. BAD, SIN, WRONG.

**EVOLUTION.** Billings 50; Chesterton 10; Congreve 3; Cuppy; Hubbard, E. 33; Hubbard, Kin 98.

**EXAGGERATION.** Billings, 112; Field 2; Gibran; Twain 98; Wilde 23.

**EXAMINATION.** Baer 20; Bierce 49; Mencken 27; Wilde 77. *See also* INVESTIGATION, QUESTION & ANSWER.

**EXAMPLE.** La Rochefoucauld 21; Twain 23; Wilde 69. *See also* IMITATION.

**EXCEPTION.** Eldridge 6; Jackson 14; Jerrold 39; Smith, S. 47.

**EXCESS.** Hubbard, Kin 108; Twain 82; Voltaire 30; Wilde 115.

**EXCHANGE.** Jerrold 23; Rowland 46. *See also* CHANGE, GIVE & TAKE.

**EXCUSE.** Franklin 1, 13; Stendhal 3. *See also* EXPLANATION, REASON.

**EXERCISE.** Depew 2; Hutchins 2; Lardner 4; Quillen 1.

**EXISTENCE.** Gourmont 3; Voltaire 16. *See also* LIVING.

**EXIT.** Fields 8; Nathan 5. *See also* DEPARTURE.

**EXPECT.** Pope 1; Whately 2; Wilde 33, 165. *See also* HOPE.

**EXPENSE.** Bailey, J. M. 3; Dewar 8; Wilde 112. *See also* COST.

**EXPERIENCE.** Bierce 51; Billings 29, 30, 31, 57; Bourget; Herold 62; Johnson 33; Lenclos 3; Maurois 1; Shakespeare 16; Shaw 33, 45; Wilde 40. *See also* HAPPEN.

**EXPERIMENT.** Darwin; Emerson 36; Ibsen 1; Mencken 2. *See also* VIVISECTION.

**EXPERT.** Butler, N. M. 1; Butler, S. 58; Russell 2.

**EXPLANATION.** Byron 8; Franklin 5; Kipling 6; Lincoln 6; Mencken 43; Schopenhauer 2; Shaw 86; Sheridan, R. B. 4, 7. *See also* DEFINITION, EXCUSE, THEORY.

**EXPURGATE.** Morley, C. 22; Nye 6. *See also* CENSORSHIP.

**EXTREME.** Hood 1; Shaw 2.

**EYES.** Allen, F. 6; Cocteau 2; Dickens 8; Forbes 2; Franklin 24; Hugo 9; Kaufman 2; Lamb 10; Leacock 2; Lichtenberg 3, 4; Morley, C. 20; O'-Malley 20; Phelps 2; Ward 2; Wells, C. 7. *See also* CRY, TEARS.

**FACE.** Ade 15; Baer 14, 29; Barrie 13; Gunther; Holmes 13; Hughes, R. 2; Leacock 4; Little 1, 16; Luce; Masefield; Montagu 2; O'Malley 40; Shakespeare 6; Smith, L. P. 4, 17; Swift 29, 36; Twain 141; Wells, C. 5; Wilde 53. *See also* COSMETICS.

**FACT.** Adams, H. 3; Canning; Gibbs, W.; Rogers 8; Sheridan, R. B. 2; Twain 26, 125. *See also* INFORMATION, STATISTICS.

**FAILURE.** Barrie 12; Curtis; Disraeli 25; Herford 33; Quarles 2; Rivarol 2; Strachey 6; Wilde 6.

**FAIR.** Johnson 14; Prentice 10; Wilde 127.

**FAITH.** Bierce 24; Billings 42; Butler, S. 78; Hubbard, E. 5; Mencken 16; Mizner, W. 13; Moore 3; Nietzsche 2, 7; Raspe; Shaw 70. *See also* BELIEF, CONFIDENCE, GOD, RELIGION, TRUST.

**FAITH, HOPE & CHARITY.** Huxley, T. H. 2; Marquis 5.

**FAITHFUL.** Ainslie; Bossuet; Franklin 42; La Rochefoucauld 69; Pope 4; Wilde 109, 161. *See also* CONSTANT.

**FAITHFUL vs. FAITHLESS.** Shaw 25; Wilde 163, 197. *See also* ADULTERY.

**FALL.** Bierce 29; Billings 92; O'Malley 20; Prentice 21; Quillen 2; Rowland 20.

**FAME.** Benchley 5; Chamfort 4; Dunne 17; Emerson 13; Hazlitt 13; Hubbard, Kin 2; Jerrold 11; Martial 3; Nye 8, 16; Shaw 67; Swift 42; Zangwill 2. *See also* GREAT, HONOR, REPUTATION.

**FAMILY.** Ade 18; Geraldy 6; Herford 1; Herold 30; Hope 2; Howe 15; Hubbard, Kin 92; Masson 5; Pope 2; Tolstoi 1; Wilde 44. *See also* CHILDREN, PARENTS & CHILDREN, RELATIVE.

**FARM.** Howe 22; Hubbard, Kin 81; Jerrold 1; Longfellow 1; Marquis 10; Martial 8; Smith, S. 6; Thoreau 12; Warner 1. *See also* CROP, LAND.

**FARMER.** Howe 10; Prentice 7; Twain 35.

**FASHION.** Bierce 25; Chamfort 3; Hazlitt 3; La Rochefoucauld 3; O'-Malley 51; Thoreau 6; Wilde 41, 42, 43. *See also* CLOTHES, STYLE.

**FAST.** Hubbard, E. 34; Mumford 5; Runyon 2; Smith, S. 34. *See also* HURRY, SPEED.

**FAT.** Billings 69; Field 4; Herford 30; Hubbard, E. 2; Lardner 5; Phelps 1; Rowland 8; Tennyson 2; Wells, H. G. 4; Whitman 4; Woollcott 1. *See also* WEIGHT.

**FAT vs. THIN.** Barrie 3; Hume.

**FATE.** Chesterton 16; Hubbard, Kin 62; Lowell, J. R. 5.

**FATHER.** Howe 20; La Fontaine 2; O'Malley 54; Russell 4; Wilde 44, 93. *See also* CHILDREN, FAMILY, PARENT.

**FAULT.** Baer 31; Beecher, H. W. 2; Billings 133; Carlyle 2; Dumas, père 6; Eliot 11; France 13; Franklin 1, 26, 47; Halifax 8; Hazlitt 8; La Roche-

foucauld 8, 18, 29, 38, 49, 51, 52;
Lytton 3; Rowland 42; Swift 40;
Talleyrand 9; Wilde 106, 190. *See also*
BLAME, COMPLAINT, CRITICISM,
MISTAKE.

**FAVOR.** La Rochefoucauld 4, 58;
Scott 3; Shakespeare 29; Twain 31,
48, 107. *See also* GRATITUDE.

**FEAR.** Howe 17; La Rochefoucauld 28,
57; Shaw 38; Stendhal 1; Sterne 6.
*See also* COWARD.

**FEAST.** Smith, L. P. 10; Smith, S. 34.
*See also* EAT, FOOD.

**FEE.** Goldberg 2; Herford 43. *See also*
PAY.

**FEELING.** Adams, F. P. 7; Butler, S.
36; Collins 1; Herold 22; Hubbard,
Kin 31; Jowett 4; O'Malley 1; Spurgeon 2; Ward 12; Wilde 49. *See also*
EMOTION, PASSION.

**FEET.** Baer 35; Coward; Dawes; Howe
11; O'Malley 21; Sousa; Twain 71.
*See also* SHOE.

**FENCE.** Ade 22; Baer 5; Brisbane;
Franklin 27; Prentice 7.

**FICTION.** Adams, F. P. 3; Billings
126; Disraeli 18; Herford 19; Twain
120, 121; Wilde 51, 57, 198. *See also*
IMAGINATION, LITERATURE.

**FIGHT.** Adler; Barrymore 15; Bierce
39; Billings 115; Dunne 20; Ibsen 2;
Voltaire 17; Ward 2. *See also*
BATTLE, PRIZE FIGHT, QUARREL,
WAR.

**FIGURE.** Canning; Skinner 3.

**FINANCE.** Pinero 1; Rogers 7. *See
also* BROKER, INTEREST.

**FINGER.** Baer 14; Franklin 4;
O'Malley 36; Spencer 2.

**FINGERNAIL.** Leacock 2; Rogers 22.

**FIRST.** Little 17; Nasby; Prentice 4;
Shakespeare 5; Walpole 6.

**FIRST & LAST.** Gourmont 18; Pascal
2; Wilde 102.

**FIRST & SECOND.** Baer 17; Franklin
35; Hugo 8; La Rochefoucauld 69;
Marshall; Rowland 22, 26, 52; Steele
3; Zangwill 6.

**FISH.** Benét; Field 2; Holmes 1; Housman; Swift 9; Thoreau 19; Twain 14;
Wells, C. 16.

**FISHING.** Ford 1; Herford 40; Hubbard, Kin 27; Johnson 5; Marquis 2;
Twain 109.

**FIVE-CENT.** Adams, F. P. 15; Chase,
I. 1; Rogers 16.

**FLATTERY.** Billings 32; Chapman 1;
Chesterfield 8, 12; Johnson 31; La
Rochefoucauld 10, 42, 59, 60; Lin-
coln 14; Mizner, W. 10; Rinehart;
Shakespeare 32; Shaw 108. *See also*
COMPLIMENT, PRAISE.

**FLEA.** Galton; Twain 25; Westcott.

**FLIGHT.** Barrymore 15; Wells, C. 12.
*See also* ELOPE, ESCAPE.

**FLIRT.** Hugo 3; Moore 13; Parker 3;
Smith, S. 13; Talleyrand 5.

**FLOOD.** Howe 14; Lamb 2; Twain 66.
*See also* SEA, WATER.

**FLORIDA.** Hubbard, Kin 27.

**FLOWER.** Beecher, H. W. 3; Mencken
10; Smith, L. P. 11; Thackeray 6;
Twain 129; White; Wilde 203; Wodehouse 7. *See also* ROSE, GARDEN.

**FLY.** Billings 55; Emerson 7; Howe 48;
Longfellow 1; Nathan 5.

**FOLLOW.** Billings 19; Chamfort 22;
Jackson 4; O'Malley 51. *See also*
PURSUE.

**FOOD.** Bierce 32; Burgess 1; Jerrold
15; Johnson 29; Lardner 1, 2; Mor-
ley, C. 14, 21; O'Malley 11, 29;
Quillen 1; Saint-Gaudens; Shaw 96;
Smith, S. 17, 31; Twain 86, 119, 143;
Voltaire 8. *See also* APPETITE,
BOARD, COOK, CROP, DIET, DI-
GESTION, EAT, FEAST, FRUIT,
MEAT, STARVATION, VEGETA-
BLE. *Also individual foods such as*
APPLE, BREAD, CABBAGE, et
cetera.

**FOOL.** Baer 26; Balzac 9; Bangs 6;
Beecher, H. W. 4; Benchley 2; Bierce
26; Billings 9, 10, 30, 61, 77, 83, 104,
108, 134; Carlyle 1; Cervantes 5;
Chamfort 15, 19; Chapman 3; Chase,
I. 4; Chesterfield 2; Colby 3; Congreve
6, 9; Cowper 1; Darwin; Delavigne;
Eliot 6; Fielding 8; Franklin 14, 25;
Frost 12; Halifax 9; Howe 27; Hub-
bard, Kin 65; Hugo 3; Inge 12;
Jackson 7, 12; Johnson 5; Jonson; La

& FUTURE, POSTERITY, PROPHECY, TIME.

**GAMBLING.** Bierce 27; Broun 6; Dewar 11; Herford 28; Hubbard, E. 25; Hubbard, Kin 126; Shaw 28; Twain 106. *See also* BET, DICE, HORSE RACE.

**GARDEN.** Davies; Hubbard, Kin 44; Kipling 1, 17; Wilde 19; Warner 6. *See also* FLOWER, FRUIT, PLANT, TREE, VEGETABLE.

**GARLIC.** Saint-Gaudens. *See also* ONION.

**GENEALOGY.** Bierce 28; Hubbard, Kin 63; Moley 1. *See also* ANCESTOR.

**GENERAL.** Clemenceau 2; Napoleon 3. *See also* ARMY.

**GENERALITY.** Ade 3; Dumas, fils 1.

**GENEROUS.** Baer 31; Billings 37; La Rochefoucauld 63. *See also* UNSELFISH.

**GENIUS.** Colton 2; Edison 1; Goethe 7; Goncourt; Herold 17; Hope 5; Hubbard, E. 10; Huxley, A. 6; Lichtenberg 1; Mizner, A. 3; Poe 1; Swift 10, 54; Talleyrand 8; Wilde 23, 48, 143. *See also* INFANT PRODIGY, TALENT.

**GENTLE.** Byron 5; Prentice 3; Voltaire 11. *See also* MODERATE.

**GENTLEMAN.** Butler, N. M. 2; Chesterfield 6; Herold 18; Mackenzie; Mencken 18; O'Malley 14; Phelps 5; Shaw 29; Smith, S. 22; West; Wilde 35, 49. *See also* CLASS, SOCIETY.

**GERMAN.** Frederick the Great 1.

**GHOST.** Baer 13; La Rochefoucauld 40.

**GIFT.** Ade 9; Butler, S. 6; Goethe 3; Lamb 18; O'Malley 15.

**GIN.** Kipling 14; Mencken 11. *See also* DRINK.

**GIRAFFE.** Butler, S. 19.

**GIVE & TAKE.** Billings 2; Mathews 2; Mencken 45; Montagu 3. *See also* EXCHANGE.

**GLASS.** Chesterton 47; Herford 35; O'Malley 49; Robinson.

**GLASSES.** Allen, F. 23; Coleridge 3; Jerrold 19, 36; Parker 3.

**GLUTTON.** Baer 4; Billings 74. *See also* EAT.

**GOD.** Allen, F. 23; Balzac 11; Bierce 45; Billings 51; Broun 3; Butler, S. 20, 29, 70; Cervantes 3; France 2; Franklin 8; Frazer; Frederick the Great 3; Gide; Gourmont 3; Heine 3; Herford 19; Herold 75; Hubbard, E. 11; Inge 1, 2; Ingersoll 3; Jackson 6; Lincoln 2; Mallock; Mencken 26; Montaigne 5; Montesquieu 2; Nietzsche 8, 9, 18, 19; Nye 12; O'Malley 16; Renan 2; Shaw 105; Smith, L. P. 16; Stendhal 3; Voltaire 16; Wilde 124, 192. *See also* ATHEIST, PROVIDENCE, WORSHIP.

**GOD vs. DEVIL.** Arnould 2; Butler, S. 4; Ellis 4; Shakespeare 34; Swift 39.

**GOD vs. MAN.** Colton 4; Conrad 1; Swift 47.

**GOLD.** Colton 2; Little 11; Walpole 1.

**GOLDEN RULE.** Dickens 5; Shaw 16, 30.

**GOLDFISH.** Allen, F. 7; Hubbard, Kin 75.

**GOLF.** Adams, F. P. 11; Rogers 28.

**GOOD.** Barrymore 2; Butler, S. 46, 66; Cervantes 1; Douglas 1; Franklin 13; Goldberg 3; Herford 34; Herold 5; Howe 32; Hubbard, Kin 41, 111; Johnson 46; Lamb 3, 17; Lincoln 4; Little 9; Mencken 23; Moore 5; Nye 7; Rousseau 1; Scott 5; Shaw 79; Smith, S. 39; Talleyrand 2; Thoreau 2, 7; Twain 11, 23, 67, 115; Voltaire 9; Ward 6, 21; Warner 4; Wilde 7, 63, 69, 93, 103; Wotton 1. *See also* KINDNESS, RIGHT, VIRTUE.

**GOOD vs. BAD.** Adams, F. P. 6; Bailey, J. M. 1; Bennett, A. 1; Billings 131; Bradley 4; Colton 12; Dewar 2; Dickens 11, 18; Emerson 15, 30; Gourmont 4; Heine 9; Herold 2; Howe 9; Hubbard, E. 20, 29; Hubbard, Kin 23, 129; Huxley, A. 1, 9; Lamb 21; La Rochefoucauld 21, 30, 41, 53; Lawrence 1; Lytton 5; Moore 19; Nathan 1; Nicolson; Plato 4; Scott 4; Shakespeare 21; Shaw 104; Socrates 2; Sterne 5; Whitman 3;

Wilde 51, 90, 183, 206. *See also*
RIGHT vs. WRONG.

GOOSE. Colbert; Nasby; Smith, S. 31.

GOSSIP. Conrad 3; Hubbard, Kin 106,
120; Rogers 29, 30; Terence 2; Wilson 3. *See also* SCANDAL.

GOVERNMENT. Beecher, L.; Bierce
42; Chamfort 6; Chesterfield 10; Emerson 6; Frederick the Great 2; Lamartine; Nathan 1; O'Malley 3;
Rogers 8; Shaw 19; Voltaire 2, 10;
Wilde 74. *See also* CIVIL SERVICE,
CONGRESS, IMPERIALISM, POLITICS, PRESIDENT, REPRESENTATIVE, REVOLUTION.

GRAMMAR. Addison 1; Ade 17;
Goldberg 4; Gourmont 5; Hugo 1;
Inge 13; Johnson 32; Morley, C. 16;
Smith, S. 36; Twain 50, 72; Ward
21; Wilde 50. *See also* LANGUAGE,
WORD.

GRANT, Ulysses S. Sherman 1.

GRATITUDE. Beecher, H. W. 5; La
Rochefoucauld 4, 58. *See also*
FAVOR.

GRAVE. Glasgow 2; Jerrold 14; Smith,
S. 19. *See also* BURY, CEMETERY.

GREAT. Hazlitt 5; Johnson 7; Masson 4; Nye 1, 16; Shaw 42. *See also*
FAME, HERO.

GREEK. Disraeli 19; Johnson 18; Shaw
32.

GRIEF. Chamfort 14; Gourmont 16;
Lamb 9; Shakespeare 4; Wilde 58.
*See also* MOURN, SAD.

GROUCH. Hubbard, Kin 113; Rowland 54. *See also* COMPLAINT.

GROW. Henderson; Jerrold 5; Wilson
2. *See also* PROGRESS.

GUESS. Hazlitt 7; Kipling 16; Rowland 17; Shaw 92; Talleyrand 10.

GUEST. Baer 9; Beerbohm 4; Hubbard, Kin 69; Jerrold 38; Shakespeare
28. *See also* COMPANY, HOST,
VISIT.

GUN. Billings 82; Shaw 8; Smith, S.
45. *See also* HUNTING.


HABIT. Herford 11; Meredith 1; Rowland 52; Twain 87; Ward 6. *See also*
CUSTOM, PRACTICE.

HAIR. Baer 34; Billings 41; Dickens
14; Herford 12; Hubbard, Kin 125;
Marquis 16; Rowland 55; Skinner 3;
Voltaire 15; Wilde 58. *See also* BALD,
BLONDE, DANDRUFF.

HAIRCUT. Roosevelt, F. D. 3; Wodehouse 7.

HALF. Billings 45; Goldberg 6; Howe
18; Little 13; Mathews 1; Prentice
6, 25; Rowland 11; Twain 24; Wilde
124; Woollcott 7.

HALO. Pinero 3; Wells, H. G. 3. *See
also* ANGEL, SAINT.

HAMLET. Barrie 6; Masson 5; Shaw
33.

HAND. Bierce 30; Howe 13; Lamb 8;
Little 4; Mencken 50. *See also* FINGER, FINGERNAIL.

HANGING. Chesterton 21; Eldridge
3; Heine 8; Jerrold 14, 34; Johnson
39; Pepys 1; Richelieu; Rogers 18;
Shakespeare 21; Shaw 42, 97; Voltaire
27; Wotton 2. *See also* CAPITAL
PUNISHMENT, ROPE.

HAPPEN. Mahaffy; Marquis 3; Shaw
22, 45; Twain 41. *See also* EXPERIENCE, LUCK.

HAPPY. Billings 79; Darrow 9; Hubbard, Kin 54; Johnson 28; Little 8;
Mencken 44; Nash 1; Nye 2; Quarles
2; Rousseau 1; Russell 3; Swift 12;
Talleyrand 8; Ward 1; Wilde 17, 94,
204. *See also* BLISS, ENJOY, PLEASURE.

HAPPY vs. UNHAPPY. La Rochefoucauld 23; Shakespeare 16; Shaw
61, 87; Tolstoi 1; Twain 99, 138;
Wilde 51.

HARD. Joad; Mencken 28; Roosevelt,
T. 3.

HARM. Fielding; Maugham 7; Munro
7; Shaw 98. *See also* DANGER,
WRONG.

HARMONY. Lamb 20; Louis XIV 2;
Shaw 53; Wilde 100. *See also* AGREE.

HARRIS, Frank. Wilde 47.

HASH. Billings 42; Cobb 14.

HAT. Addison 4; Allen, F. 8; Baer
30; Barrymore 15; Lytton 6; Twain
84.

HORSE SENSE. Hubbard, Kin 136.
See also COMMON SENSE.

HOSPITAL. Baudelaire 1; Emerson 32.
See also NURSE, PATIENT.

HOST. Beerbohm 4; Huxley, A. 7.
See also GUEST.

HOTEL. Billings 6; Shaw 31; Twain
67; Ward 10.

HOUSE. Ade 8; Franklin 30; O'Malley
49; Smith, L. P. 2; Thoreau 15. See
also HOME.

HOUSEKEEPING. Hubbard, Kin 43;
Wade 3.

HUMAN NATURE. Bagehot 3; Ervine 2; Galsworthy 1; Masson 2;
Milne; Ward 15.

HUMAN RACE. Beecher 9; Emerson
8; Fischer 6; Mencken 51; Twain 39.

HUMILITY. Billings 76; Burton 3;
Helps 1; Holmes 12; Russell 1;
Shaw 11, 59.

HUMOR. Billings 114; Levant 6;
Little 2; Rogers 27; Strachey 5; Twain
99, 102. See also COMEDY, JEST,
JOKE, SENSE of HUMOR, WIT.

HUMORIST. Allen, F. 12; Herold
22; Masson 17.

HUNTING. Smith, S. 45; Wilde 35.
See also GUN.

HURRY. Edison 3; Herford 25;
Jackson 16; Stevenson 4. See also
FAST, SPEED.

HUSBAND. NOTE: This word has not
been cross-referenced because it occurs very often.

HYPOCRISY. Behn 2; Billings 44;
Hazlitt 1; La Rochefoucauld 7, 48;
Sterne 3; Wilde 80, 98. See also
AFFECTATION.


ICE. Billings 92, 120. See also COLD.

IDEA. Bradley 2; Butler, S. 41; Cham-
fort 17, 19; Coleridge 1; Disraeli 6;
Eldridge 1; Gourmont 14; Holmes 19;
Jackson 1; Johnson 35; Lincoln 3;
Marquis 6; Renard; Swift 24; Thoreau
20; Voltaire 15, 32. See also BELIEF,
THOUGHT.

IDEAL. Chesterton 42; Emerson 37;
Galsworthy 4; Howe 12; Jackson 6;
O'Malley 43; Rowland 25; Shaw 39,

98; Smith, L. P. 19; Tarkington 1;
Thoreau 4; Wade 3. See also PER-
FECT.

IDIOT. Chekhov 4; O'Malley 38;
Shaw 78; Twain 59, 96. See also
FOOL, STUPID.

IDLE. Bagehot 8; Billings 60, 110, 111;
Haliburton 3; Jerome 3; Lamb 17;
Little 15; Lytton 9; Ovid 3; Prentice
29; Rascoe 2; Schopenhauer 3; Shaw
58. See also LEISURE, LOAF.

IGNORANCE. Bentham; Bierce 20,
24, 52; Billings 47, 125; Brandeis;
Coleridge 6; Disraeli 6; Eliot 5;
Hobbes; Hope 3; Hubbard, Kin
122; Jackson 15; Mizner, A. 8; Mumford 6; Renan 1; Rogers 3; Spencer 1;
Twain 5, 18, 88; Voltaire 7, 23; Wilde
64, 70, 97. See also LEARNING vs.
IGNORANCE.

ILL. See DISEASE, SICK.

ILLITERATE. Chesterton 46; Twain 18.

ILLUSION. Rowland 22; Voltaire 18.

IMAGE. Baer 11; Herold 75; Jerrold 8.
See also MIRROR, PICTURE.

IMAGINATION. Adams, F. P. 3;
Johnson 38; Mencken 30; Pinero 1;
Sheridan, R. B. 2. See also FICTION.

IMITATION. Franklin 43; Goldsmith
4; Tree; Voltaire 26. See also EX-
AMPLE.

IMMIGRATION. Rogers 12; Wilson 5.

IMMORAL. Smith, L. P. 17; Twain
81; Wilde 21, 37; Woollcott 1. See
also INDECENT, SIN, VICE,
WRONG.

IMPERIALISM. Roosevelt, T. 4; Shaw
18; Voltaire 13. See also GOVERN-
MENT, INTERNATIONAL.

IMPORTANT. Johnson 3; Wilde 91,
179.

IMPOSSIBLE. Emerson 10; Mahaffy;
Santayana 4.

IMPROPER. Maugham 2; Smith, L. P.
10. See also INDECENT, WRONG.

IMPROVE. Munro 3; Priestley; Spurgeon 1. See also PROGRESS, RE-
FORM.

INCOME. Billings 63; Munro 5; Nash
4. See also PAY.

INCOME TAX. See TAX.

**INDECENT.** Bradley 6; Mencken 51; Shaw 13; Wilde 65. *See also* IMMORAL, IMPROPER, OBSCENE.

**INDEPENDENCE.** Rogers 17; Santayana 3. *See also* FREEDOM.

**INDIGESTION.** Hugo 5; Lenclos 1; O'Malley 18; Stevenson 4. *See also* DIGESTION, DYSPEPSIA.

**INDIGNATION.** Hubbard, E. 29; Wells, H. G. 3. *See also* ANGER.

**INDISCRETION.** Butler, S. 7; La Rochefoucauld 70; Smith, S. 20; Wilde 144, 209.

**INFANT PRODIGY.** Hubbard, Kin 118; Huxley, A. 6. *See also* CHILDREN, GENIUS.

**INFERIOR.** Chesterfield 7; Martial 9. *See also* WORSE.

**INFIDELITY.** Baer 30; Bierce 53; La Rochefoucauld 70. *See also* FAITHFUL vs. FAITHLESS.

**INFINITE.** Renan 1; Shakespeare 8; Voltaire 19.

**INFLATION.** Adams, F. P. 15; Henderson; Herold 3; Shakespeare 17. *See also* COST OF LIVING.

**INFORMATION.** Howe 39; Smith, L. P. 1; Twain 56. *See also* ENCYCLOPEDIA, FACT, KNOWLEDGE, TELL.

**INGRATITUDE.** Beecher, H. W. 5; Louis XIV 1.

**INHERITANCE.** Burke 4; Hubbard, Kin 52; Lavater 2; Martial 4; Nash 2; O'Malley 45; Twain 20. *See also* HEIR.

**INJUSTICE.** *See* JUSTICE vs. INJUSTICE.

**IN-LAW.** Howe 28; Ward 8. *See also* MOTHER-IN-LAW, RELATIVE.

**INNOCENT.** Hubbard, Kin 77; Wilde 209.

**INQUEST.** Mencken 48; Rowland 21.

**INSANE.** Bierce 49; Colby 5; Heine 14; Mann, H. 2; Montaigne 5; Prentice 14; Saint-Gaudens; Twain 39, 54. *See also* FOOLISH, MENTAL INSTITUTION.

**INSECT.** *See individual insects such as* ANT, BEDBUG, BEE, et cetera.

**INSOMNIA.** Adams, F. P. 9; Baer 6. *See also* SLEEP & WAKE.

**INSPIRATION.** Chesterton 20; Dumas, père 4; Edison 1.

**INSTINCT.** Butler, S. 69; Moore 9; Munro 4; Wilde 189.

**INSULT.** *See* ABUSE, RUDE.

**INSURANCE.** *See* LIFE INSURANCE.

**INTELLIGENCE.** Adams, H. 1; Ade 12; Gourmont 7; Herold 8, 25, 67; Howe 8; Matthews; Mencken 30; Russell 7; Smith, S. 10; Wilde 165, 190. *See also* BRAINS, CLEVER, KNOWLEDGE, MIND, SENSE, UNDERSTANDING, WISDOM.

**INTENTION.** Lytton 5; Rowland 12; Shaw 15; Wilde 49. *See also* DESIGN, PLAN.

**INTEREST.** Billings 39, 102; Franklin 45; Inge 14; Stendhal 4. *See also* BANK, FINANCE.

**INTERESTING.** Burgess 2; Disraeli 21; Leacock 6; Twain 107.

**INTERNATIONAL.** Bierce 39; Rogers 15. *See also* DIPLOMACY, IMPERIALISM.

**INTERRUPTION.** Ade 5; Morley, C. 20. *See also* CONVERSATION.

**INTRODUCTION.** Mizner, W. 3. *See also* BEGIN.

**INTUITION.** Hughes, R. 1; Jackson 16; Nathan 6.

**INVENTION.** Billings 1, 84; Butler, S. 34; Gourmont 7; Hoffenstein 2; Jerrold 33; Rogers 25; Swift 22; Thoreau 8; Voltaire 16; Wells, C. 11.

**INVESTIGATION.** Herford 42; Mizner, W. 33; Rogers 2. *See also* EXAMINATION.

**INVITATION.** Mizner, A. 2; Wilde 47, 73.

**IRELAND.** Little 6; Mahaffy; Moore 8.

**IRISH.** Johnson 14; Moore 12; Nicolson; O'Malley 12, 23; Shaw 84; Wilde 205.

**ITALY.** Smith, S. 11; Twain 16.

**ITCH.** Jerrold 11; Lover; Montaigne 3. *See also* SCRATCH.

**JAMES, Henry.** Guedalla 7; Wilde 57.

**JAZZ.** Herold 9; Sousa. *See also* MUSIC.

**JEALOUSY.** Fielding 9; Wells, H. G. 3.

**JERUSALEM.** Ellis 7.

**JEST.** Burke 3; Rowland 54; Sheridan, R. B. 2. *See also* FUN, JOKE.

**JEW.** Prentice 1; Shakespeare 17.

**JEWELRY.** Barrie 3; Eldridge 3; Herford 18; Hubbard, Kin 26; La Bruyère 7; Spencer 2. *See also* DIAMOND.

**JOKE.** Ade 13; Beecher, H. W. 8; Dewar 4; Eastman 2; Howe 31; Lowell, J. R. 5; Rogers 8, 23; Shaw 75; Strachey 5. *See also* FUNNY, HUMOR, JEST, STORY, WIT.

**JONAH.** Edison 2; Paine.

**JOURNALISM.** Greeley 2; Nye 11; Pulitzer; Wade 4; Wilde 31, 74, 107. *See also* NEWSPAPER, WRITING.

**JOURNALIST.** Bennett, A. 3; Ibsen 1; Simonds; Wilde 14. *See also* EDITOR, WRITER.

**JUDAS.** Smith, S. 23.

**JUDGE.** Colton 5; Dewar 6; Hughes, C. E. 2; La Bruyère 3; Mencken 27; Twain 79. *See also* COURT, JUSTICE.

**JUDGMENT.** Bennett, A. 2; Howe 3, 61; Jerrold 32; La Bruyère 7; La Rochefoucauld 2. *See also* CRITICISM, OPINION.

**JURY.** Frost 10; Jerrold 20; Mencken 39; Spencer 1; Twain 18. *See also* COURT, JUSTICE.

**JUSTICE.** Baer 18; Chamfort 13; Colton 4; Dickens 3; Douglas 1; La Bruyère 3; La Rochefoucauld 16; O'Malley 2. *See also* COURT, JUDGE, RIGHT.

**JUSTICE vs. INJUSTICE.** La Rochefoucauld 16; Mencken 21. *See also* RIGHT vs. WRONG.

**KILL.** Arp; Kingsley 3; Prentice 19; Shakespeare 5. *See also* CAPITAL PUNISHMENT, HANGING, MURDER.

**KINDNESS.** Herford 5; Herold 6, 7; Hubbard, Kin 59; Jerrold 12, 18; Nye 7; Smith, L. P. 5; Smith S. 2. *See also* GOOD.

**KING.** Bismarck 1; Frederick the Great 3; O'Malley 30; Shaw 55. *See also* ROYALTY, RULE.

**KISS.** Carlyle 3; Gourmont 18; Little 1; Mencken 50; Meredith 4; Morley, C. 5; Rowland 26, 29, 44; Shakespeare 30; Swift 22; Toscanini. *See also* CARESS.

**KNAVE.** *See* FOOL vs. KNAVE, RASCAL.

**KNEEL.** Bierce 12; Kipling 17; O'Malley 37.

**KNOT.** Roosevelt, F. D. 2; Rowland 27. *See also* TIE.

**KNOWLEDGE.** Auerbach; Austen 2; Barrie 5; Bierce 52; Butler, N. M. 1; Butler, S. 42; Gourmont 13; Halifax 5; Hubbard, Kin 56; Huxley, T. H. 1; Lowell, A. L.; Lowell, J. R. 10; Maeterlinck 1; Mencken 5, 43; Mizner, W. 8; Mumford 7; Prentice 6; Rogers 1; Shaw 101; Stephens 2; Talleyrand 10; Twain 76, 80; Undset; Wilde 13, 55, 97, 120, 216; Yeats-Brown. *See also* ENCYCLOPEDIA, HIGHBROW, INTELLIGENCE, LEARN, UNDERSTANDING, WISDOM.

**LAMB.** Billings 117; Smith, S. 33. *See also* SHEEP.

**LAND.** Emerson 17; Warner 5; Wilde 89. *See also* FARM, GARDEN, PROPERTY.

**LANGUAGE.** Behn 3; Benchley 1; Franklin 15; Goethe 6; Lichtenberg 2; Mencken 37; Morley, C. 10; O'Malley 53; Rogers 11; Sandburg 2; Shaw 17, 51; Twain 90, 101, 135; Wilde 50, 171. *See also* GRAMMAR, GREEK, LATIN, PROSE, SLANG, SPEECH, STYLE, WORD, WRITING.

**LAST.** Rowland 47, 55. *See also* FIRST & LAST.

**LATE.** Hubbard, Kin 66; Lucas 3; Mencken 33; Twain 97; Wilde 59, 202. *See also* PUNCTUAL.

**LATIN.** Heine 5.

**LATITUDE & LONGITUDE.** Ade 20; Thoreau 16; Twain 110. *See also* EARTH, EQUATOR.

**LAUGH.** Baer 2; Billings 59; Chamfort 6; Franklin 38; Little 10; Mencken 39; Wilde 90. *See also* AMUSE, ENJOY, FUNNY.

**LAW.** Baer 15, 18; Billings 27, 101; Chamfort 21; Cicero 1; Colton 4; Coolidge 3; Darrow 7, 10; Dickens 10; Dunne 6; France 9; Frost 14; Halifax 4; Howe 33; Hughes, C. E. 1; Jerrold 26; Johnson 24; Mizner, A. 8; Poe 3; Rogers 23; Russell 5; Smith, S. 44; Twain 108; Woollcott 1. *See also* COURT, JUDGE, TEN COMMAND-MENTS.

**LAW STUDENT.** Mencken 27. *See also* SCHOLAR.

**LAWSUIT.** Frost 15; Mizner, A. 7; Twain 43; Voltaire 1, 21. *See also* COURT.

**LAWYER.** Bentham; Billings 27; Brougham; Choate; Colton 5; Darrow 7; Dickens 11; Franklin 9; Frost 10; Halifax 4; Hays 2; Howe 25; Hubbard, E. 19; Hubbard, Kin 15; Huneker 5; Irving 4; Jefferson 1; Jerrold 28; Johnson 16; Lamb 4; Martial 5; Mizner, W. 14; O'Malley 52; Rowland 27; Shakespeare 5; Shaw 93; Steele 3. *See also* COURT.

**LAXATIVE.** Billings 2; Flammarion; Huxley, A. 2. *See also* DRUGS.

**LAZY.** *See* IDLE.

**LEADER.** Ellis 5; Herold 19; Jackson 4; Rogers 13; Twain 19.

**LEARN.** Balzac 10; Butler, S. 55; Carroll 2; Cato 2; Clemenceau 1; Hegel 2; Herold 8; Pope 3; Shaw 45; Wells, C. 18. *See also* EDUCATION, KNOWLEDGE.

**LEARN vs. TEACH.** Billings 31; Shaw 11; Wilde 38. *See also* EDUCATION, SCHOOL.

**LEARNING vs. IGNORANCE.** Franklin 15, 25; Gourmont 17; Herold 31. *See also* SCHOLAR.

**LECTURE.** Bierce 34; Ward 14. *See also* PUBLIC SPEAKING, SPEECH.

**LEG.** Bierce 15; Roosevelt, F. D. 4; Smith, S. 9.

**LEISURE.** Cowper 2; Dunne 19; Herford 25; Hubbard, Kin 3; Shaw 87. *See also* IDLE.

**LEND.** Addison 11; Franklin 22; Gibbs, P.; Mizner, W. 16; Twain 37.

**LENT.** Bailey, J. M. 2; Fuller 2.

**LETTER.** Byron 9; Chekhov 5; Colby 1; Hubbard, E. 35; Morley, C. 18; Pascal 4; Rousseau 3; Shaw 39; Steele 4; Thoreau 21. *See also* CORRE-SPONDENCE, WRITING.

**LEVITY.** Landon 3; Smith, S. 47. *See also* AMUSE, FUN, PLEASURE.

**LIAR.** Bangs 1; Broun 7; Herford 20; Lincoln 11; Marquis 2; Rogers 28; Shaw 60. *See also* LIE.

**LIBERAL vs. CONSERVATIVE.** Bierce 14; Billings 40. *See also* PO-LITICAL PARTY, POLITICS.

**LIBERTY.** *See* FREEDOM.

**LIBRARY.** Butler, S. 33. Holmes 7; Masson 16. *See also* BOOK.

**LICENSE.** Jerrold 37; Little 14; Maurois 2.

**LIE.** Arbuthnot 1; Aristotle 1; Bangs 4; Billings 17; Burgess 8; Butler, S. 28, 55; Dewar 2; Disraeli 22; Dunne 7; France 5; Gay 2; Herford 10; Hubbard, Kin 25; Jackson 5; Little 13, 16; Loomis 1; Mizner, A. 10; Mizner, W. 11; O'Malley 34, 48; Prentice 4; Rowland 29, 42; Shaw 27; Twain 79, 89, 139; Wells, C. 1; Wilde 134; Wotton 1. *See also* LIAR, PERJURY.

**LIE vs. TRUTH.** Billings 11, 112; Butler, S. 3; Byron 2; Chamfort 8; Emerson 38; Herford 20; Hope 4; Ingersoll 4; Jerome 2; Mencken 25, 46; Nietzsche 5; Shakespeare 33; Smith, L. P. 7; Strachey 3.

**LIFE.** Baudelaire 1; Billings 62; Butler, S. 1, 11, 39, 40, 69; Dunne 8; France 16; Gilbert 5; Gourmont 5; Henry 1; Herold 3, 21, 28; Holmes 14; Hubbard, Kin 35; Huneker 7; James, W. 2; Kettering; Kierkegaard; Lytton 7, 8; Mizner, W. 38; Moore 7; Morley, C. 10; Mumford 4; Norris; Santayana 7; Schopenhauer 2; Smith, S. 14; Stendhal 2; Swift 46; Twain 24, 89; Voltaire 20; Walpole 7; Wilde 91, 131. *See also* BIOGRAPHY, LIVING.

**LIFE & DEATH.** Barrymore 2; Browne 1; Butler, S. 14; Choate; Cocteau 2; Eldridge 5; Fielding 4; Gourmont 2; Greeley 2; Heine 9; Hubbard, E. 4; James, H. 2; Lichtenberg 5; Maeterlinck 2; Mizner, W. 17; Prentice 19; Rogers 6; Shakespeare 31; Stevenson 11; Twain 74; Voltaire 28; Wilde 147. *See also* BIRTH & DEATH.

**LIFE INSURANCE.** Herford 44; Howe 47; Hubbard, Kin 30.

**LIGHT.** Chesterton 46; Lang 2; Wilson 4.

**LIMIT.** Hubbard, E. 10; Napoleon 2. *See also* END.

**LINE.** Butler, S. 5; Chesterton 4; Cobb 3.

**LION.** Balzac 14; Billings 117; Prentice 1; Shaw 47, 98; Tennyson 1.

**LIQUOR.** Harris 1; Kipling 5; Lamb 13; Mizner, A. 1; Swift 2; Ward 10. *See also* BOTTLE, DRINK, PROHIBITION, TEETOTALER, TEMPERANCE. *Also individual liquors such as* BEER, CHAMPAGNE, GIN, et cetera.

**LISTEN.** Chesterfield 3; Hardy; Herold 34; Howe 42; Hubbard, Kin 85; Mizner, W. 8; Nye 9; Stephens 1. *See also* ATTENTION, HEAR.

**LITERATURE.** Ade 10; Carlyle 6; Chase, I. 2; Disraeli 25; Lewis 1; Lover; Moore 19; Shaw 51; Voltaire 28; Wallace; Wilde 31. *See also* BOOK, FICTION, STYLE, WRITING.

**LITTLE.** *See* SMALL.

**LITTLE vs. MUCH.** Shaw 26; Twain 27. *See also* SMALL vs. LARGE.

**LIVING.** Carlyle 7; Emerson 19, 39; Ertz 2; Fischer 4; Herold 64; Howe 18; Hubbard, Kin 44; Huneker 5; Marquis 4; Moore 15; Munro 5; Shaw 118; Swift 6, 23; Thoreau 14; Voltaire 4; Wells, C. 18. *See also* COST OF LIVING, LIFE, LIFE & DEATH.

**LOAF.** Howe 10, 24; Shaw 29, 63. *See also* IDLE, LEISURE.

**LONDON.** Pitt 1; Shelley; Wilde 92, 156, 162, 203.

**LONELY.** Barrymore 5; Burgess 3; Chekhov 1; Hubbard, Kin 68; La Bruyère 1; Lucas 1; Masson 4; Maurois 4; Morley, C. 14; Nye 2; Pepys 2; Thoreau 5, 9; Twain 11; Whistler 3.

**LONG vs. SHORT.** Nietzsche 11; Pascal 4; Thoreau 17; Wilde 132. *See also* SIZE.

**LONGEVITY.** Herold 47; Shaw 10. *See also* OLD AGE.

**LOSE.** Bailey, J. M. 6; Billings 73; Butler, S. 68; Churchill 2; Hubbard, Kin 46, 126; Rowland 22; Sargent. *See also* WIN or LOSE.

**LOUD.** Rowland 37; Wilde 72. *See also* NOISE.

**LOVE.** NOTE: This word has not been cross-referenced because it occurs very often.

**LOVE vs. HATE.** La Rochefoucauld 9; Macaulay, T. B. 2; Marquis 7; Swift 53.

**LOW.** Billings 67; Little 5; Morley, C. 5.

**LUCK.** Butler, S. 21; Leacock 8; Mizner, W. 23; Montaigne 8; Swift 41. *See also* FORTUNE, HAPPEN.

**LUNATIC.** *See* INSANE, MENTAL INSTITUTION.

**LUNCH.** Baer 28, 32. *See also* EAT.

**LUNT, Alfred.** Coward.

**LUXURY.** Adams, F. P. 16; Hubbard, Kin 123. *See also* COMFORT.

**LUXURY vs. NECESSITY.** Holmes 9; Rowland 29; Wilde 172.

**MACAULAY, Thomas Babington.** Smith, S. 28.

**MAIL.** Billings 14; Hubbard, Kin 87. *See also* LETTER.

**MAJORITY.** Butler, S. 14; Delavigne; Disraeli 15; Glasgow 1; Howe 27; Mann, H. 2; Twain 29. *See also* MANY vs. FEW, MINORITY.

**MAN.** NOTE: This word has not been cross-referenced because it occurs very often.

**MAN vs. ANIMAL.** Butler, S. 1, 44; Herford 11; Herold 41; Marquis 8; Osler 2; Palmerston 1; Plato 3; Pope 4; Smith, A.; Twain 77; Voltaire 1.

**MANAGEMENT.** Hubbard, Kin 62; Shaw 23. *See also* BUSINESS.

**MANNERS.** Burgess 1; Franklin 37; Herford 13; James, H. 1; Twain 61; Wilde 14. *See also* BEHAVIOR, BREEDING.

MANUSCRIPT. Herford 25; Johnson 46. *See also* BOOK, PRINT.

MANY vs. FEW. Shaw 14; Stendhal 1. *See also* MAJORITY, MINORITY.

MARRIAGE. NOTE: This word has not been cross-referenced because it occurs very often.

MARTYR. Eldridge 1; Shaw 67; Spurgeon 4. *See also* BELIEF, DEATH.

MAXIM. Macaulay, T. B. 1; Shakespeare 24; Twain 64, 92. *See also* PROVERB, RULE.

MEAN. Barrie 9; Billings 37; Field 3; Howe 29; Hubbard, Kin 121; Shaw 68; Wilson 3.

MEANING. Prentice 17; Voltaire 33. *See also* AMBIGUITY, DEFINITION.

MEASLES. Billings 64; Field 3; Jerome 4; Jerrold 21; Kingsley 2; Ward 3. *See also* DISEASE.

MEDICINE. Billings 8; Eliot 5; Franklin 11; Osler 2; Shaw 34; Voltaire 3. *See also* DISEASE, DRUGS, LAXATIVE, SICK.

MEEK. Hubbard, Kin 52; Twain 20. *See also* PATIENCE.

MEMORY. Barrie 2; Billings 61; Carroll 1; Cobb 4; Franklin 6; Halifax 1; Howell; La Rochefoucauld 2, 67; Lincoln 11; Morley, J. 3; Nye 15; O'Malley 17; Sheridan, R. B. 2; Stevenson 7; Twain 28; Wilde 101. *See also* REMEMBER.

MENTAL INSTITUTION. Chesterton 26; Ellis 3, 7; Nietzsche 2. *See also* ASYLUM.

MEREDITH, George. Wilde 105.

MICHELANGELO. Twain 16.

MIDDLE AGE. Adams, F. P. 11; Cobb 12; Hecht 1; Hubbard, Kin 6; Marquis 18; Shaw 21. *See also* AGE.

MILK. Billings 58; Blackie; Emerson 29; Fields 7; Herford 5; Masson 11; Mencken 11; Thoreau 19. *See also* COW.

MIND. Allen, F. 14; Burbank 2; Dickens 9; Herford 6; Jackson 3; Johnson 39; Macaulay, T. B. 3; Morley, C. 23; Phelps 1; Rogers 22; Santayana 2; Shaw 27; Smith, L. P. 1, 10. *See also*

BODY & MIND, BRAINS, INTELLIGENCE, NARROW-MINDED, OPEN-MINDED, PSYCHOLOGY.

MINORITY. Gibbon 1; Smith, S. 27. *See also* MAJORITY, MANY vs. FEW.

MIRACLE. Hubbard, E. 22; Huneker 2; Paine; Shaw 70; Voltaire 31; Woollcott 9.

MIRROR. Chesterton 47; Guedalla 6; Rabelais 2. *See also* IMAGE.

MISERY. Billings 121; Herold 27; Mizner, A. 12; Shakespeare 22; Walton 1. *See also* UNHAPPY.

MISFORTUNE. Benét; Billings 75; Colton 9; Gilbert 2; Jerrold 29; La Rochefoucauld 12, 26, 45; Lowell, J. R. 6; Marquis 3; Martial 6; O'Malley 54; Wilde 106, 166. *See also* ADVERSITY, FORTUNE vs. MISFORTUNE.

MISS. Twain 128; Walton 1.

MISSIONARY. Billings 13; Buck; Wilde 177. *See also* CONVERT, RELIGION.

MISTAKE. Allen, F. 11; Bennett, J. G.; Bierce 40; Billings 81; Collins 1; Franklin 7; Gilbert 6; Herold 44; Jackson 15; Kipling 6; Mencken 24; Nietzsche 20; Russell 2; Wheatley; Wilde 40, 110. *See also* BLUNDER, ERROR.

MISTRESS. Moore 6; Nietzsche 4; Wycherley 3.

MISUNDERSTAND. Cocteau 5; Darrow 5; France 7; Wilde 142. *See also* WRONG.

MODEL. Goldsmith 4; Joubert 1. *See also* DESIGN.

MODERATION. Shakespeare 24; Twain 124. *See also* GENTLE, TEMPERANCE.

MODESTY. Agate 1; Herford 27; Mencken 55. *See also* CHASTITY, PRUDERY.

MONEY. NOTE: This word has not been cross-referenced because it occurs very often.

MONKEY. Beecher 9; Billings 50; Congreve 3; Hubbard, E. 33; Twain 93.

**MOORE, George.** Chase, I. 2; Wilde 50.

**MORALITY.** Bennett, A. 7; Chesterton 4; Herold 51; Hugo 5; James, H. 1; Macaulay, T. B. 2, 6; Mencken 13; Russell 8; Shaw 20; Smith, L. P. 17; Stevenson 5; Strachey 4; Twain 58, 65, 81; Wells, H. G. 3; Wilde 98, 108. *See also* RIGHT vs. WRONG, VIRTUE.

**MORNING.** Lamb 22; Rowland 40. *See also* DAY.

**MORTGAGE.** Ade 8; Hubbard, Kin 61. *See also* PROPERTY.

**MOSQUITO.** Little 4; O'Malley 4; Poe 1; Skinner 1.

**MOTHER.** Baer 23; Barrymore 9; Butler, S. 61; Chesterton 29; Disraeli 1; Frost 12; Goethe 3; Hubbard, Kin 79, 130; Lucas 2; Michelet; O'Malley 34; Wilde 5. *See also* CHILDREN, FAMILY, PARENT.

**MOTHER-IN-LAW.** Ade 13; Billings 6, 25; Butler, S. 56, 61; Rowland 49. *See also* IN-LAW, RELATIVE.

**MOTHER vs. DAUGHTER.** Sheridan, R. B. 1; Wilde 12. *See also* FAMILY.

**MOTION PICTURES.** *See* MOVIES.

**MOTIVE.** Barrie 9; La Rochefoucauld 62; Wilde 176.

**MOURN.** Martial 4; Nye 4; Rowland 41. *See also* GRIEF, SAD.

**MOUTH.** Adams, F. P. 8; Bierce 17; Edison 2; Holmes 1; O'Malley 21; Prentice 5; Sandburg 1. *See also* KISS, TEETH, TONGUE, YAWN.

**MOVIES.** Allen, F. 23; Baer 24; Ervine 1; Levant 2; Mizner, W. 15, 25; Wilder. *See also* HOLLYWOOD.

**MULE.** Ade 6; Billings 81; Ingersoll 7. *See also* ASS.

**MURDER.** Byron 5; Collins 3; Dickens 2; Karr 2; Shaw 2, 109, 111; Wallace; Wilde 110. *See also* KILL, POISON.

**MUSIC.** Addison 3; Ade 21; Billings 82; Butler, S. 75, 77; Colby 4; Fontenelle 1; Heine 11; Herold 24; Hubbard, Kin 9; Huneker 1; Johnson 30; O'Malley 31; Romberg; Rossini 1; Shaw 76, 80; Smith, L. P. 18; Twain 123; Wilde 67, 72, 206. *See also* COMPOSITION, JAZZ, OPERA, SING, TUNE.

**MUSICAL INSTRUMENT.** Allen, F. 17; Rogers 20; Shaw 10, 76; Smith, S. 31. *See also* VIOLIN.

**MYSTERY.** Smith, L. P. 14; Smith, S. 39. *See also* SECRET, SKELETON-IN-CLOSET.

**NAKED.** *See* NUDE.

**NAME.** Bierce 45; Byron 16; France 2; Herford 7, 13; Holmes 8; Hubbard, E. 16; Hubbard, Kin 120; Mencken 17; Mizner, W. 18; Swift 41; Wade 1; Wilson 5; Zangwill 3. *See also* AUTOGRAPH, TITLE.

**NAPOLEON.** Baer 30; Hugo 8; Huxley, A. 5.

**NARROW-MINDED.** Allen, F. 6; Chesterton 22; Forbes; Swift 45. *See also* PREJUDICE.

**NASTY.** Shaw 83; Swift 24; Wallace.

**NATION.** Aldington; Metternich; Rogers 26; Voltaire 10.

**NATURAL.** Howe 37; La Rochefoucauld 20; Wilde 15.

**NATURE.** Balzac 9; Billings 81, 83; Cowley; Gilbert 6; Inge 13; Jackson 15; Johnson 24; Voltaire 3; Wells, C. 2.

**NEAT.** Herold 70; Morley, C. 1. *See also* CLEAN.

**NECESSITY.** Billings 84; Butler, S. 34; Holmes 9; Hubbard, Kin 29; Mencken 53; Voltaire 30; Wells, C. 6. *See also* LUXURY vs. NECESSITY.

**NECK.** Eldridge 3; O'Malley 19; Rogers 18.

**NEIGHBOR.** Aretino 1; Baer 5; Billings 56, 80; Bradley 5; Chesterton 5; Franklin 27; Howe 34; Macaulay, T. B. 2; Moore 18; Nietzsche 13; O'Malley 5, 42; Prentice 6, 12; Shaw 7; Wilde 174.

**NERO.** Herford 36.

**NERVOUS.** Herold 2; Korzybski; Mizner, W. 27; Rowland 14; Shaw 94.

**NET.** Spurgeon 1; Johnson 25; Swift 49.

**NEW.** *See* OLD vs. NEW.

NEW ENGLAND. Benét; Twain 46.
NEW YORK. Brush 2; Dunne 18; Herold 66, 68; Marquis 10.
NEWSPAPER. Ade 6; Baer 22; Howe 39; Hubbard, E. 6; Hubbard, Kin 122; Jefferson 2, 3; Rogers 1; Thoreau 8. *See also* JOURNALISM, PRESS.
NIETZSCHE, Friedrich Wilhelm. Guedalla 6.
NIGHT. Hubbard, Kin 128; Nathan 4. *See also* EVENING.
NOAH. Twain 66.
NOBLE. Twain 115; Wilde 176.
NOISE. Cowper 3; Hoffenstein 2; Johnson 30; Twain 50, 85, 112. *See also* ECHO, LOUD.
NONSENSE. Addison 3; Fadiman 2; Franklin 25; Howe 22; Montaigne 7; Nietzsche 8; Pitt 2. *See also* FOOLISH.
NOSE. Claudel; Coleridge 7; Gay 3; Moley 1; Pascal 3; Phelps 2; Spencer 2; Twain 114; Welles 3. *See also* SMELL.
NOTHING. Allen, F. 4; Butler, S. 22; Franklin 32; Gilbert 1; Hubbard, E. 32; Huneker 1; Maurois 1; O'Malley 19, 23, 31, 36; Pope 1; Prentice 8; Richter 2; Shakespeare 8; Shaw 28; Twain 32.
NOVEL. Adams, F. P. 3; Galsworthy 1; Moore 1; Wilde 130, 150. *See also* BOOK, LITERATURE, STORY.
NUDE. Bismarck 1; Bradley 6; Hutchins 1; Jerrold 3; Lin Yutang; Montagu 2; Prentice 2; Rogers 9; Smith, S. 26; Thoreau 10; Wade 2.
NUISANCE. Ellis 6; Zola 2.
NUN. *See* CONVENT.
NURSE. Dunne 5; Jerrold 35; Lardner 3; Twain 140. *See also* CURE, HOSPITAL, PATIENT.

OBSCENE. Shaw 77; Whitman 2. *See also* INDECENT.
OBSERVE. Mizner, W. 35; Montagu 2; Shakespeare 25. *See also* SEE.
OBSTINATE. La Rochefoucauld 51; Sterne 5.
OFFENSE. Bierce 46; Rostand. *See also* NUISANCE, SIN.

OFFICIAL. Louis XIV 1; Nathan 1; Wilson 2. *See also* CIVIL SERVICE, GOVERNMENT.
OLD. Balzac 11; Bierce 48; Lamb 24; Pascal 5; Prentice 3; Rowland 34; Swift 6, 13; Wilde 103. *See also* AGE, OLD vs. NEW.
OLD AGE. Baruch; Billings 121; Coleridge 5; Disraeli 23; Emerson 14; Franklin 2, 41; Johnson 22; Swift 39. *See also* LONGEVITY, YOUTH vs. AGE.
OLD MAID. *See* SPINSTER.
OLD vs. NEW. Colby 5; Hood 5; Inge 12; Jerrold 4; Pascal 5; Shakespeare 3; Thoreau 6; Wycherley 3; Zangwill 3.
ONION. Bailey, J. M. 7; Franklin 34; Huneker 7. *See also* GARLIC.
OPEN. Lichtenberg 3; Nathan 4.
OPEN-MINDED. Bradley 2; Chesterton 27; Dewar 9; Joubert 3.
OPERA. Chesterfield 11; Herold 34; Mencken 37; Rossini 2; Stephens 1. See also MUSIC, SING, VOICE.
OPERATION. Fischer 1; Gourmont 1; Thomas. *See also* DOCTOR.
OPINION. Bierce 41; Billings 26; Chesterton 28; Gilbert 7, 9; Hecht 1; Hubbard, Kin 82; Inge 6; Joubert 3; La Rochefoucauld 24; Lowell, J. R. 4; Ruskin 2; Tolstoi 2; Shaw 19; Twain 27, 54, 62; Wade 5; Wilde 10, 18. *See also* BELIEF, DOGMATISM, IDEA, JUDGMENT, PREJUDICE, THOUGHT.
OPPONENT. Johnson 36; Smith, S. 37; Twain 54; Wotton 4; Wycherley 4. *See also* ARGUMENT, DEBATE, ENEMY, RESISTANCE.
OPPORTUNITY. Bierce 37, 38; Lang 1; Rowland 6; Shaw 65; Wells, C. 14.
OPTIMISM. Bradley 3; Chesterton 33; Ellis 3; Lardner 5; Nathan 5.
OPTIMIST vs. PESSIMIST. Bennett, A. 5; Cabell 1; Twain 80.
ORATOR. Dunne 21; Franklin 10; Montesquieu 3; Tennyson 1. *See also* PUBLIC SPEAKING.
ORIGINAL. Inge 8; Johnson 46; Moore 12; Rowland 36; Shaw 35; Twain 127; Voltaire 26.

**OSTRICH.** Wells, H. G. 1.
**OX.** Longfellow 1; Thurber 4.
**OYSTER.** Munro 6.

**PACKAGE.** Baer 17; Ruskin 4; Smith, L. P. 9.
**PAIN.** Baer 25; Herold 17, 49; Huneker 8; Maeterlinck 1; Mizner, A. 3. *See also* PLEASURE vs. PAIN, SUFFER, TOOTHACHE.
**PAINT.** Ade 8.
**PAINTING.** Herbert; Wilde 213. *See also* PICTURE, PORTRAIT.
**PARENT.** Hubbard, Kin 66; Moore 7; Wilde 166. *See also* FATHER, MOTHER.
**PARENTS & CHILDREN.** Darrow 2; Dickens 13; Goldberg 6; Mencken 41; Nash 1; Russell 4; Shaw 100; Wells, C. 13; Wilde 25, 45. *See also* FAMILY.
**PARIS.** Chamfort 14; Walpole 10.
**PARLIAMENT.** Bagehot 1, 8; Wilde 213. *See also* CONGRESS.
**PARROT.** Rogers 30; Swift 52.
**PARTY.** Hubbard, Kin 137; Mencken 49; Wodehouse 4. *See also* POLITICAL PARTY.
**PASSION.** La Rochefoucauld 11; Moore 9; Rowland 32; Wilde 132. *See also* EMOTION, FEELING.
**PAST.** Arnould 1; Butler, S. 20; Dunne 13; Lytton 10; Mallock; Santayana 9. *See also* HISTORY, TIME.
**PAST & FUTURE.** Wilde 71, 133, 186.
**PAST & PRESENT.** Repplier; Wilde 81, 93.
**PASTIME.** Allen, F. 10; Wotton 3. *See also* AMUSE, SPORTS.
**PATH.** Adams, F. P. 8; Hubbard, E. 26; Hubbard, Kin 40. *See also* ROAD, WAY.
**PATIENCE.** Bierce 34; Hubbard, Kin 60; Kelland; Kipling 3. *See also* MEEK.
**PATIENT.** Herold 13; Holmes 25; Twain 33; Voltaire 3. *See also* DISEASE, DOCTOR, NURSE, SICK.
**PATRIOTISM.** Burgess 6; Byron 15; Cabell 2; Coolidge 4; Hubbard, Kin 51; Mencken 23; Nye 1; Prentice 32; Shaw 18, 78, 81, 122; Strachey 4.
**PAWN.** Pinero 1.
**PAY.** Allen, F. 1, 20; Hubbard, Kin 34, 97, 101; Mizner, A. 16, 18; Roche 2; Sinclair; Wilde 48, 87. *See also* EARN, INCOME.
**PEACE.** Bierce 39; Chesterfield 9; Chesterton 13; Gay 3; Montague; Prentice 23; Wade 5.
**PEANUT.** Pollock 3; Wilde 149.
**PERFECT.** Butler, S. 31; Chamfort 1; Goldsmith 2; Maugham 1; Sévigné 3; Zola 2. *See also* IDEAL.
**PERFUME.** Billings 32; Hubbard, E. 27; Moore 9. *See also* SMELL.
**PERJURY.** Dewar 2; O'Malley 34. *See also* LIE, SWEAR.
**PERSIST.** Billings 14; Sterne 5; Wells, C. 14.
**PESSIMISM.** Arlen 2; Bradley 4; Shaw 83. *See also* OPTIMIST vs. PESSIMIST.
**PET.** Galton. *See also* ANIMAL, CAT, DOG.
**PHILANTHROPIST.** Jerrold 10; Wilde 211. *See also* CHARITY.
**PHILOSOPHER.** Bierce 49; Cicero 2; Collins 6; Fontenelle 2; Frederick the Great 2; Goethe 6; Goldsmith 5; Huxley, A. 2; Marquis 9; Mencken 44; Nietzsche 12; Pascal 6; Shakespeare 26; Sienkiewicz; Socrates 2; Thoreau 22.
**PHILOSOPHY.** Adams, H. 2; Collins 6; Emerson 12; Herold 21; Hubbard, E. 11; La Rochefoucauld 26; Lichtenberg 2; Moore 7; Newton; Santayana 6; Swift 48; Voltaire 33.
**PICASSO, Pablo.** Herbert.
**PICTURE.** Allen, F. 7; Butler, S. 2, 49; Munro 8; Rogers 2. *See also* IMAGE, PAINTING, PORTRAIT.
**PIE.** Spurgeon 1; Swift 27.
**PIG.** Burgess 2; Dickens 9; Harris 3; Ingersoll 1; Prentice 19; Thoreau 24.
**PIGEON.** Spurgeon 1.
**PIN.** Allen, F. 6; Billings 71; Jerrold 7; Prentice 22; Swift 34.
**PIPE.** Lamb 12. *See also* SMOKING, TOBACCO.

**PIRATE.** Leacock 2; Mencken 15. *See also* THIEF.

**PITY.** Billings 94; Cobb 1; Gourmont 16. *See also* SYMPATHY.

**PLACE.** Billings 99; Palmerston 2.

**PLAGIARISM.** Coleridge 2; Disraeli 17; Inge 8; Mizner, W. 33; Moore 17; O'Malley 25; Parker 4; Swift 8.

**PLAN.** Bierce 6; Billings 24; Hubbard, Kin 96. *See also* DESIGN, INTENTION.

**PLANT.** Butler, S. 36; Emerson 1; Fabre; Smith, L. P. 11. *See also* FLOWER, FRUIT, GARDEN, TREE, VEGETABLE.

**PLATITUDE.** Bierce 5; Shaw 116; Strachey 2. *See also* DULL.

**PLAY.** *See* CARDS, CIRCUS, FUN, OPERA, PASTIME, SPORTS, THEATER.

**PLAYTHING.** Augustine 2; Mizner, W. 5; Nietzsche 17; Walpole 9.

**PLEASANT.** Hubbard, Kin 57; Mizner, W. 35. *See also* AGREEABLE.

**PLEASE.** Johnson 42; La Fontaine 2; La Rochefoucauld 6; Lincoln 1; Shaw 90; Twain 34. *See also* AGREEABLE, CHARM, CONTENT, SATISFACTION.

**PLEASURE.** Bagehot 9; Bierce 1; Billings 46; Byron 10; Chamfort 14; Darrow 6; Dunne 19; Herold 23, 57; Hugo 6; Jerrold 14; Johnson 48; La Rochefoucauld 59; Little 15; Montagu 1, 3; Rostand; Rowland 29, 33; Twain 81, 92; Voltaire 18; Wilde 121, 154, 163; Wycherley 3. *See also* BUSINESS vs. PLEASURE, ENJOY, FUN, HAPPY.

**PLEASURE vs. PAIN.** Johnson 20; Macaulay, T. B. 4.

**PLUMBING.** Baer 8; Morley, C. 6; Shaw 33.

**POCKET.** Bierce 17; Hubbard, Kin 91, 97; Spurgeon 2.

**POET.** Aristotle 1; Cocteau 5; Eastman 1; Mizner, A. 18; Plato 5; Thomas; Wilde 140.

**POETRY.** Beecher, H. W. 6; Irwin; Lamb 24; Macaulay, T. B. 3; Marquis 13; Martial 1; Montaigne 10; Nye 6;

Wilde 20, 125, 168, 182. *See also* FREE VERSE, PROSE vs. POETRY.

**POISON.** Billings 24; Brush 3; Wilde 125. *See also* DRUG, MURDER.

**POLICE.** Adams, F. P. 14; Bierce 50; Frost 15; O'Malley 38; Stevenson 6.

**POLITE.** Bailey, J. M. 4; Billings 95; Bismarck 2; Burdette 2; Hood 4; Howe 21; Little 13. *See also* BEHAVIOR.

**POLITICAL PARTY.** Arbuthnot 1; Rogers 13; Whately 4. *See also* DEMOCRATIC PARTY, LIBERAL vs. CONSERVATIVE, REPUBLICAN PARTY.

**POLITICIAN.** Cameron; Clarke; Gunther; Ibsen 1; Inge 9; Lloyd George; Luce; Morley, J. 3; O'Malley 36, 44; Roosevelt, T. 6; Simonds; Ward 6. *See also* REPRESENTATIVE, STATESMAN.

**POLITICS.** Adams, H. 3; Chamfort 13; Disraeli 10; Dunne 22; Einstein 2; Hubbard, Kin 14, 77, 87; Franklin 7; Leacock 3; Lincoln 10; Moley 2; Morley, J. 1; Rogers 19; Shaw 98; Stevenson 9; Ward 18. *See also* LIBERAL vs. CONSERVATIVE, GOVERNMENT.

**POLYGAMY.** Billings 115; Kreisler; Ward 19, 20. *See also* BIGAMY.

**POOR.** *See* POVERTY.

**POPULAR.** Einstein 1; Huxley, A. 5; Twain 34.

**PORTRAIT.** Dali; Dickens 17; Sargent. *See also* PICTURE.

**POSITIVE.** Bierce 40; Phelps 2. *See also* DOGMATISM, SURE.

**POSSESSION.** Billings 79; Emerson 17; Gourmont 10; Prentice 20; Roche 1. *See also* PROPERTY.

**POSTERITY.** Addison 5; Ade 14; Ingersoll 7; Mumford 3. *See also* FUTURE.

**POSTPONE.** Billings 20; Howe 38; La Bruyère 3; Marquis 12; Wilde 76.

**POVERTY.** Beecher, H. W. 6; Behn 1; Billings 36, 68, 89, 97; Dickens 12; Dunne 11; Herold 58; Hubbard, Kin 53, 68, 107; Jerome 5; Jerrold 38;

Marquand; Mizner, A. 2; Mizner, W. 22; Moore 15; Nietzsche 6; Pitt 3; Rabelais 1, 4; Shaw 56; Smith, S. 35; Tolstoi 3; Twain 38; Welles 3; Wilde 145. *See also* RICH vs. POOR.

**POWER.** Johnson 24; Mizner, W. 20; Mumford 7.

**PRACTICE.** Austen 1; Billings 105; Franklin 28; Hazlitt 14; Mizner, A. 8; Osler 3; Twain 57, 59; Warner 4. *See also* CUSTOM.

**PRACTICE vs. PREACH.** Holmes 22; Russell 1, 8; Shakespeare 13; Swift 48.

**PRAISE.** Franklin 47; Hubbard, Kin 32; Johnson 26; La Rochefoucauld 39; Morley, C. 4; Shakespeare 19; Voltaire 28. *See also* COMPLIMENT, FLATTERY.

**PRAYER.** Augustine 1; Barrie 13; Beecher, L.; Butler, S. 43, 73; Colton 7; Farquhar 1; Heine 1; Herold 37; Ingersoll 11; Montaigne 6; O'Malley 37; Plato 4; Renan 2; Shaw 12; Smith, S. 15; Swift 4, 43; Voltaire 25; Wilde 141, 181. *See also* BLESSING, WORSHIP.

**PREACH.** Franklin 32; Johnson 43; Lincoln 17; Morley, C. 15; Smith, S. 8, 38, 43; Twain 32. *See also* PRACTICE vs. PREACH.

**PREACHER.** Rowland 54; Selden; Shaw 7; Spurgeon 4. *See also* CLERGY, SERMON.

**PREGNANCY.** Henderson; Herold 55; Moore 8. *See also* BABY.

**PREJUDICE.** Bierce 41; Burbank 1; Huneker 8; James, W. 1. *See also* NARROW-MINDED, OPINION.

**PRESENT.** Adams, F. P. 7; Franklin 1; Mencken 45; Wilde 165. *See also* GIFT, PAST & PRESENT, TIME.

**PRESIDENT.** Chase, S. P.; Darrow 8; Fadiman 1; Hubbard, Kin 109; O'Malley 46; Phillips; Sherman 3; Twain 90; Wilde 74.

**PRESS.** Barrie 10; Butler, S. 48; Wilde 81. *See also* NEWSPAPER, PRINT.

**PRICE.** *See* COST, COST of LIVING, VALUE, WORTH.

**PRIDE.** Billings 91, 100; Burton 3; Franklin 49; Herold 5; Howe 44; Voltaire 19. *See also* BOAST, DIGNITY.

**PRINCIPLE.** Adler; Austen 1; Butler, S. 24; Franklin 45; Hubbard, Kin 119; Shaw 18; Twain 94; Wilde 59. *See also* BELIEF, TRUTH.

**PRINT.** Byron 16; Lincoln 12. *See also* BOOK, MANUSCRIPT, NEWSPAPER.

**PRISON.** Johnson 17; O'Malley 38; Rogers 19; Shaw 49, 73; Sherman 3; Thoreau 12; Wilde 135. *See also* CRIME.

**PRIVATE vs. PUBLIC.** Billings 123; Hay, I.; Herold 60.

**PRIVILEGE.** Lowell, J. R. 9; Scott 2. *See also* ADVANTAGE, FAVOR.

**PRIZE FIGHT.** Mencken 50; Mizner, W. 12.

**PROBLEM.** Adams, H. 2; Shaw 86. *See also* QUESTION.

**PROFESSION.** Ade 10; Bryce; Stevenson 9. *See also* CLERGY, LAW, MEDICINE, TEACH.

**PROFESSOR.** Auden; Lewis 1; Moore 19; Thoreau 22. *See also* COLLEGE, TEACHER, UNIVERSITY.

**PROFIT.** Churchill 2; Dunne 7; La Rochefoucauld 50; Nietzsche 13.

**PROFOUND.** Eldridge 6; Prentice 1.

**PROGRESS.** Ellis 6; Huxley, A. 4; Rousseau 2; Shaw 1. *See also* GROW, IMPROVE.

**PROHIBITION.** Bangs 2; Masson 12. *See also* DRINK, LIQUOR.

**PROMISE.** Hazlitt 12; Hubbard, Kin 112; Jerrold 37; La Rochefoucauld 57; Swift 27.

**PRONUNCIATION.** Broun 4; Morley, C. 10; Twain 113; Wade 1. *See also* ACCENT, SPEECH.

**PROOF.** Butler, S. 63; Mencken 48. *See also* TRUTH.

**PROPERTY.** Chesterton 44; Gourmont 10; O'Malley 5; Shaw 28; Swift 5. *See also* ESTATE, HEIR, INHERITANCE, LAND, MORTGAGE, POSSESSION, WEALTH.

**PROPHECY.** Billings 23; Lowell, J. R. 3. *See also* FUTURE.

**PROPHET.** Halifax 1; Morley, C. 17; Schlegel; Shakespeare 12; Walpole 6.

**PROSE.** Chase, I. 2; Molière 4; Smith, L. P. 6. *See also* LANGUAGE.

**PROSE vs. POETRY.** Little 14; Nichols 1; Wilde 105

**PROSPERITY.** Goethe 2; Hubbard, Kin 42; Rogers 26. *See also* FORTUNE, SUCCESS.

**PROTESTANT.** Inge 5.

**PROVERB.** Herold 52; Spencer 3. *See also* MAXIM.

**PROVIDENCE.** Butler, S. 57; Ruskin 5; Twain 103. *See also* GOD.

**PRUDERY.** Butler, S. 26; Hugo 7. *See also* MODESTY, PURITAN.

**PSYCHOLOGY.** Deeping 2; Galsworthy 1; Masson 8. *See also* MIND.

**PUBLIC.** Broun 4; Burke 2; Butler, S. 58; Chamfort 15; Hood 5; Hubbard, Kin 39; Lincoln 4; Lytton 7; Montaigne 1; Wilde 143, 216. *See also* PRIVATE vs. PUBLIC.

**PUBLIC SPEAKING.** Adams, F. P. 1; Butler, S. 22; Hubbard, Kin 17, 124; Nye 1, 9; Twain 69; Warner 7. *See also* LECTURE, ORATOR.

**PUBLICITY.** Baer 14; Bangs 1; Dewar 7; Johnson 15; Nathan 2; Rogers 14.

**PUBLISH.** Ade 14; Franklin 39; Marquis 13; Morley, C. 18; Shaw 112.

**PUN.** Baer 28; Lamb 12, 27; Levant 6; Poe 4; Swift 28. *See also* WIT.

**PUNCTUAL.** Lucas 1; Mizner, A. 6, 17; Walker, J. 1; Wilde 59. *See also* EARLY.

**PUNISHMENT.** Bentham; Billings 127; Chamfort 6; Frederick the Great 2; Hubbard, E. 19; Mencken 39; Shaw 60; Voltaire 27; Wilde 181. *See also* PURGATORY.

**PURGATORY.** Chamfort 2, 20; Lincoln 15. *See also* HELL.

**PURITAN.** Chesterton 35; Macaulay, T. B. 4; Mencken 34; Rogers 12. *See also* PRUDERY.

**PURSUE.** Burgess 4; Rowland 23; Sterne 2; Twain 84; Wells, H. G. 2; Wilde 35. *See also* FOLLOW.

**PUSH.** Dewar 5; Jowett 3.

**QUARREL.** Chesterton 19; Conrad 4; Hubbard, Kin 81; Meredith 3; Shaw 121; Sheridan, R. B. 7; Swift 26; Ward 17. *See also* ARGUMENT, BATTLE, FIGHT.

**QUESTION.** Eliot 1; Joubert 2; Pollock 2. *See also* PROBLEM.

**QUESTION & ANSWER.** Cervantes 7; Sienkiewicz; Wilde 144. *See also* EXAMINATION.

**QUIET.** Baer 28; Bagehot 4; Dickens 1; Thoreau 14. *See also* CALM, SILENCE.

**QUOTATION.** Bunner; Shaw 15, 52; Welles 2. *See also* REPEAT.

**RACE.** *See* HORSE RACE, HUMAN RACE.

**RADIO.** Allen, F. 22, 25; Herold 4; Mizner, W. 37; Wade 3.

**RAILROAD.** Roosevelt, T. 5. *See also* TRAIN.

**RAIN.** Frost 1; Jerrold 12; Phelps 4; Twain 9. *See also* WEATHER.

**RAKE.** Macaulay, T. B. 5; Shaw 63. *See also* SEX.

**RANK.** Mencken 3; Thoreau 10; Wilde 89. *See also* CLASS.

**RASCAL.** Carlyle 5; Napoleon 2; Shaw 21, 46, 88; Thoreau 23; Wilde 153. *See also* FOOL vs. KNAVE, VILLAIN.

**RAT.** Nye 15.

**RAZOR.** Hubbard, Kin 24; Smith, S. 46.

**READING.** Billings 61; Butler, S. 53; Chesterton 41; Colton 13; Disraeli 24; France 19; Hazlitt 9; Hobbes; Holmes 19; Jefferson 2; Jerrold 25; Lamb 28; Levant 3; Lincoln 12; Marquis 17; Martial 1; Masson 16; Mencken 5, 22; Mizner, W. 11, 39; Phelps 3; Rogers 10; Schopenhauer 1; Shaw 9, 116, 120; Smith, L. P. 6; Twain 15; Wilde 31, 195, 208. *See also* ILLITERATE.

**REAL ESTATE.** *See* LAND, PROPERTY.

**REASON.** Billings 43; Butler, S. 32, 69; France 11; Franklin 3, 10; Inge 3; Jackson 16; Moore 20; O'Malley 47; Shakespeare 15; Swift 44; Wilde 96.

RIGHT vs. WRONG. Billings 23, 40; Chesterfield 4; Chesterton 29, 35, 42; Haliburton 2; Hazlitt 14, 17; Herford 14; Herold 36; Howe 36; Longfellow 2; Moore 20; Pollock 2; Shaw 74; Stevenson 10; Wells, C. 3. See also CONSCIENCE, GOOD vs. BAD, JUSTICE vs. INJUSTICE, MORALITY, VICE vs. VIRTUE.

ROAD. Billings 98; Herford 8; Herold 59; Smith, L. P. 19. See also PATH, WAY.

ROBBER. See PIRATE, STEAL, THIEF.

ROMAN. Disraeli 19; Heine 5; Voltaire 13. See also ROME.

ROMANCE. Disraeli 18; Shaw 64; Wilde 78, 102, 114, 167, 169. See also COURTSHIP.

ROME. Herford 36; Montaigne 1. See also ROMAN.

ROOSEVELT, Theodore. Dunne 14.

ROPE. Baer 19; Rogers 18; Roosevelt, F. D. 2. See also HANGING.

ROSE. Barrie 2; Jerrold 7; Karr 3; Twain 56. See also FLOWER.

ROYALTY. Bismarck; Burke 3; Fabre. See also KING.

RUDE. Billings 49; La Rochefoucauld 68; Smith, S. 21.

RUIN. Billings 62, 98; Rowland 43; Voltaire 21; Wilde 28, 169.

RULE. Cobb 10; Eldridge 6; Gourmont 5; Lamb 5; Thoreau 1. See also KING, MAXIM.

RUM. Billings 99; Byron 14. See also LIQUOR.

RUN. Pollock 1; Rabelais 5.

RUSSIA. Churchill 5.

RUT. Glasgow 2; Hubbard, Kin 132.

SACRIFICE. Holmes 22; Jackson 11; Maugham 7; Rowland 15; Shaw 88; Ward 8; Wilde 145.

SAD. Hugo 6; Ward 7. See also GRIEF, HAPPY vs. UNHAPPY, MOURN.

SAFE. Billings 101; La Rochefoucauld 19; Mencken 49; Shaw 47.

SAINT. Bierce 43; Colton 14; Mizner, W. 19; Wilde 133. See also HALO.

SAME. See ALIKE.

SAMSON. Franklin 36.

SANE. Mann, H. 2; Stevenson 1.

SATIRE. Colby 3; Franklin 39; Lamb 19; Swift 29; Voltaire 28; Walpole 8.

SATISFACTION. La Rochefoucauld 17; Martial 6; Shaw 97. See also CONTENT, PLEASE.

SAVAGE. Billings 82; Franklin 37; Twain 102; Wilde 177. See also WILD.

SAVE. Bailey, J. M. 1; Churchill 3; Cobb 13; Herold 40, 77; Hood 2. See also ECONOMY.

SCANDAL. Fielding 5; Meredith 5; Nye 18; Wilde 128. See also GOSSIP.

SCARCE. La Bruyère 7; Lewis 2.

SCENERY. Twain 86; Woollcott 8.

SCHOLAR. Hazlitt 18; Macaulay, T. B. 5; Nietzsche 23; Shaw 32, 58. See also LAW STUDENT, LEARNING vs. IGNORANCE.

SCHOOL. Ade 10, 17; Benton; Billings 30; Butler, S. 66; Chesterton 2; Goldberg 4; Hubbard, Kin 2, 118; Mencken 41; Twain 52, 59, 68. See also LEARN, TEACH, TEACHER.

SCIENCE. Butler, S. 63; Chesterton 36; Dunne 5; Lamb 11; Newton; Shaw 34, 86.

SCOT. Johnson 21, 29.

SCRATCH. Lover; Montaigne 3; Zangwill 4. See also ITCH.

SEA. Jerrold 2, 22; Steinbeck.

SEASICK. Baer 29; Billings 91; Butler, S. 51.

SECRET. Balzac 10; Chesterfield 2; Franklin 20, 44; Hubbard, E. 30; La Fontaine 1; Lamb 3; La Rochefoucauld 15, 18; Nye 16; Shaw 92; Smith, S. 39; Voltaire 35; Wilde 113, 212, 214. See also MYSTERY, SKELETON-IN-CLOSET.

SEDUCTION. Bennett, A. 4.

SEE. Billings 65; Johnson 44; Mumford 9; Rowland 40; Shaw 5; Wilde 44, 53; Zangwill 6. See also OBSERVE.

SELF. Colby 3; Howe 46; Hubbard, Kin 131; Johnson 2; Landon 1; La Rochefoucauld 24, 55, 56; Levant 2; Masson 2, 3; Montaigne 6; Shaw 6.

**SELF-DECEPTION.** France 8; La Rochefoucauld 55, 71; Wilde 78.

**SELFISH.** Austen 1; Beecher, H. W. 7; Parkhurst. *See also* CONCEIT, EGOTISM, VANITY.

**SELF-MADE MAN.** Billings 100; Cowper 4; Holmes 6; Hubbard, Kin 76; Nye 12.

**SELL.** Butler, S. 2; Leacock 7; Mencken 23; Ruskin 3; Stevenson 2; Wells, C. 8. *See also* AUCTIONEER, BARGAIN, BROKER.

**SENSE.** Allen, F. 25; Herold 66, 67; La Rochefoucauld 61; Metternich; Pitt 2. *See also* COMMON SENSE, HORSE SENSE.

**SENSE of HUMOR.** Inge 2; Wilde 114. *See also* HUMOR.

**SENTIMENTAL.** Herold 32; Kingsley 2.

**SEPARATION.** Chesterfield 9; Colton 4; Hubbard, E. 18; Hubbard, Kin 90; Munro 5; Shaw 17; Twain 131.

**SERIOUS.** Butler, S. 54; Chesterton 49; Herold 28; Johnson 19; La Rochefoucauld 29; Montaigne 7; Rowland 12; Smith, S. 47; Strachey 5; Wilde 91, 173.

**SERMON.** Beecher, H. W. 6; O'Malley 18; Rabelais 3. *See also* PREACHER.

**SERVANT.** Bailey, J. M. 5; Barrie 4; Frost 5; Hubbard, Kin 92; Johnson 38; Shaw 57. *See also* BUTLER.

**SEW.** Jerrold 7.

**SEX.** Barrymore 13; Beerbohm 1; Billings 51; Butler, S. 50; Brush 1; Cobb 7; Franklin 36; Gourmont 9, 11; Herold 20, 69, 80; Hoffenstein 1; Johnson 34, 38; Lenclos 2; Nietzsche 23; Russell 9; Smith, L. P. 11; Smith, S. 1; Talleyrand 5; Wilde 214. *See also* RAKE.

**SHAKESPEARE, William.** Bunner; Moore 1; Nye 6; Shaw 15; Ward 20; Welles 2.

**SHAME.** Hubbard, Kin 53; La Rochefoucauld 32; Mencken 55; Shaw 72, 110; Twain 77; Wilde 21.

**SHAPE.** Ade 12; Morley C. 3.

**SHARP.** Irving 2; Jerrold 28; Moore 13.

**SHAW, Bernard.** Herold 30; Munro 1; Wilde 16; Zangwill 1.

**SHEEP.** Balzac 14; Inge 6; O'Malley 22, 44; Stendhal 4; Twain 117. *See also* LAMB.

**SHINE.** Benchley 3; Herford 37; Kaufman 2.

**SHIRT.** Jerrold 27; Lardner 4.

**SHOE.** O'Malley 37; Prentice 15. *See also* FEET.

**SHOPPING.** Hubbard, Kin 46. *See also* BUY.

**SHORT.** Barrymore 16; Bennett, A. 7; Lincoln 10. *See also* BREVITY, LONG vs. SHORT.

**SICK.** Bierce 54; Cobb 9; Emerson 31; Herold 37; Ingersoll 10; Jerrold 38; Lawrence 2; Little 17; Shaw 41; Smith, S. 38. *See also* DISEASE, DOCTOR, HOSPITAL, PATIENT, SEASICK.

**SIDE.** Lamb 4; Montesquieu 2; Palmerston 1; Pollock 2; Prentice 9; Sévigné 1; Twain 3, 29.

**SILENCE.** Adams, F. P. 8; Baer 24; Benchley 1; Billings 103, 104; Burdette 4; Chesterfield 3; Chesterton 37; Coolidge 2; Eliot 3; Goethe 4; Hardy; Hazlitt 11; Herford 24; Huxley, A. 3; Johnson 8; Lang 1; Little 11; Lowell, J. R. 1; Morley, J. 5; O'Malley 21; Prentice 23; Schopenhauer 3; Shaw 13; Skinner 2; Smith, S. 28; Wilde 56. *See also* QUIET, SPEECH vs. SILENCE.

**SIMPLE.** Gourmont 14; Herold 15; Wilde 154.

**SIN.** Augustine 3; Beecher, H. W. 10; Bierce 43; Billings 12, 80, 133; Byron 10; Crane; Dickens 13; Eldridge 4; Emerson 36; France 14; Hubbard, E. 3; Hubbard, Kin 73; Karr 4; Korzybski; Little 9; Madariaga; Mencken 24, 26; Morley, C. 15; Nietzsche 18; Ovid 2; Rowland 36, 54; Shakespeare 3; Twain 14, 103; Wells, C. 4, 9, 17; Wilde 24, 133. *See also* CONFESSION, EVIL, IMMORAL, VICE, WRONG.

**SINCERE.** Congreve 7; Wilde 85. *See also* HONESTY.

**SING.** Adams, F. P. 13; Ade 11; Butler, S. 77; Chesterton 31; Coleridge 4; Frederick the Great 1; Glass; Grant; Herford 39; Herold 34; Hubbard, Kin 130; Kipling 1; Romberg; Rossini 2; Sterne 1; Ward 7. *See also* MUSIC, OPERA, TUNE, VOICE.

**SISTER.** Billings 116; Butler, S. 71; Kipling 10.

**SIT.** Benchley 3; Wilson 1; Wylie.

**SIZE.** Billings 55; Glasgow 3; Lincoln 13. *See also* LONG vs. SHORT, SMALL & LARGE.

**SKELETON-IN-CLOSET.** Barrymore 12; Butler, S. 52; Mizner, W. 27. *See also* SECRET.

**SKEPTICISM.** Huxley, A. 2; Nietzsche 7. *See also* DOUBT.

**SKIN.** Allen, F. 19; Beecher, H. W. 8; Nietzsche 21; O'Malley 22; Twain 68, 130.

**SKUNK.** O'Malley 13.

**SLANG.** Bierce 44; Sandburg 2. *See also* SPEECH.

**SLAVERY.** Lincoln 16; Shaw 19.

**SLEEP.** Adams, F. P. 9; Auden; Bennett, A. 9; Inge 5; Mizner, W. 24; Rabelais 3; Smith, S. 43; Stephens 1; Twain 112. *See also* BED, DREAM.

**SLEEP & WAKE.** Balzac 3; Heine 4; Herford 26; Little 6; Maugham 6; Mizner, W. 7; Nietzsche 14; Rowland 4; Thurber 1; Twain 142. *See also* INSOMNIA, WAKE.

**SMALL.** Allen, F. 19; Chesterton 38; Johnson 47; Ruskin 4; Thoreau 15.

**SMALL & LARGE.** La Rochefoucauld 49; O'Malley 41; Swift 56; Voltaire 19. *See also* LITTLE vs. MUCH, SIZE.

**SMELL.** Allen, F. 13; Goethe 1; Gourmont 15; Howe 16; Hubbard, E. 27. *See also* GARLIC, NOSE, ONION, PERFUME.

**SMILE.** Depew 1; Herold 38; Lardner 6; Twain 141.

**SMOKE.** Allen, F. 24; Emerson 23; Prentice 19; Twain 82, 116, 142. *See also* CIGAR, CIGARETTE, PIPE, TOBACCO.

**SNAKE.** Billings 57; Shaw 71.

**SOAP.** Burgess 4; Ingersoll 9; Rinehart; Twain 100. *See also* WASH.

**SOCIALISM.** Hubbard, Kin 133.

**SOCIETY.** Balzac 6, 9; Billings 72; Byron 12; Chamfort 16; Dewar 7; Emerson 32; Jackson 13; La Rochefoucauld 25; Lavater 1; Ruskin 1; Saltus 3; Shaw 37; Talleyrand 4; Wilde 10, 153, 156, 205. *See also* CLASS, GENTLEMAN.

**SOFT.** Roosevelt, T. 3; Rowland 37.

**SOLDIER.** Jerrold 40; Mencken 52; Napoleon 3. *See also* ARMY, WAR.

**SOLOMON.** Barrymore 10.

**SON.** Hubbard, Kin 79, 115; Prentice 12; Rowland 19. *See also* CHILDREN.

**SONG.** *See* SING.

**SOPHISTICATION.** Herold 63, 66; Rowland 32.

**SORROW.** *See* GRIEF, SAD, REGRET.

**SOUL.** Beecher, H. W. 3; Butler, S. 60; Dewar 1; Haldane 2; Herold 40; Holmes 17; Renan 2; Ward 12. *See also* BODY & SOUL, SPIRITUAL.

**SOUP.** O'Malley 29.

**SPACE.** Lamb 15; Nye 19.

**SPEECH.** Benchley 6; Cobb 8; Fénelon; Fielding 7; France 3; Herford 21, 39; Howe 31; Hubbard, Kin 58; Montaigne 1; Moore 12; Morley, J. 4; Parker 2; Shakespeare 8; Voltaire 32. *See also* FREEDOM of SPEECH, LANGUAGE, PRONUNCIATION, PUBLIC SPEAKING, SLANG, TALK, TONGUE, VOICE, WHISPER, WORD.

**SPEECH vs. SILENCE.** Emerson 34; Franklin 40; Frost 7. *See also* CONVERSATION, TALK vs. LISTEN.

**SPEED.** Cocteau 3; Herford 30. *See also* FAST, HURRY.

**SPELLING.** Twain 45, 113; Ward 11. *See also* WORD.

**SPEND.** Agate 2; Hubbard, Kin 110; Rascoe 1.

**SPICE.** Morley, C. 16, 21; Shaw 52.

**SPIDER.** Swift 19.

**SPINSTER.** Balzac 13; Chamfort 11; Ferber; Loomis 2; Moore 11; Russell 5. *See also* CELIBACY.

**SPIRITUAL.** Bierce 13; Herold 49; O'Malley 18. *See also* SOUL.

**SPOIL.** Wilde 4, 114; Zangwill 4.

**SPOONS.** Emerson 22; Johnson 10.

**SPORTS.** Broun 3; Hubbard, Kin 43; Jackson 8; Jerrold 24; Little 2; Macaulay, T. B. 4; Masson 9; Ruskin 6; Shaw 109; Swift 9. *See also individual sports such as* BASEBALL, CARDS, CRICKET, et cetera.

**SPRING.** Hubbard, Kin 26; Nye 18; Richter 1; Rowland 16, 20; Walpole 3.

**STAND.** Adams, F. P. 13; Adams, H. 4; Little 16; Quillen 2; Twain 71.

**STAR.** Eliot 2.

**STARVATION.** Jerrold 10; Lenclos 1; Wilde 177.

**STATESMAN.** Clarke; Hubbard, Kin 51; Lincoln 4; Lloyd George; O'Malley 44; Phillips; Twain 58. *See also* POLITICIAN.

**STATISTICS.** Disraeli 22; Lang 2; Nye 15; Shaw 43; Strachey 3. *See also* FACT.

**STATUE.** Baer 11; Cato 1; Hubbard, Kin 86; Sibelius.

**STEAL.** Baer 12; Butler, S. 11; Howe 5; Jerrold 40; Rogers 7; Roosevelt, T. 5. *See also* PIRATE, PLAGIARISM, THIEF.

**STEELE, Richard.** Macaulay, T. B. 5.

**STEIN, Gertrude.** Fadiman 3.

**STEP.** Jerrold 31; Rowland 50.

**STINGY.** Billings 74, 124.

**STOCKINGS.** Johnson 34; Rowland 37.

**STOMACH.** Cato 3; Field 4; Halsey 1; Herford 17; Hubbard, Kin 103; Hugo 5; Mizner, A. 9; Prentice 16; Swift 2.

**STONE.** Herford 37; Morley, C. 17.

**STORK.** Allen, F. 9; Hubbard, Kin 1; Mizner, W. 22; Quillen 4.

**STORY.** Cobb 4; Howe 9; Hubbard, Kin 23; Irving 1; O'Malley 14; Thoreau 17; Twain 48; Wells, C. 8; Zangwill 2. *See also* JOKE, NOVEL.

**STRANGE.** Twain 12, 120, 121.

**STRANGER.** Burdette 2; Shakespeare 14.

**STRIKE.** Kipling 4; Mencken 18; Shakespeare 10.

**STRONG.** Runyon 2. *See also* POWER.

**STRONG vs. WEAK.** Deffand; La Rochefoucauld 11; Masson 10.

**STUDY.** Butler, S. 18; Masson 2; Shaw 58; Wells, H. G. 2. *See also* EDUCATION, LEARN, SCHOLAR, SCHOOL.

**STUPID.** Butler, S. 25; Chesterton 9; Gourmont 7; Heine 14; Herold 7; Hubbard, E. 10; La Bruyère 9; Napoleon 2; Nietzsche 11; Russell 7; Smith, S. 39; Thurber 4; Wilde 85, 176. *See also* DULL, FOOL, IDIOT.

**STYLE.** Allen, F. 8; Chesterton 24; Mizner, W. 9; Smith, S. 24; Tolstoi 2; Wilde 191. *See also* FASHION, WRITING.

**SUBWAY.** Strunsky.

**SUCCESS.** Billings 106; Collins 2; Congreve 2; Dewar 13; Disraeli 4; Eldridge 2; Fadiman 1; Helps 2; Hubbard, Kin 103; Hugo 1; La Bruyère 2, 9; La Rochefoucauld 37; Little 12; Marquis 14; Mizner, W. 7; Quarles 2; Shaw 89; Twain 5, 73, 111, 143; Wilde 9, 115. *See also* FORTUNE, PROSPERITY, SELF-MADE MAN, TRIUMPH, WIN.

**SUFFER.** Darrow 5; Renard; Swift 20. *See also* GRIEF, PAIN.

**SUICIDE.** Billings 107; Collins 3; Hubbard, Kin 24. *See also* DEATH, KILL.

**SUMMER.** Emerson 7; Hubbard, Kin 99; Prentice 21; Walpole 4.

**SUN.** Eliot 4; Rogers 9; Smith, L. P. 15; Twain 9.

**SUNDAY.** Beecher, H. W. 10; Deeping 3; Ertz 2; Farquhar 2; Little 9; Swift 43; Twain 65.

**SUPERIOR.** Balzac 2; Mencken 3; Shaw 81; Socrates 4.

**SUPPER.** Chamfort 10.

**SUPPLY.** Billings 4; Shaw 79.

**SUPPORT.** Landon 2; Lang 2; Lytton 1; Rowland 52; Sherman 1.

**SURE.** Bierce 40; Kipling 16; Lowell, J. R. 8; Phelps 2. *See also* POSITIVE.

**SURPRISE.** Mizner, W. 32; Twain 6; Voltaire 14; Wilde 215. *See also* UNEXPECTED.

**SUSPENSE.** Deeping 1; Swift 19.

**SUSPICION.** Billings 15; Emerson 22; Johnson 10; Mizner, W. 6; Wilde 120. *See also* DISTRUST.

**SWEAR.** Burton 1; Mizner, A. 6; Nye 11; Shaw 44; Twain 40, 132. *See also* PERJURY.

**SWEAT.** Edison 1; Huneker 5.

**SYMPATHY.** Howe 23; Hubbard, Kin 104; Jowett 2; Wilde 8. *See also* PITY.

**TABLE.** Burgess 1; Gilbert 4; Swift 5.

**TACT.** Cocteau 4; Mizner, W. 12; Talleyrand 4.

**TAIL.** Hood 1; Nathan 2.

**TALENT.** Agate 1; France 8; Goncourt; Mizner, W. 12; Scott 1; Zangwill 3. *See also* ABILITY, GENIUS.

**TALK.** Colby 4; France 17; Heine 6; Holmes 24; Howe 42; Jefferson 1; Johnson 6; La Rochefoucauld 27, 56; Maugham 3; Mizner, A. 4; Mizner, W. 24; Molière 4; O'Malley 31; Plato 6; Prentice 9; Sévigné 2; Sitwell; Swift 7; Twain 7; Walpole 9; Wilde 72; Wodehouse 4. *See also* CONVERSATION, SPEECH, TELEPHONE.

**TALK vs. LISTEN.** Bierce 8; Disraeli 20; Hugo 9; La Bruyère 5; Morley, C. 19; Rowland 48; Wilde 200, 205, 206. *See also* CONVERSATION, SPEECH vs. SILENCE.

**TAPEWORM.** Nye 14; Twain 90.

**TASTE.** Adams, F. P. 6, 14; Bennett, A. 1; Emerson 26; Howe 16, 48; Jowett 4; Little 1; Shaw 16, 35.

**TAVERN.** Douglas 2; Greeley 1; Mizner, W. 4; Swift 31. *See also* DRINK, LIQUOR.

**TAX.** Adams, F. P. 4; Colbert; Dewar 12; Nye 17; O'Malley 22; Rogers 28; Twain 130; Wade 6; Warner 5.

**TAXICAB.** Baer 3; Herold 59.

**TAXIDERMY.** Herold 19; Hubbard, Kin 27; Twain 130.

**TEA.** Blackie; Fielding 5; Holmes 20; Lincoln 7; Twain 63.

**TEACH.** Billings 31; Butler, S. 17; Fischer 3; Franklin 14; Halifax 9; Hubbard, E. 24; Maurois 1; Shakespeare 13; Shaw 36; Talleyrand 4; Twain 25, 115. *See also* EDUCATION, LEARN vs. TEACH.

**TEACHER.** Ade 21; Herold 24; Mencken 42. *See also* PROFESSOR, SCHOOL.

**TEARS.** Holmes 5; La Rochefoucauld 55; Mizner, W. 20. *See also* CRY, EYES.

**TEETH.** Allen, F. 21; Franklin 38; Leacock 2; Prentice 24; Rowland 22; Shaw 76; Swift 13; Twain 1, 114. *See also* DENTIST, TOOTHACHE.

**TEETOTALER.** Butler, S. 65; Chesterton 8; Kipling 5, 14; Shaw 48. *See also* ABSTINENCE, TEMPERANCE.

**TELEPHONE.** Chase, I. 1; Maugham 3; Shaw 77; Thurber 3. *See also* CONVERSATION.

**TELL.** Herold 12; Kipling 13; Prentice 6; Whistler 2. *See also* INFORMATION.

**TEMPER.** Emerson 26; Gibran; Hubbard, E. 29; Wilde 96; Ybarra. *See also* ANGER.

**TEMPERANCE.** Johnson 1; Ward 10. *See also* ABSTINENCE, MODERATION, TEETOTALER.

**TEMPTATION.** Bagehot 5; Bierce 1, 38; Billings 15; Butler, S. 16; Herold 79; Shaw 65, 103; Twain 105; Wilde 7, 22, 62, 139, 157.

**TEN COMMANDMENTS.** Macaulay, T. B. 2; Marquand; Masefield; Mencken 40.

**TENNIS.** Adams, F. P. 11; Frost 19.

**TESTIMONIAL.** Fishbein; Hubbard, Kin 32.

**TEXAS.** Sheridan, P.

**TEXT.** Rowland 54; Schopenhauer 2.

**THEATER.** Ade 5; Barrymore 3; Ervine 2; Herold 63; Howe 37; Nathan 4; Shaw 117; Wilde 52, 193; Woollcott 8. *See also* ACTING, ACTOR, AUDIENCE, COMEDY, MOVIES, OPERA, TRAGEDY.

**THEOLOGY.** Mencken 43; Morley, C. 13; Smith, S. 37; Voltaire 1. *See also* BELIEF, GOD, RELIGION.

**THEORY.** Marquis 9; Masson 12; Rochester 1. See also EXPLANATION.

**THIEF.** Chesterton 44; O'Malley 25. *See also* PIRATE, STEAL.

**THIN.** *See* FAT vs. THIN.

**THINK.** Bierce 9; Burbank 1; Colby 2; Collins 1; Holmes 24; Hubbard, E. 31; Hubbard, Kin 28; James, W. 1; Karr 1; Lippman; Marquis 7; Masson 10; Mencken 34; O'Malley 12; Rabelais 6; Russell 6; Schopenhauer 1; Shakespeare 15; Shaw 24; Sitwell; Wilde 195; Wilson 1. *See also* REASON, THOUGHT.

**THOUGHT.** Butler, S. 64; Colton 6; Heine 2; Herold 71; Marquis 15; O'Malley 1, 51; Reade; Thoreau 8. *See also* BELIEF, IDEA, OPINION.

**TIE.** *See* KNOT.

**TIGER.** Shaw 109.

**TIGHT.** Prentice 15; Wodehouse 5.

**TIME.** Agassiz; Barrymore 13, 14, 16; Billings 122; Chesterfield 5; Franklin 16; Frost 12, 17; Haliburton 5; Heine 5; Herford 41; Herold 32; Hubbard, Kin 3; Johnson 6; Lamb 15; La Rochefoucauld 26; Macaulay, R.; Morley, J. 2; Nietzsche 16; Rowland 19; Shaw 22, 58; Stendhal 2; Warner 3; Wilde 59; Woollcott 7. *See also* CLOCK, DAY, FUTURE, PAST, PAST & FUTURE, PAST & PRESENT, PRESENT, TODAY & TOMORROW, TOMORROW, WATCH, YEAR.

**TIRED.** Butler, S. 39; Byron 6; Chesterton 41; Dumas, fils 4; Sterne 2; Twain 78: Wilde 104.

**TITLE.** Barrie 6; Colman (younger).

**TOAD.** Billings 24.

**TOAST.** Jerome 6; Rowland 45.

**TOBACCO.** Coleridge 7; Lamb 22; Toscanini; Zola 2. *See also* CHEWING TOBACCO, CIGAR, CIGARETTE, SMOKING.

**TOLERANCE.** Prentice 31; Wilde 143.

**TOMBSTONE.** Lamb 19; Little 16; Morley, C. 17. *See also* EPITAPH.

**TOMORROW.** Auerbach; Broun 5; Burdette 3; Herold 26; Whistler 1; Wilde 76. *See also* TIME, TODAY & TOMORROW.

**TONGUE.** Chapman 2; Chesterfield 3; Huxley, A. 8; Irving 2; Lang 1; O'Malley 53; Osler 3; Sheridan, R. B. 1; Smith, L. P. 5; Swift 13; Twain 28. *See also* MOUTH, SPEECH.

**TOOTHACHE.** Franklin 23; Shakespeare 26. *See also* TEETH.

**TOP.** Emerson 18; Nye 19; Twain 114.

**TOWN.** Hubbard, Kin 106; Quillen 3. *See also* CITY, VILLAGE.

**TRAGEDY.** Beerbohm 2; Byron 1; Wilde 5, 82, 163. *See also* THEATER.

**TRAIN.** Chesterton 32; Herold 75, 78; Hubbard, Kin 31. *See also* RAILROAD.

**TRAINING.** Morley, C. 2; Twain 119.

**TRAP.** Adams, F. P. 8; Billings 16.

**TRAVEL.** Allen, F. 7; Benchley 4; Chesterton 22; Herford 8, 50; Herold 60; Shaw 40; Swift 43; Thoreau 11; Twain 55; Walpole 10. *See also* TRIP.

**TREAT.** Hubbard, Kin 92; Prentice 30.

**TREE.** Baer 16; Shaw 23; Undset.

**TRICK.** Hubbard, E. 5; La Rochefoucauld 65. *See also* CHEAT, DECEIT.

**TRIP.** Ade 16; Arlen 1. *See* TRAVEL.

**TRIUMPH.** Johnson 33; La Rochefoucauld 26; Mencken 30. *See also* SUCCESS.

**TROUBLE.** Barrymore 13; Billings 53; Brush 1; Franklin 17; Herford 23; Herold 57; Hubbard, Kin 71; Inge 14; Jerrold 35; Marquis 15; Moore 18; Twain 41, 115. *See also* BOTHER, WORRY.

**TROUSERS.** Kaufman 2; Masson 18; Nye 8; O'Malley 37; Smith, S. 5; Vorse.

**TRUST.** Ainslie; Dunne 15; Johnson 37; Leacock; Nash 3; Rowland 31; Wilde 122; Rabelais 7. *See also* CONFIDENCE, CREDIT, FAITH.

**TRUTH.** Aretino 1; Bennett, A. 3; Billings 4, 126; Bradley 6; Cavour; Chesterton 30; Churchill 4; Collins 6; Fischer 3; Gibran; Goldberg 3; Gourmont 12; Holmes 21; Huneker 6; Ibsen 2; Jefferson 3; Jerrold 17; Kipling 13; La Rochefoucauld 41; Lytton 4; Mathews 1; Morley, C. 21; Phillips; Prentice 2, 13; Raspe; Santayana 6; Shaw 7, 75, 102, 112; Thoreau 18; Twain 47, 83, 120, 121, 133; Wilde 68, 84, 88; Wotton 4. *See also* HONESTY, LIE vs. TRUTH, PROOF.

**TRY.** Adams, F. P. 16; Santayana 5.

**TUNE.** Hubbard, Kin 9; Lamb 20; Schumann. *See also* MUSIC, SING.

**TURKEY.** Balzac 12.

**TURN.** Herford 17; Mizner, A. 9; Rowland 16; Shaw 84; Smith, L. P. 12.

**TWINS.** Billings 75, 113.

**UGLY.** Baer 11; Chesterfield 8, 12; Haldane 1; Heine 13; Mencken 49; O'Malley 50; Wilde 41, 98, 148. *See also* BEAUTY vs. UGLY.

**UMBRELLA.** Frost 1; Jerrold 12; Twain 9.

**UNDERSTANDING.** Butler, S. 10; Chesterfield 12; Disraeli 7; Fontenelle 1; France 7; James, H. 1; Molière 3; Moore 10; Pope 3; Shaw 42; Sinclair; Smith, S. 9; Stephens 2; Twain 7; Walpole 2; Wilde 187, 207; Zangwill 5. *See also* INTELLIGENCE, KNOWLEDGE, WISDOM.

**UNDERTAKER.** Billings 95; Martial 2; Twain 74. *See also* BURY, FUNERAL.

**UNEXPECTED.** Roche 1; Shaw 45; Wilde 165. *See also* SURPRISE.

**UNHAPPY.** Arnould 1; Herold 72; Hurst 1; La Rochefoucauld 6; Lawrence 1; Munro 4; Socrates 3; Wilde 122. *See also* HAPPY vs. UNHAPPY, MISERY, SAD.

**UNITED STATES.** *See* AMERICA.

**UNIVERSE.** Emerson 33; Morley, C. 13. *See also* WORLD.

**UNIVERSITY.** Beerbohm 3; Chekhov 3; Howe 1; Lowell, A. L.; Masson 14. *See also* COLLEGE.

**UNSELFISH.** Billings 18; Jackson 10; Munro 6; Nietzsche 13. *See also* GENEROUS.

**USE.** Irving 2; Roche 1; Wotton 2.

**USELESS.** Adams, F. P. 1; Ade 19; Franklin 11; O'Malley 26, 30; Prentice 28; Shaw 106; Voltaire 27.

**VACATION.** Hubbard, E. 23; Hubbard, Kin 38, 99. *See also* REST.

**VALUE.** Billings 106; Franklin 21, 33; La Rochefoucauld 19; Swift 17; Wilde 29. *See also* COST, WORTH.

**VANITY.** Bennett, A. 8; Billings 5; Cobb 11; Franklin 12; La Rochefoucauld 3, 42, 44, 52, 64; Shakespeare 29; Stevenson 11; Twain 125; Wilde 167. *See also* CONCEIT, EGOTISM.

**VEGETABLE.** Butler, S. 15; Hubbard, Kin 35, 137; Inge 6; Twain 119. *See also* FOOD, GARDEN, PLANT.

**VENUS.** Heine 12; Moore 21.

**VERSE.** *See* POETRY.

**VICE.** Bagehot 5; Butler, S. 18; Dunne 16; Emerson 27; Franklin 48; Hazlitt 14, 16; Hubbard, Kin 88; Lamb 23; La Rochefoucauld 66; Sévigné 3; Smith, S. 40; Wilde 54. *See also* EVIL, IMMORAL, SIN.

**VICE vs. VIRTUE.** Billings 66; Dickens 13; Johnson 10; La Rochefoucauld 7; Lincoln 8; Molière 1; Nietzsche 3; Whately 4. *See also* GOOD vs. BAD, RIGHT vs. WRONG.

**VILLAGE.** Colton 3; Smith, S. 42. *See also* TOWN.

**VILLAIN.** Howe 37; Jerrold 39. *See also* FOOL vs. KNAVE, RASCAL.

**VIOLIN.** Herford 36; Kreisler; Lytton 7; Roosevelt, F. D. 3.

**VIRTUE.** Billings 11, 105; Geraldy 5; Hazlitt 4; Heine 13; Holmes 12; Jerome 5; La Rochefoucauld 14, 19, 34, 43, 44; Lenclos 3; Mencken 47; Nye 2; Shaw 46, 103; Strachey 1; Swift 39; Twain 12, 122; Voltaire 12, 31; Wilde 32, 174. *See also* CHASTITY, GOOD, GOOD vs. BAD, MORALITY, VICE vs. VIRTUE.

**VISIT.** Franklin 22; Howells; Molière 2; O'Malley 28; Pain 1; Santayana 1; Twain 40. *See also* COMPANY, GUEST, HOST.

**VIVISECTION.** Ibsen 1; Mencken 2. *See also* EXPERIMENT.

**VOICE.** Bierce 40; Johnson 45; Sherman 2; Smith, L. P. 18; Wade 3. *See also* SING, SPEECH.

**VOTE.** Henry 2; Inge 9; Mann, H. 2; Nathan 1. *See also* ELECTION.

**VULGAR.** Hazlitt 3; Jerrold 32; Twain 104; Wilde 10, 11, 107, 170.

**WAGNER, Richard.** Rossini 3; Twain 123; Wilde 72.

**WAIT.** Bradley 1; Edison 3; Frost 17; Hubbard, Kin 16, 95; Jerrold 17; Kelland; Lucas 3; Mizner, A. 6; O'Malley 2.

**WAITER.** Herold 28.

**WAKE.** Ade 2; Howe 10. *See also* SLEEP & WAKE.

**WALK.** Allen, F. 16; Roosevelt, F. D. 4; Thurber 2.

**WAR.** Bismarck 2; Clemenceau 2; Heine 11; Hubbard, Kin 86; Jerrold 16; Mencken 28; Morley, C. 22; Prentice 32; Rogers 21; Twain 19; Ward 8. *See also* ARMY, BATTLE, GENERAL, SOLDIER.

**WASH.** Howe 13; Prentice 11. *See also* BATH, CLEAN, SOAP, WATER.

**WASHINGTON, D.C.** Wilson 2.

**WASTE.** Mansfield; Shaw 95; Twain 139.

**WATCH.** Johnson 6; Shakespeare 10. *See also* CLOCK, TIME.

**WATER.** Bangs 2; Blackie; Chesterton 14, 15; Fischer 5; Housman; Kipling 14; Lamb 2, 13; Masson 12; Mizner, A. 14; Mizner, W. 20; Prentice 15; Smith, S. 46; Steinbeck; Twain 124; Wilde 36. *See also* BATH, FLOOD, WASH.

**WAVE.** Skinner 3; Steinbeck.

**WAY.** Frost 2; Holmes 15; O'Malley 52; Rowland 43; Shakespeare 3; Wade 4. *See also* PATH, ROAD.

**WEAK.** La Rochefoucauld 51. *See also* STRONG vs. WEAK.

**WEALTH.** Billings 35; Franklin 19; La Rochefoucauld 19; O'Malley 16; Roche 1; Smith, L. P. 16; Smith, S. 26. *See also* PROPERTY, RICH.

**WEATHER.** Auerbach; Baer 9; Byron 4, 17; Frost 1; Hubbard, Kin 12; Johnson 40; Lowell, J. R. 7; Shakespeare 27; Swift 35; Twain 46, 144; Warner 2. *See also* RAIN.

**WEDDING.** Jerrold 15; Rowland 15, 45. *See also* BRIDE.

**WEIGHT.** Prentice 34; Quillen 1; Rowland 8. *See also* FAT.

**WELCOME.** Baer 9; Shakespeare 28.

**WHIP.** Twain 68.

**WHISPER.** Joubert 4.

**WHISTLER, James McNeill.** Wilde 182.

**WHITMAN, Walt.** Little 14.

**WHOLE.** Billings 45; Leacock 4.

**WIDOW.** Ade 20; Burgess 7; Cervantes 6; Franklin 34, 35; Gay 1; Haliburton 4; Holmes 5; Howe 6, 47; Hubbard, Kin 67; La Bruyère 10; Lamb 9; Loomis 2; Rowland 10; Wilde 58.

**WIDOWER.** Howe 47; Rowland 41; Shaw 66.

**WIFE.** NOTE: This word has not been cross-referenced because it occurs very often.

**WILD.** Smith, S. 8; Swift 32. *See also* SAVAGE.

**WILL.** Holmes 15; Mizner, A. 7; Mumford 1; O'Malley 27, 52; Prentice 13; Rabelais 4; Voltaire 1.

**WILL POWER.** Lamb 10; O'Malley 27.

**WIN.** Ade 1; Dewar 11; Wilde 127, 151.

**WIN or LOSE.** Rogers 21; Thackeray 5; Voltaire 21.

**WINDOW.** Moore 3; Rolland 49; Ward 12.

**WINE.** Baudelaire 3; Bierce 22; Blackie; Ertz 1; Goethe 5; Jerrold 19, 36; Johnson 42; Wilde 36. *See also* DRINK.

**WINE, WOMEN, & SONG.** Adams, F. P. 10; Luther 2.

**WINTER.** Barrie 2; Byron 4; Nye 18.

**WISDOM.** Barrymore 10; Billings 57; Churchill 1; Coleridge 1; Eldridge 2; Hurst 2; Lamb 25; Landor; Little 3; Mencken 35; Smith, S. 7; Stephens 2;

Twain 139; Wilde 195. *See also* FOOLISH vs. WISE, INFORMATION, INTELLIGENCE, KNOWLEDGE, UNDERSTANDING.

**WISH.** Franklin 17; Lowell, J. R. 5; Nicolson; Woollcott 7. *See also* DESIRE.

**WIT.** Bennett, A. 6; Congreve 7; Landon 3; La Rochefoucauld 1, 68; Maugham 2; Moore 13; Pope 3; Rowland 54; Shakespeare 10; Swift 11, 52, 55. *See also* COMEDY, EPIGRAM, HUMOR, PUN, REPARTEE.

**WOLF.** Inge 6; Quillen 4.

**WOMAN.** NOTE: This word has not been cross-referenced because it occurs very often.

**WORD.** Barrymore 8; Butler, S. 22, 70, 77; Chesterton 36; Cobb 6; Congreve 8; Ford 2; Franklin; Lincoln 3; Martial 5; Nye 7; O'Malley 15; Prentice 28; Shakespeare 9; Smith, S. 24; Swift 8, 36; Thoreau 8; Twain 17, 45, 101; Wells, C. 1. *See also* LANGUAGE, PRONUNCIATION, SLANG, SPEECH, SPELLING, TALK.

**WORK.** Baer 6, 7; Billings 86; Darrow 3; Dunne 2, 17; Frost 4, 13, 18; Halifax 6; Herold 2, 26; Hubbard, Kin 10, 72; Jerome 1, 3; La Bruyère 9; Leacock 8; Lincoln 9; Marquis 4; Mencken 20; Prentice 10; Nye 12; Rascoe 2; Rowland 51; Sandburg 1, 2; Voltaire 4; Warner 3; Wilde 155; *See also* BOSS, BUSINESS.

**WORLD.** Balzac 1; Beckford; Billings 44, 108; Bradley 3; Browne 3; Burdette 1; Cabell 1; Collins 8; Emerson 18; Hazlitt 7; Howe 18; Hubbard, E. 34; Hubbard, Kin 128, 129; La Fontaine 2; Montaigne 4; Moore 4; Pascal 3; Quarles 2; Shaw 53; Wilde 21, 124, 193, 194, 195. *See also* EARTH, UNIVERSE.

**WORM.** Cobb 15; Montaigne 5. *See also* TAPEWORM.

**WORRY.** Adams, F. P. 9; Burdette 3; Frost 9, 13; Herold 46; Inge 14; Mizner, W. 34; O'Malley 23; Scott 2; Shaw 73. *See also* TROUBLE.

**WORSE.** Arlen 2; Moore 17; Ruskin 3; Terence 2; Wilde 55, 66. *See also* BEST & WORST, INFERIOR.

**WORSHIP.** Frazer; Montagu 5; Wilde 192. *See also* CHURCH, GOD, PRAYER, RELIGION.

**WORTH.** Ade 4; Disraeli 13; Herford 32; Johnson 44; Twain 32. *See also* COST, VALUE.

**WRITER.** Colby 5; Coleridge 6; France 20; Hecht 2; Maugham 5; Prentice 17; Rascoe 2; Shaw 116; Twain 83. *See also* AUTHOR, EDITOR.

**WRITING.** Ade 14; Baer 27; Beerbohm 5; Benchley 5; Carlyle 6; Cobb 7; Colton 11; Disraeli 24; Emerson 30; Franklin 39; Gibbon 2; Goldsmith 2; Hazlitt 9; Hurst 1; Johnson 27; Karr 4; Lamb 24; Landor; Marquis 17; Martial 1; Maurois 3; Moore 19; Nathan 3; Pascal 2; Prentice 11; Richelieu; Rogers 10; Smith, S. 49; Vorse; Walpole 2; Wilde 50, 57; Zola 1. *See also* AUTOGRAPH, COMPOSITION, ILLITERATE, LETTER, PLAGIARISM, STYLE.

**WRONG.** Billings 9; Darrow 9; Disraeli 6; Houssaye; Hubbard, E. 35; Johnson 35; Kipling 4; La Rochefoucauld 33; Lichtenberg 2; Moore 20; Shaw 64, 86; Stevenson 5; Thurber 3; Wilde 180; Woollcott 9. *See also* CRIME, EVIL, IMPROPER, JUSTICE vs. INJUSTICE, MISUNDERSTAND, RIGHT vs. WRONG, SIN.

**YAWN.** Chesterton 48; Rowland 13; Stendhal 2.

**YEAR.** Bennett, A. 9; Deeping; Emerson 3; Lichtenberg 1; Mizner, W. 38; Rowland 19; Schopenhauer 2; Shakespeare 11.

**YES & NO.** Billings 90; Cervantes 2.

**YIELD.** Talleyrand 5; Wilde 139, 157.

**YOUTH.** Barrie 5; Billings 134; Burgess 5; Chesterton 49; Disraeli 3; Herford 34; Herold 44; Jackson 3; Jowett 1; Kipling 2; Shakespeare 35; Shaw 95; Smith, L. P. 4, 18; Spencer 4; Wade 6, 199.